Self, Interaction, and Natural Environment

Self, Interaction, and Natural Environment: Refocusing Our Eyesight

Andrew J. Weigert

State University of New York Press

Published by
State University of New York Press, Albany

© 1997 State University of New York

Printed in the United States of America

For information, address State University of New York Press,
State University Plaza, Albany, NY 12246

Production by Cynthia Tenace Lassonde
Marketing by Bernadette LaManna

Library of Congress Cataloging-in-Publication Data

Weigert, Andrew J.
    Self, interaction, and natural environment : refocusing our
eyesight / Andrew J. Weigert.
        p.   cm.
    Includes bibliographical references and index.
    ISBN 0-7914-3259-9 (alk. paper). — ISBN 0-7914-3260-2 (pbk. :
alk. paper)
    1. Environmentalism—Social aspects.   2. Human ecology.   3. Man—
Influence of environment.   4. Man—Influence on nature.   I. Title.
    GE195.W43   1997
    304.2—dc20
                                                        96-32486
                                                          CIP

10 9 8 7 6 5 4 3 2 1

For Seeing

Karen's and Sheila's

Earth

Contents

Acknowledgments

Permission to reproduce revised versions of the following materials is gratefully acknowledged:
"Transverse Interaction," pp. 353–363 in Volume 14, No. 3, *Symbolic Interaction*; and "Lawns of Weeds," pp. 80–96 in Volume 25, No. 1, *The American Sociologist.*

Much appreciated and warmly patient help in typing and preparing the manuscript came from the Decio Clerical Services Office of the University of Notre Dame, especially Cheryl Reed and Sherry Reichold. Clarity and camaraderie came from colleagues of an Enviro-Sub-Group of the Joan B. Kroc Institute for International Peace Studies. Steve Zavestoski helped gather data and offered inspiration. Andy Downs provided support, competence, and good cheer in the final stages of preparation. Special regards go to Robert "Mac" McIntosh for mentoring me in things ecological. As always, the sustaining love of my "earthmate" Kathleen and our daughters, Karen and Sheila, to whom this book is dedicated, motivates and challenges me.

Introduction. Natural Environments Are Real and Seen

The Civil War was drawing to a bloody close and the final stage in the "Winning of the West" was set with the golden spike linking the railroad from the Atlantic to the Pacific. The manifest destiny of the American Revolution was replayed to the tunes of a war for union and a free citizenry. After the victory of the industrialized North, these United States set out to fulfill the founding values of Expansion, Control, and Progress. The frontier disappeared and states emerged from sea to shining sea. The 1860s are remembered as a founding period of American economic, moral, political, and geographical history.

In the year 1864, however, a book of a different tone was published. George Perkins Marsh raised perhaps the first American voice directly to address the dependency of human life on a sustaining natural environment as the basic issue of his time. Marsh was a self-taught interpreter of human-environment interaction. What he saw motivated him to try to teach fellow Americans how to look at nature—not a simple task. He saw the cultural imperatives of Expansion, Control, and Progress grounded in a more basic Dependency on nature.

In masculinist Victorian prose, he made it clear that we never simply see what we look at. True, the eye is but an organ that takes what comes to it through colored light. Were we mere animals, all we would have to do is open our eyes' shutters, aim, and focus. As humans, however, we see much more than what the light imprints on our retinas. What we knowingly see is colored, shaped, and interpreted by the "eye" behind our eyes, that is, by our "mind's eye," the cultured eye evolving not from genes but from society. Marsh noted that, unlike animals, the human observer can acquire new powers of sight that go beyond what the eye receives. Learning to see nature anew is a difficult though not impossible task. It was mightily needed in his time. He wrote:

1

the power most important to cultivate, and, at the same time, hardest to acquire, is that of seeing what is before him. Sight is a faculty; seeing, an art. The eye is a physical, but not a self-acting apparatus, and in general it sees only what it seeks. . . . it is agreed on by all hands that the power of multifarious perception and rapid discrimination may be immensely increased by well-directed practice. This exercise of the eye I desire to promote, and, next to moral and religious devotion, *I know of no more important practical lessons in this earthly life of ours . . . than those relating to the employment of the sense of vision in the study of nature.* (Marsh, 1864/1965: 15–17, emphasis added)

Marsh was prophetic. What he saw as a need in his time is an imperative in ours. One hundred and thirty years after Marsh wrote, we recognize that societies are struggling for an adequate view of human-environment relations. We now know that industrial society produces increasing risks along with greater goods and services (Beck, 1992). Consumption drives modern economies and simultaneously generates waste and pollution. Growing populations underwrite prosperity in one context and threaten it in another. Scholars are scientifically tracking the data through which we can see what is really going on. Or can we?

Two books published in 1995 give us point-counterpoint. The Worldwatch Institute has published a yearly volume since 1984 entitled *State of the World.* In his opening chapter, Lester Brown reviews trends in population, food, water, and climate. His conclusion is that "in various ways, nature's limits are beginning to impose themselves on the human agenda, initially at the local level, but also at the global level" (1995: 5). By contrast, the Competitive Enterprise Institute published a volume entitled *The True State of the Planet* with articles on basic environmental issues. In his prologue, editor Ronald Bailey argues that, "Moving forward can increase resources and wealth. . . . if something does go wrong, our increased knowledge and greater economic resources can be mobilized to solve the problem" (1995: 5). Brown sees natural limits where Bailey sees technological problems. Whom to believe?

In spite of different diagnoses, both Brown and Bailey appear to look through similar lenses of ecological processes, life-support systems, scientific data, population dynamics, institutional definitions, and personal motivation. Neither one would argue that we can go on with business as usual assuming that the earth can support human populations that continued to double every forty to forty-five years at increasing rates of personal consumption. Beneath the differences, then, lie shared lenses for seeing human-environment relations. There are shared views on what are relevant data and the obligation to obtain, interpret, and act on such data. Subsequent differences of policy and prior differences of ultimate values are joined and clarified in the light of agreements. This book is an exercise in seeing human-environment relations through lenses and concepts that I hope all can share in the service of mutual understanding and cooperative living.

I use the term *eye-sight* to continue Marsh's "practical lesson." It refers to the mix of physical reality and social interpretation that makes up what we think we see when we look at the natural environment. Environmental movements in northern Europe teach "a new way of seeing" that informs our knowledge and pragmatic responses to what we think we see (Jamison et al, 1990: 5). New eye-sight is basic to the collective identities that members of environmental movements experience. New eye-sight re-presents human-physical environment relations in terms of dependency and sustainability. These ideas are basic to control and development. We cannot control what we cannot sustain; we can develop only to the limits of our dependency. Seeing ourselves as dependent on a sustainable environment reframes how we look at pollution, public health threats, and conflicting definitions of the environment. This framing elicits new values, motives, and feelings within individual and collective life. A central cognitive and moral challenge is to understand how, in fact, we are relating to our physical environment and how we are to act responsibly on that understanding.

This book offers social psychological lenses to carry on Marsh's challenge of learning to see adequately. My choice of issues grows out of their importance and my concern. I present environmental descriptions with a layperson's knowledge of scientific data. I build the intellectual perspective with the tools of my scholarly practice: a life-long concern with everyday reality as seen through a sociological social psychology rooted in the symbolic interactionist and phenomenological traditions. I call this perspective "pragmatic social constructionism."

Organism versus Symbol: From Progress to Paradox

Eye-sight is a bastardized word. It combines two contrary realities into one construction. Yet, it is apt for indicating the single reality constructed in what we take to be the neutral act of seeing. As a sighted person, just close and open your eyes focused on this book and you experience the unquestioned unity of everyday eyesight. You see color, hue, and shape as a single book; and you know that visual object to be the same thing as the resisting, stiff, and not too heavy object in your hands. Through eye-sight, you see the "book"—even though the organic eye does nothing of the sort. Eye knows no book; only I do. Centuries of philosophical dialectics debated primary and secondary qualities of things and whether we ever "see" anything, or indeed know anything as it is in inself, apart from its relationships to our organs or senses that grasp objects as things in themselves.

The givenness of eye-sight comes through material structures and processes of a bodily organ, an "eye." An eye results from millennia of evolutionary changes in organisms crawling on a shore from the molecular soup. Those organisms responded to the sun's rays, like the eye of a trilobite or horseshoe crab responding to the unchanging laws of light and sight over four hundred million years ago (Eisley, 1978: 54, 122). So an eye is a totally material organ whose functioning is explained in the language of physical science. The structure and functioning of the eye selects objects from phenonemena as naturally physical as the eye itself. The eye is totally in nature in the physical meaning of the phrase. The human eye is an eye in the same way as the eye of an eagle, except it is not as farsighted, or more precisely, far-focused. Yet, through instruments like the far-focused telescope and the near-focused microsope, the physical range of the human eye is mightily extended. Instrumentally extended eyes bring new sights like an ever-expanding milky way and ever tinier atoms—all objects of faith in our world of everyday eye-sight.

I prefer "focus" to "sight" in discussing the eagle's eye. "Sight" has the notion of an interpretive power that is not reducible to the physical processes of focusing lenses or eyes. Sight refers to an interpretive power that constructs new visual objects and transforms these into things, real things out there in the real world. For the human eye, sight emerges from symbolic ways of seeing indicated by the way we talk about what we think we see. It depends on how we "eye" the object, cockeyed or otherwise. How we eye objects depends on how we learn to see them, that is, to actively look at, talk about, and frame sensory objects as meaningful visual wholes (Arnheim, 1969).

The organic eye takes a limited range of sensory input from the environment. Sight, by contrast, is symbolically freed from the limits of the here, the now, and the this. Sight, as symbolically empowered, is potentially infinite: we "see" whatever its symbolic apparatus configures as meaningful from the eye's raw material. What we see is shaped by the "relatively natural view" of the everyday world in which we live (Schutz, 1962). This everyday world is not the physically given world of the dog or eagle. It is a symbolically constructed world that selectively grasps the physical world in terms of our values, motives, and intentions. It is a socially constructed world that answers to culturally pragmatic needs as we understand them, not necessarily as they really are.

As experienced, the environment is, in part, a platonic world of formal meanings constructed through the creative power of eye-sight. It is a *theoretical* world, that is, a world we construct through the way we look at it. Theory is a way of seeing, and all seeing is in part theoretical (Kuhn, 1970).

The brute organic eye does not see. The person sees through the frames and words that structure the environment, select the object, and make up its meanings. This mix of given and constructed reality is the complex object of eye-sight. It is also a general theme in post-modern critiques of taken-for-granted foundations guaranteeing what and how persons know anything of cultural importance, including themselves (Gergen, 1991). My themes are more particular: I look at implications of eye-sight for interpreting the physical environment, for the emergence of a new self, and for paradoxes of intentions and outcomes. The way we act on the environment even has implications for the brute physical eye: consider the probabilities of a link between ozone depletion, wavelengths of relatively unfiltered sunlight, and rates of cataract growth over human eyes. Our actions may reduce our eye-sight.

Meaningful objects we see around us are wholes, totalities, or *gestalts*. Totalities that we think we see, including our own self-images, dissolve into particular parts only under analytic scrutiny. If a person I immediately recognize as my lover enters the room, the person I recognize is not the outcome of a series of inferences or chains of connected dots that gradually take the shape of my lover's nose, face, hair, and body. Recognition affirms that total person as my lover, not as a bundle of molecules and atoms I infer to be my lover. Meaningful wholes are not constructed by individuals. As culturally meaningful, they are shared social productions. They are generated by social processes; sustained as plausible by group activities or legitimating authorities; and transmitted through socializing agents such as families, schools, and media.

Totalities are objectified in the symbols and images of interaction, language, and artifact. They function as typical unquestioned elements of a collective worldview that bestows the aura of reality on personal experience. Even though it looks flat to me, I think I know with certainty that the earth is round because every meaningful assertion I hear about its shape assumes its roundness. How could I possibly question what is the unquestioned assumption of all meaningful talk and thought about the earth's shape? Put simply, I could not and still be considered normal (even though it really looks flat)!

Are there other taken-for-granted assumptions about the earth that render my experience socially meaningful? This book assumes that American culture encodes our consciousness with a dominant response to that question: Western eye-sight is framed by the assumption that events are discrete, linear, repeatable, and progressive. My conviction, however, is that a systemic gestalt that sees events as mutual, cyclic, discontinuous, and contingent is more adequate. Indeed, new data demand a systemic view to complement linear thinking. The thesis of this book is that we moderns need a systemic or ecological framework for interpreting earthly events, experiences, and dynamics. The question is, How can we learn such a

framework? My response is that we must learn to: see everyday circumstances and actions differently; generate a new self-understanding; and
learn a new ecological paradigm, that is, a more adequate way of thinking
and talking about our relationship to the physical environment.

A few years before Marsh published his book, Charles Darwin's *On the
Origin of the Species* marked such a deep shift in eye-sight that it is still going
on and has yet to play out its full implications for our cultural self-understanding (Eisley, 1978). A simplistic reduction of this struggle over eye-sight
is creationism versus evolution. This debate is too narrow for our purpose.
Our theme is ecological eye-sight, namely, a way of seeing informed with
scientific-based data on the probabilities that our actions affect the dependency and sustainability of human life. Ecological understanding is central to
the struggle over paradigms for interpreting the human condition. This book
contributes to the struggle by refocusing our eye-sight. The hope is that
more adequate ecologically informed frameworks will lead to stronger motivation for acting as environmental citizens. Such motivation eventually
includes learning when and how to subordinate nation-state citizenship to a
more basic and universal environmental citizenship.

This book is not about philosophy or ethics, though it contains
everyday concerns that have philosophical and ethical implications. I do
not ask how society is possible nor what is a good society. I am interested
in the everydayness of the key question, How do we perceive our relationship with the natural environment? I approach this issue through a sociology of knowledge aimed at understanding some social processes that
construct the objects of experience, in our case, the natural environment
framed as the earth. The informing image is the National Aeronautics and
Space Administration (NASA) photo of the Big Blue Marble, the from-outer-
space sight of the earth as a single whirling blue-white ball with no socially
constructed national boundaries.

The Big Blue Marble is the image of the twenty-first century. It is as the
primary visual analogue for all sensory eyeings and socially constructed
sightings. In simple terms, visual aesthetics in everyday life—that is, sightings informed by feelings, motives, and values—need to have the Big Blue
Marble as the background as we frame our lives. The Big Blue Marble
becomes the backyard in which we live as environmental citizens, just as a
nation's mythic history works as a backyard for an emotional sense of
national citizenship and patriotic identity.

The Same Eyes See Many Sights

We talk about what we see. Talk frames and focuses seeing. Seeing
informed by talk, then, structures our thinking. Within environmental

discourse, frequently heard lemmas tell us: Think like a mountain (Leopold, 1970); Think globally, act locally; and Think globally, act globally. Taken literally, these lemmas make no sense: mountains and globes do not think, and no one can take the perspective of a mountain or globe. If we substitute earth for globe, we are hardly better off. Of course, someone reminds us that globe is simply a metaphor for thinking ecologically about the systemic forces at work in the natural environment. Yet, this supposed clarification darkens the issue further: no one knows how the total natural environment works, no one knows all the laws of ecology. Even worse, no one on earth even sees the earth, nor the biosphere, nor any natural system as such. Not even orbiting astronauts saw these; they merely eyed the planet Earth from a sufficient distance to capture it as a single visual object. They never saw the earth as a functioning system of ecosystems, a biosphere, which is what the upper case "E" for Earth as a proper noun calls to mind.

Today's ecological lemmas realize empirical and supposedly demythologized secular versions of traditional and religious sayings. Such lemmas are derived from and point toward inherited world views that ground our unquestioned sense of what is real. Our world view underlies belief statements about everyday realities. Lemmas locate motives and interpretations within acceptable accounts that display the moral legitimacy of our actions to ourselves and to others who challenge us (Lyman and Scott, 1970). These acceptable accounts motivate and empower us to believe in what we and others think are reasonable actions in a real world. As a result, we think, feel, and decide our lives in ways that we and others accept as moral and reasonable rather than unaccountably absurd.

What a consolation it is! If you and I accept my reasons for writing this book as telling how we shape what our senses select from the world into real objects that justify our lives, then together we are constructing a moral and physical world and sharing true knowledge about it. Imagine, the truth is that we must think like mountains! Only thus would our lives mesh with the grounded reality of the earth. I take these lemmas as secular translations of inherited religious discourse. They build on the human condition as socially and ecologically empirical, not as prophetically or apocalyptically transcendent. The lemmas lead us to empirical frameworks for interpreting experience.

Traditional religious sayings tell us to judge events and motives from the point of view of a transcendent eternity, *sub specie aeternitatis.* Or, they place us imaginatively in our graves to see how events look from the angle of a supine corpse. Or, more abstractly, they ask us to see our life as God sees it: how does my life look through God's sight? Do I believe that this God acts in and guides all events in terms of an unknowable divine plan for the earth and all who dwell in it? This is wholistic thinking based on transcendent non-empirical categories. As powerful as these religious perspectives are, they are too individualistic, just as, it seems to me, our use of ecological lemmas is. It is true that eyes are always and only the eyes of individual organisms. Yet, the structures and functions of sensory receptivity are generically the same for categories of sighted individuals, and at a somewhat more abstract level, the same for all humans. In some trivial way, we all *eye* the same things. In a powerful and problematic sense, though, we do not all *see* the same things. The eyes have it, but it is not the same sight. We see different sights shaped by socially constructed empirical or transcendent ways of talking and thinking. We often believe that our ways enable us to see the world as it really is.

Sights, in other words, refer to socially constructed objects that we assume inform and direct my actions as socially meaningful to me and to relevant others as well. Lemmas point to an underlying worldview that works as the background against which the things our eyes see become the sighted objects we think we know. In other words, lemmas trigger the everyday behavioral ways in which we realize how and why we act realistically, truthfully, and morally. These perennial issues are not just constructions of moralists in the business of selling primers on living the good life. They are also templates of daily life.

My approach to these perennial questions comes from American pragmatic philosophy informing the sociological tradition (Mead, 1934). The sociological social psychology known as "symbolic interaction" works with a threefold grounding of the hows and whys of human action: we act toward things as though we are responding to meaningful objects; the reality of meaningful objects emerges from interaction with others for whom they are objects; and, objects and their meanings are precariously sustained, occasionally changed, and ever created by interpretations we put upon them (Blumer, 1969; Weigert, 1983).

The organizing content of this book is types of interaction and their interpretations that generate the meaningful objects of our experience and constitute our social and physical worlds. The sights we see, in a word, are constructions built through interaction with the things and people available through our eyes and other senses. Sociological social psychologists provide many analyses of social interaction generating both interpersonal realities like personal identities, feelings, or self, and institutional realities such as groups, nation states, or international organizations. Just as the seemingly solid structure of a brick building is made up of arrangements of individual bricks that do what bricks do all day, so too, the seemingly solid structures of society are made up of the interactions of persons who do what moral members do all day, or, at least, what they are expected and occasionally forced to do—until further notice is served and dashed expectations interrupt our lives.

A Focus on What's Coming

This book focuses on a universal mode of interaction that is sorely needed but underdeveloped. My thesis is driven by the conviction that sociological social psychology is a necessary perspective for making sense out of a definitive challenge of our time: interactions among the three realities of self, society, and natural environment. For this reason, the discussion builds on what I call "transverse interaction," that is, interaction between self and natural environment.

Consider an analogy with medical talk of "diagnosis" and "prognosis." These Greek roots refer to doctors use of medical frameworks to interpret patient knowledge of mere symptoms by linking them to what is really going on in patients' bodies. The doctor places the symptoms in a category that also indicates both "causes" of the ill health and "likelihoods" of future health developments. A strong scholarly tradition within social psychology recognizes that lay persons use basically the same logic as scientists, doctors, and clinicians. Everyone describes, categorizes, explains, and interprets events in such a way as to understand past causes and anticipate what current events will bring next. Lay persons use different concepts, sources of data, methods of evidence, and explanatory frameworks. Yet all of us diagnose everyday situations to weigh different prognoses of future events, and most importantly, to decide what to do next.

Rather than words with Greek roots, I use the Anglo-Saxon phrase *seeing through* to refer to lay persons' versions of theoretical and empirical interpretive processes for placing events and anticipating futures implicated in our everyday actions. I use the term *throughsight* to capture the practical lesson of seeing through human-environment relations with frameworks and evidences more adequate to the modern condition.

Seeing through is also one of the practical lessons of a sociological perspective and a decisive contribution of a sociological imagination (Berger, 1963: 30ff.; Mills, 1961). Changing the frames through which we see changes both what we see now and what we expect next. Eventually, it changes how we reflexively see ourselves. Eye-sight is powerful.

I try to unpack part of this power in the following chapters. Chapter 1 discusses the fundamental idea of "interaction." I believe that well-socialized and intelligent contemporaries tend to build understandings of how the world works on an individualistic idea of human action, that is, that behavior issues from the free decisions of individuals and effects changes in other individual persons or objects. This individualistic version of human action masks the reciprocal impact of the other's response on self. Furthermore, it tends to understand interaction as a rather arbitrary piecing together of the prior realities of individual acts, so that interaction is a sort of fictional construction, much like understanding society as a fiction or mere word rather than a reality in its own right. Secondly, an individualistic reading of interaction explains it by reducing it to the prior reality of each individual's behavior. In sum, an individualistic version sees individual action as real and interaction as a construction and, as a result, explains interaction by reducing it to individual behavior.

Contemporary explorations of systems, ecology, institutions, and environmental dynamics, however, include the idea of interaction as the starting point from which individual actions are derivations and abstractions. In chapter 1, I develop the idea of interaction within the American pragmatic sociological tradition to set the conceptual and interpretive setting for the rest of the book. Readers less interested in conceptual foundations can skip it, but the rest of the discussion relies on the logic and linkages developed in chapter 1.

Chapters 2 through 6 point out anomalous and sometimes jarring features of contemporary life that challenge us to see through them to a more adequate understanding of human-environment interaction. Chapter 2 contains ways we see, name, and interpret the natural environment. Chapter 3 points to technological extensions of our animal ability to affect changes in the environment that react back upon us, that is, it looks at the growing number of "trippers" by which we make the environment act for our convenience, at least for a time. Chapter 4 lists "inversions" of inherited feelings toward and conventional interpretations of objects that make up our everyday surroundings. Chapter 5 brings the tools and particulars of previous chapters to see through those pieces of earth many of us think we control, namely, "lawns," and to generate a better understanding of the why and what of the grasses surrounding suburban homes, businesses, and recreational areas. Chapter 6 is a first step toward a Primer Paradigm linking key ideas into a framework for seeing through our interaction with the environment so that we can think about and motivate ourselves to build environmental citizenship.

By the end of these chapters, we share the tools of an interactionist framework and awareness of key aspects of human-environment relations such as: names, trippers, perceptual inversions, lawns of weeds, and a Primer Paradigm for seeing through our actions to their environmental responses. Finally, with these shared tools and awareness, chapter 7 argues that we need to refocus and see through to a new sense of self as an interactor in fundamental environmental dynamics that hold the sustainability of human life in the balance. A new self comes from reflexive awareness of ourselves interacting with new others within new conditions for survival. This new sense of self provides the foundation for workable environmental identities from which we see through inherited ideas and evaluate their adequacy as best we can in our everyday interactions for a sustainable world.

We need to bring transverse interaction into our sense of self-under-standing. This involves learning to respond to self as related to the natural environment. In transverse responses, persons become aware of themselves in a self-conscious way as environmentally related. As social psychologists teach, we acquire different senses of self by responding to ourselves in different types of interaction. These acquired or imposed senses of self then lead to socially constructed identities that give content and meaning to our lives. The self who each of us is today results from the buildup of relationships and interactional responses in situations within the institutional arrangements and natural environments that generate, sustain, and define who we are.

The experience of a twenty-year-old marine, for example, challenges us to re-sight human-natural environment interaction. During an atomic bomb test explosion, he crouched in a trench that was whipping like a snake. He later remembered that, "I *could see the bones* in my elbow. I'm looking *with my eyes shut*, and it was just as clear as could be" (quoted in Gallagher, 1993: 75, emphasis added). Imagine *shutting* your eyes, yet *seeing* the bones in your elbow! This experience raises a central question for our time: will new ways of seeing our interaction with physical nature generate a new environmental self? Will this new sense of self as constantly interacting with the environment ground new environmental identities adequate for citizenship in tomorrow's world? And what kind of eye-sight will know this new self-identity? Our journey starts with a focus on self-environment interaction, then moves toward a Primer Paradigm for seeing interaction with the natural world, and ends with a new sense of an environmentally identified self.

1

Transverse Interaction: Re-Sighting Self-Environment Relations

Nouns dominate individualistic American culture. Each of us believes my individual existence is the foundational reality and grounding value of life. I believe that I see: individual things, animals, and persons; single events; separate acts; bounded and marked territories; private property; small numbers of events in short sequences with timed beginnings and endings. All these individual realities that I believe I see are united around my individual self. I am the 0,0 center around which I frame the world of individuals I see and know. In a word, Americans live in a hyperindividualistic world because that is, in fact, the way we see it. True believers in this individualized world argue that we live in a hyperindividualistic world because that is the way it truly is, and because that is the way the world is, that is the way we see it. The dominant cultural response is that hyperindividualism is realism.

In this cultural perspective, the world is nothing but aggregates of individual beings, acts, events, times, and territories. Larger realities, such as institutions, communities, nations, societies, cultures, histories, species, or ecological systems are taken to be mere words used as shorthand references to aggregates of individuals. Names for such "larger realities" are just nominal, constructed, or artificial references to the really real individual elements. Society and community are not real; they are just names we give to aggregates of individuals, each of whom sees and lives in a personal world, makes individual rational decisions, and personally acts rightly and for the good of all on the basis of these decisions. Society or community is an imagined or statistical pattern of real individual actors, actions, and moral decisions. Even interaction between two persons is seen as two autonomous individuals behaving toward each other so that each can attain personal goals. Interaction as a collective or joint reality is seen as an overlay, a construction put over two really separate individuals and their behaviors. Interaction is constructed out of individual acts, like a building built with bricks that exist prior to and then make up the building. When the building is torn down, the individual bricks remain. Because the world is made up of autonomous individuals and behavioral bricks, that is the way we see it. The bricks are real; the building is a temporary and derived construction. Our hyperindividualistic eye-sight gives us the truth. Any other sighting is error. Today, however, other experiences are balancing this view.

A hyperindividualistic way of seeing makes it difficult if not impossible to see environmental responses to our actions. The environment is not an object or thing that any individual, as an individual, can grasp through the eyes or other senses in a single perception. We never see the environment as a whole responding to us. Yet, we know that there are gradual environmental responses to every behavior, no matter how small and unnoticeable (Graumann and Kruse, 1990). The perceptual problem is clear, though no solution is in sight. We need a new way of seeing ourselves in relation to the environment so that we can generate a more adequate sense of environmental insight. Rachel Carson told us how to see in the opening sentence of her substantive analyses in *Silent Spring*: "The History of Life on earth has been a history of interaction between living things and their surroundings" (1962/1994: 5).

This chapter develops a way of seeing through new glasses. The glasses contain lenses that focus our eyes on environmental issues within a framework of *systematic interactionism* that enlarges individualistic time and space. Systematic interactionism looks at issues in a range of *time frames*, including the long-term time frame of ecological forces playing themselves out. Aldo Leopold told us to "think like a mountain" and take the long-term view. As the Iroquois motto professes, policy decisions by the elders must consider the impact on the next seven generations.

Systematic interactionism also varies the *spatial focus*, from the habitat of the smallest organisms in the soil to the habitable space of earth's life-support systems. An apt metaphor for this spatial point of view is to imagine the earth as an encapsulated life-supporting spaceship within which all humans live together. Thinking in a wider range of time-space coordinates means we must interpret more extensive data dealing with statistical and empirical outcomes of cumulative actions.

Of course, no individual is capable of such large-scale seeing. The power of empirical thinking about the physical world grows within disciplined institutions such as natural and social sciences, engineering design, and systems analysis. For individuals, large-scale seeing involves *faith* in scientific authorities, religious teachers, or cosmologists. Faith in environmental forces is not limited to revealed, divinely inspired, or inerrant biblical texts about transcendent realities. Secular faith is based on methodologies, evidences, inferences, and ever-reformable texts produced by communities of empirical scientists studying how the Earth supports our lives. Since we live by commonsense faith in objects and processes we do not see, we must all *choose*, or let someone else choose for us, how to imagine the environment and our relationships with it (cf. Berger, 1980).

As Heraclitus would say, everything is in process of connecting to everything else. Earthly reality is a single seamless system of interacting dynamics and ever-forming and reforming parts. In a metaphoric sense, this view of reality that frames us as passengers on a single Spaceship Earth is the world view informing our discussion. Seen through this frame, moderns are today experiencing a "reversal of sight," a re-sight of objects, events, and persons as interacting parts of life-support systems. Realities we were taught to see through hyperindividualistic frames are now re-sighted as interacting parts of dynamic systems. Earthly life is first of all ecological. As such, we more adequately understand it in relationship to contexts that are themselves in flux. Reality is dynamic, that is, events in process, processes that at first glance appear as orderly objects and events. The phrase, systematic interactionism, in intended to highlight a dynamic understanding of what appear as orderly objects.

The perspective of this book builds on the insight that the meanings of things, persons, and objects arise from interaction (Baldwin, 1986; Blumer, 1969; Mead, 1934). Social psychologists have given long and deep attention to meanings constructed within the social life process, that is, to "social and cultural meanings." They have somewhat ignored meanings constructed with reference to and by the world that is there, to "natural meanings." Indeed, a key modern move is to expand everyday understandings of meaning to include natural meaning as a prior context and constant consequence of social meanings. Natural meanings emerge from interaction with the environment. I focus attention, then, both on mixed interaction with the natural world that is there and on symbolic interaction with other persons through which we fashion understandings of both social *and* physical worlds.

Studies of social meanings and everyday practices give us needed insight into symbolic interaction. They are not, however, exhaustively adequate for the foundation of human interaction that depends on a supportive environment. We need to include transverse interaction to bring an ecological perspective into social psychology. On the other hand, merely behavioral or naturalistic studies of human intervention in nature do not exhaust the meanings of transverse interaction. Moderns need a combined symbolic-naturalistic frame for inquiry (Bennett, 1993). A pragmatic social constructionism combines behavioral naturalism and symbolic realism to study the interface between constructed social selves and naturalistic others. This chapter focuses on interaction and, specifically, transverse interaction between humans and the natural environment.

Systematic interaction always requires an "other" as a cogenerator of meaning. Isolated individuals as such cannot make their own private meanings socially real unless relevant others validate them. Meanings derive from self-other interaction. In the next section, I expand the idea of other to include a thing, person, event, or symbol to which meanings refer; in which they exist; and around which they are patterned. As a result, meaningful objects are socially constructed. Meanings are always about something grasped as other than self.

To understand natural environment, we learn to think of it as an other in systematic interaction with self. In short, we re-sight the meanings we give to environment as other by taking account of our interaction with it and its responses to our actions, whether we are aware of them or not. As we unpack self-environment interaction, we realize that meanings are more fundamentally in nature than in society. Naturalistic meanings ground and eventually support or destroy social meanings. Just as society is prior to the individual, so nature is prior to society. Individuals are born into ongoing societies, and societies are formed within ongoing environments. Ambiguities and challenges in the modern situation highlight the order of dependencies: nature and society come before and continue beyond individuals.

Systematic interactionism includes transverse interaction with particular environments that have implications for our shared environment. Just as social interactionists note that individuals think of themselves, their motives, and their actions in terms of a generalized social other that represents anticipated organized responses to individual actions, so too, I argue that in an ecological age we are learning to think of meaning in terms of the anticipated responses of the environment as a generalized natural other. Moderns come to see, think, and act in terms of a "generalized environmental other." The idea of generalized environmental other recognizes the order of dependencies: nature → society → individual. The interactional processes also make us aware of the impact of individuals: individual → society and individual → nature.

As modern persons become more powerful biospheric actors, the translation of natural meanings into adequate social meanings becomes more important. Today, new instruments orbit the Earth and relay new information and new images of natural meanings. Even the term *ecology* is barely a hundred years old (McIntosh, 1986). Earthly data beamed from orbiting satellites are hardly twenty-five years old. These concepts and data create an awareness of environmental responsibility. For the first time in history, we must think about the concepts, images, and irony involved in the fit, or lack of it, between social and natural meanings. The chances of desirable human survival teeter in the balance of the fit.

Individual meanings, what you and I know, never equal the knowledge available in social meanings. Furthermore, social meanings never exhaust natural meanings. We never know all the responses that nature is making. Paradoxically, however, social meanings are all we have in our struggle to grasp natural meanings. We are, as it were, first dealt those social meanings that dominate our historical moment on stage. History, science, and art, however, offer alternative ways of interpreting the present and imagining various futures. We must choose which meanings we shall believe in and live by and hope that the consequences of these meanings sustain an environment that continues to support us. An ironic pathos lies in the fit between natural and social meanings. The Sartrean dictum is that humans are "condemned to be free." I add that they are condemned both to be free *and* to know that their freedom to choose is always based on partial ignorance and contingency. This ironic pathos deepens in modern awareness of environmental outcomes.

The pathos hides in the gaps between social meanings and natural meanings (see chapter 2). Social meanings reside in constructed social objects and interpretive schema based on our trust and faith in culture and authority. Natural meanings, on the other hand, are a mix of cosmic processes and social meanings. This cosmic-social mix locates understandings of the world that is there in the realm of natural faith objects. They do not refer to transcendent constructions like the eschatological eternity or wheel of rebirth of religious believers, but actually and ironically to the world that is under our feet and in our lungs, mouths, and stomachs. Like the eternal world, however, individuals cannot see natural events as systemic realities, because these realities lie beyond our sensory range. Atmosphere, ozone layer, ecosystems, and the life-support cycles of carbon, water, nitrogen, or oxygen lie outside the framing power of individual minds, eyes, and ears. Natural systems are known only because experts with institutional ways of knowing tell us so. Key questions for contemporaries always include, Says who? Whom do we believe? How should I act?

Wide and deep changes in the social meanings through which we know the environment define our time. If I may oversimplify an issue discussed in the next chapter, there are three worldviews through which contemporaries typically see the natural environment. The first is rapidly disappearing, namely, a traditional worldview based on low technology links with the environment seen as interwoven with a sustainable local way of life. It is a worldview we may know as linked to "primitive," tribal, or autochthonous ways of living in long-term sustainable interaction within the local habitat. Traditional worldviews inform the long success, until now, of natives in the Amazon jungle or pygmies in the rain forests of central Africa for five thousand years, or as long as we have written reference (Turnbull, 1962).

A second and contrasting worldview dominates industrialized nations and modernizing sectors of developing societies. This worldview frames natural environment through markets, technology, and desire in support of large-scale production and expanding consumption. This industrial world-view is based on short-term utilitarian values that drive contemporary lifestyles and national policies as signs and means of Progress. It is eliminating traditional world views in the light of rain forests ablaze and logs aground.

Recently, new world views are emerging, or new renditions of older frameworks, especially and paradoxically in industrialized nations. A core value in these new-old world views gives priority to sustaining the natural environment rather than to economic growth through increasing population, production, and consumption (Dunlap et al, 1993; Inglehart, 1990; Olsen et al, 1992). These attitudes reflect a "postmaterialist" set of values growing from awareness that environmental degradation is a humanly produced threat to our lives and the lives of our children.

Different ways of seeing the environment lead to general questions. How do we believe we know how things work in the natural environment? How can people with different ideologies arrive at a shared understanding? One pathway is to share relevant data concerning the *empirical workings* of the environment. With data in hand, we can discuss how we are to respond to accepted environmental facts. A different response is to believe that we have *divinely revealed* truth about the natural environment and how we should act. Or, we believe that we have an adequate framework within a *rational worldview* for guiding how we should act toward the environment, even if our data and knowledge are incomplete. A postmodernist may say that contemporary society is characterized by simulated and uncertain stories about nature and moral narratives about how we should act.

Traditional societies had a kind of "hands-on" or "tacit" knowledge about nature, that is, knowledge carried by our senses in direct contact with the physical world, much the way a blind person knows the world in a limited but direct way by tapping a delicate cane on the ground in front of her (cf. Polanyi and Prosch, 1975). In contrast, the postmodern person knows only images, signs, stories, and authorities' dicta with no direct touching of the natural world. A powerful version of this mediated and uncertain way of seeing is "virtual reality," a sensory experience that carries appearances of reality, but which in fact is an array of images with no sensory or certain link to physical realities. Virtual reality breaks the sensory tacit links to the natural environment; it is nothing but a simulation, a similitude, of the real world. Virtual reality is a reality, but not the reality it appears to be. Virtual reality can even contradict direct experience of the world that is there, putting ambiguity between us and nature. In virtual reality, the only pathway to the natural world is the appearance that the programmer puts into the software now downloading through our senses and into our brains' virtual minds. Individuals can: believe and act as though they "live" in virtual reality; acquire a "virtual identity"; have "virtual sex" with "virtual others"; and form "virtual communities" existing in the cyberspace and time of "cyberia" (e.g., Rheingold, 1993).

The honest response to the question about how the natural world works is that we simply do not know enough about environmental dynamics to think and act so that we make the world we intend or sustain the one that we have (Miller, 1994). For the everyday citizen, postmodern ways of knowing increase the cognitive distance between the world that is ✓ there and institutional means for knowing that world. This distance is illustrated by the break between the experience of virtual reality—a "sensed" reality carried by dots on a screen that elicit images and sensations generated by computer software with no intrinsic links with the world that is there; and the experience of natural reality—a sensed reality entering our bodies through images and sensations generated by physical things, that is, tacit hands-on knowledge about the physical environment.

The virtual break between seeing and reality and the inability of individuals' senses to know ecological dynamics make the links between social meanings and natural meanings a definitive issue of our time. Peter Berger (1980) argues that contemporary religion in pluralistic societies brings believers face-to-face with a supermarket of options from which they must choose what to believe and how to live the good life. As a salient source of worldviews, religion illustrates how individuals relate to other faith objects as well. Individuals' perceptions and interpretations of the natural environment are faith dynamics. We who live in a postmodern context must choose a framework through which we believe we know the natural world and how to act toward it and toward others who share it.

Never before has an empirical and self-aware choice of a world view been a general task for humans in their struggle to understand the world and live sustainably within it. It is now! We must make these choices in the face of ignorance and uncertainty. There is not likely to be a time at which humans believe that all the data are sufficiently known to guide a sustainable moral life in the face of environmental challenges. Contemporaries must learn to act, not on the basis of empirical, divine, rational, or scientific *certitude*, but on reasonable yet contingent moral, faith-based commitment to one or another framework for knowing and living in the world. Do we choose business as usual as the way to a world for our childrens' children, or is now a moment of critical searching for new ways of living?

A contemporary, you or I, must choose a framework for seeing the natural world. The moral and rhetorical purpose of this book is to argue that a more inclusive and shared way of seeing, a framework of systemic transverse interaction, is needed in our time. I assume that a re-sighting to this kind of seeing alters the dominant hyperindividualist and consumptionist frame at the core of Western and American culture. Within a systemic transverse interactionist framework, particular behaviors of isolated individuals are not the foundation blocks from which we construct sustainable institutions and societies. Rather, it is the reverse. I accept systemic transverse interaction as the foundational empirical framework. Person as individual and action as particular are abstractions that we select out of the fundamental world and the social life process dependent on that world.

This re-sighting not only reframes how we see. It turns the cultural world upside down. Through this inverted frame, the biosocial life process generates individuals. Individuals as such do not generate the biosocial life process, though we reproduce it and introduce changes. If individuals destroy supportive ecosystems, the species they support are transformed or go extinct. Of course, individuals in their subjectivities do experience self as fundamentally individual and real. As living organisms, however, individuals are totally dependent on often out-of-awareness dynamics of energy, air, water, food, acidity, and temperature for their existence, not just as individuals but as populations that sustain individuals. Species go extinct because their populations fall below a critical level, not because the last two individuals decide not to reproduce. Individuals die, species become extinct. Extinction is a systemic collective outcome. In this framing, we see the *team* losing the World Series, not the individual batter who strikes out with the tying and winning runs on base with two outs in the bottom of the ninth inning of the seventh game.

From a systemic transverse interactionist standpoint, individuals are temporary forms in the coming together at birth of physical realities that recombine into other forms at death. Individuals live a limited organic time; populations live a far longer collective time. Both depend on supportive environmental dynamics. These dynamics are central to an interactionist framework which sees environment as an interactional other. George H. Mead's self-other paradigm generates a naturalistic social psychology. His perspective is grounded in an assumed "world that is there," and a to-be-explained "social life process" of symbolic interaction among selves and others. Irreducible social processes emerge through symbolic interaction. Analysis of these processes starts with the social act as the basic unit. Mead recognized natural and cultural types of the social life process illustrated by the differences between ants and humans. He worked toward a naturalism that included human social organization based on significant symbols irreducible to, yet dependent on, natural physical processes. "Self interacting with other" is the foundational paradigm that undergirds the social interactionist tradition. The next section presents a simplified schema of types of interaction with a focus on interaction between humans and the natural environment, or transverse interaction.

Types of Interaction: Looking for Transverse Interaction

Analysts of self-other interaction use dichotomies such as: biologic and reflective, nonsignificant and significant, behavioral and communicative, nonsymbolic and symbolic, natural and social, or signal and symbolic (Goffman, 1974; Mead, 1934: 81; 1982; Blumer, 1969; Weigert, 1983). George H. Mead's metaphor of animals engaged in a "conversation of gestures" exemplifies the first term in each dichotomy. Two dogs fighting illustrate gestural interaction between animals that do not use symbols. The second term in the dichotomies refers primarily to humans interacting in a situation through shared meanings generated in social actions. We see this type of interaction everyday in casual conversations, formal courtroom proceedings, or the deference and authority between doctors and patients. Such interaction takes on deep importance in critical situations that redefine the path of a person's life (Denzin, 1989).

Mead provocatively anchors his naturalistic evolutionary account by arguing that human interaction develops from the physical processes constituting nonhuman life (e.g., 1982: 116). Yet, he argues against reductionism by positing emergent social processes that demand their own explanation so that, paradoxically, physical processes generate types of social interaction and organization that cannot be totally explained by the laws governing their genesis (e.g., 1934: 30; cf. Baldwin, 1986). The same central nervous system cannot explain different moral meanings.

Social scientists often study the many modes of symbolic interaction (Reynolds, 1990). There are also studies of mixed interaction, nonsymbolic and symbolic, between people and their pets, even therapeutic pets (Rochberg-Halton, 1986). Symbol users teach simians and other species to manipulate symbols and engage in proto-social acts with their human teachers. Animals, in turn, manipulate humans in many ways from goring them to licking their wounds. Mixed interaction between humans and animals generates mixed shared meanings with one-sided interpretations of what is shared, since only humans write or talk about it later. Scholars appear comfortable interpreting mixed interaction. It yields well to the anthropocentric perspective of analysts and their audiences.

Today's population and technological developments make transverse interaction increasingly important. Mead told students about the humble ox. An ox's internal "bacteriological laboratory" (1934: 131) is a natural mechanism that physically links the organism with selected elements of natural surroundings, thus constructing a supportive "environment" for that ox-form (1934; 1982: passim). Animals have internal mechanisms enabling them to select their interactive environment out of the physical world. For biologic individuals such as nonsymbol-using oxen, the mechanism is totally in the natural world—physiologically, neurologically, anatomically. For humans, however, selective mechanisms include symbolic constructions that have no evolutionary or natural functional guarantees. Symbols add another level of psychological functionalism to the organism (Cook, 1993). The symbolic realm adds potential infinity and eventual pathos to humanly selected environments. The possibility of dysfunctional or self-destructive interaction that may destroy the ability of the environment to support the interactors' survival also arises. Natural pathos emerges with symbols.

In Mead's example, the ox transforms the brute physicalness of grass into a new object, "grass-as-food." Grass in itself is not food. It becomes food through its physical relationship to an animal with selective impulses toward, and a mechanism for, filling its stomach with grass that it digests and changes into its body. The ox "eats" grass, that is, makes grass into its body, but not intentionally. The ox's supportive environment is realized through an objective perspective and enacted through an interactional mechanism built into oxen without self-awareness on their part.

Symbol-using humans selectively construct their environments through cognitive and emotional processes that guide action on the natural world by transforming it into cultural categories. Grass and hamburger are grasped by organisms and made into oxen or human food for the body. Natural environments are constructed by society and made into suburban lawns and gross national products. Regardless of the symbolic content of cognitive and emotional processes, it is only what we do that gets into the natural stream shaping the empirical future and that sustains the social life generating that future. Actions are fateful in a deeper causal sense than mere ideas or symbols. It is through action that symbol users make the world real, regardless of what they think or intend. Ironic, unforeseen, unintended, and pathetic outcomes of interaction become physical realities—even for self-conscious knowers, sometimes against their own best intentions.

Action is primary in the genesis of the human species and in the probabilities of its survival. Action is the biophysical foundation of human life. Modern life, however, is characterized by technologically extended ways of seeing and acting through powerful and disjunctive instruments. Instruments that break the links between what we see and what is really there take away the tacit or tactile ground for what we think we know. Contemporaries risk losing the tacit dimension of knowing the environment through the senses and their extensions. Compare the cane of the blind walker, glasses for the nearsighted, or hearing aids for the near deaf with the virtual contact of computer simulations. Rather, as exemplified by the reconstruction of sensory similitudes through virtual objects that appear real but have no certain link to the world that is there, moderns believe in a natural reality and, more fateful still, interact with it through instruments that have no direct contact with that world. Increasingly, human actions have effects that many individuals do not know and do not intend, or do know and do not intend but must do, and thus cannot avoid the outcomes they foresee but do not intend. Consider the automobile commuter who wishes she did not have to pollute the air in order to get to work. This systematic interactional dilemma characterizes modern life in developed societies and the plans of developing societies (see "trippers" in chapter 3).

Types of Interaction: A Listing

This section presents a listing of types of interaction to glimpse the scope and to clarify the sense in which I use the term, although the particular nuance emerges from the immediate context. Social scientists widely analyze human communication and interactional patterns, as in studies of families, race relations, or bureaucratic encounters. In spite of its bulk, however, social scientists have overlooked the relevance of Mead's ox and its selective biological mechanisms for interacting with grass and transforming it into grass-as-food. Building on the parallelism of nonsymbolic interaction between biologic individuals and symbolic interaction between self-conscious actors, transverse interaction refers to a universal type of interaction between living forms and the natural environment.

Consider these types of interaction:

Human interacting meaningfully with Human = Symbolic Interaction
Human interacting with Ox = Symbolic-Signal, or Mixed Interaction
Ox interacting with Ox = Non-symbolic or Signal Interaction, e.g., Conversation of Gestures
Human interacting with Environment = Transverse Symbolic Interaction
Ox interacting with Environment = Transverse Signal Interaction
Environment interacting with Environment = Physical Interaction.

The types are listed in analogical order starting with human interactors, rather than in a genetic or evolutionary order. Each type of interaction except the last is part of a social act in the broad sense of interactors forming new objects through impulses, gestures, symbols, and responses. Each interactional order is interpreted as a totality that is studied as an emergent and functioning dynamic among actors that grounds the possibilities of their existence (Mead, 1934: 8; cf. Goffman, 1983). Furthermore, each type of interaction is interrelated with all others in the real world, although analysts perforce must select and abstract aspects of the totality. Eventually, all interaction that concerns immediate human survival constitutes the biosphere, the realm of living dependencies, as far as we know.

Today's awareness is beginning to recognize the wide scope of interaction within the biosphere as the ultimate empirical context for making sense of even our personal lives. The tools for knowing, or more accurately, believing in a total system of interaction and its implications for self and society range from measuring instruments beneath and beyond the earth to imaginative scenarios of temperature and climate change into the next century. Scientists depict scenarios for anticipating actual futures through the same computer potentiality that produces virtual realities with no intended link to tomorrow's conditions.

The primary analogue for a social act is human-human interaction, and the most derived type is organism-environment interaction. Mead states that a social act involves the response of one form to another that shares the same environment. The way interactors share the environment varies significantly with technological transformation of the channels of interaction. Computer technology introduces virtual human-human interaction in which there is no tacit link between self and other. In virtual communication, the body is not available. There is no grounding of personal identity beyond computer visuals that have no validated link to a biological individual. Just as virtual interaction and virtual communities emerge, ecologists and environmental scientists are enlarging our understanding of the real processes linking humans and the natural world. The range of interaction even within each type continues to grow with expanding channels of communication informing social life and more complex ways of collecting and interpreting data about the natural world. Throughout the changes, I emphasize that even social acts performed within a selected environment always have effects beyond it: every animal affects the world that is there, as well as the social life process within which its selectivity primarily operates. Just as human sensation carries more knowledge of the world than senses know, so each action affects the world more than individual or collective actors know.

These are types of social interaction in a broad naturalistic sense. The interacting organism, to the extent that the organism knows anything, is simultaneously two "things" at once—Mead's basic notion of sociality. The organism both is itself interpreting surroundings as signs eliciting its responses, and takes account of the other whose anticipated responses guide the first organism's behavior. The behaving organism, as it were, "takes" the role, attitude, gesture, reaction, or, in general, the anticipated response of the other.

Different terms refer to responses specific to each type of interaction. Physicalistic responses within the world that is there are "reactions," as in physical or chemical reactions. Responses by nonsymbol-using organisms are "behaviors"; those by symbol-using organisms are behaviors-plus-intentions, or "actions." The level of response self must "take" is situationally specific to the type of interaction, for example, the bureaucratic logic of an institution; the role of a social actor; the intending attitude of an individual actor; the gesturing attitude of a nonsymbol-using organism; or the determined physical reaction of an inanimate other. The complexity of human-environment interaction derives from the fact that humans can act toward two or more others at different levels of reality simultaneously. Types of interaction emerge from different objective perspectives on the one natural world that paradoxically grounds many social life processes and from the different social and psychological worlds within which persons live.

Our discussion focuses on human-environment interaction, that is, transverse symbolic interaction, or simply, transverse interaction. Transverse interaction combines categories that scholars usually separate: intentional action and inanimate reaction; assumed freedom and a realm of determinism; individual response and systemic interaction; personal motives and institutional logics; the social life process and the world that is there. Looked at through a physical frame, such interaction falls within the natural science of ecology. Seen through a symbolic frame, it falls within the disciplines that study human constructions of reality and motives, for example, individual and social psychology, anthropology, and in general, the semiotic and social disciplines. This book moves toward an ecological social psychology, that is, a study of ways in which humans frame and interpret their relationships with the natural environment (Catton and Dunlap, 1978; Howard, 1993).

An Interactional Other Codefines Meaning

The idea of transverse interaction helps us interpret the ways we speak about and act toward the environment. Mead, for example, saw the engineer as an exemplar of rational human-environment interaction. Imagine an engineer designing a bridge that will physically do what bridges are supposed to do even though the engineer is neither a bridge, nor the outcropping of rock over the river, nor the feet or wheels that will cross the bridge. Yet, the successful engineer somehow takes the attitude of all of these simultaneously if that bridge is to span the river while walkers and wheels cross over. As Mead said:

> An engineer who is constructing a bridge is talking to nature in the same sense that we talk to an engineer. There are stresses and strains there which he meets, and nature comes back with other responses that have to be met in another way. *In his thinking he is taking the attitude of physical things.* He is talking to nature and nature is replying to him. (1934: 185, italics added)

We continue the engineer's discussion with nature whenever we cross the bridge, perhaps with a touch of fear as we wonder whether it is like the Bridge of San Luis Rey.

Although we too address physical things at times (Cohen, 1989), such interaction does not imply that we or the engineer are hearing voices. Communicating is an activity before it is a vocality. What we do becomes what we communicate. Thus do nature's reactions "tell us" what we are doing. Meaning is in nature more basically than it is in symbols. Indeed, the temporal lag between humanly intended outcomes and nature's reactions, as well as differences between intention and responses, make it difficult in practice and impossible in principle for us to know all the natural meanings of our actions. Hence the ever-present pathos of interaction in which we do more than we intend. Society's laws and social graces recognize this gap. Sometimes society holds us responsible for outcomes we did not intend by declaring us "negligent," that is, failing at foresight that a normal person is legally expected to have. Social disclaimers and excuses right the wrongs committed in the social life process, but they are literally meaningless within the physical world. Nature is unforgiving in the face of interactional pathos: it reacts to what we do regardless of what we intend. This truism gains importance each time we flip a switch.

Transverse interaction engages us with an environmental other. To understand self conceptually and empirically, it is necessary to develop the other engaged in the interaction (Hughes, 1962). Scholars have studied various others such as: generalized, significant, reference, authoritative, intimate, confirming, labelling, victimizing, oppressive. Each particular other, with the structured exception of the generalized other, is usually taken to be another symbol-using individual on an analytic par with the self. Self and other, then, are often taken as interpretive pairs on the same level of symbolic use, like two humans.

The environmental other in transverse interaction, however, exists at two levels. It comes to us, first, as a *constructed* other, that is, a perceptual object seen from self's perspective looking through cultural lenses. Self anticipates a constructed environment's reactions by analogy with taking the role of human others and expecting them to respond in typical ways as they normally do. The environment, however, is also a *nonconstructed* other that reacts through naturalistic causal patterns that are only partially seen through cultural lenses (cf. Greider and Garkovich, 1994; McCarthy, 1984). A crucial aspect of contemporary environmental awareness is that constructed meanings increasingly include physical "substructured" meanings that are foundational to symbolic meanings. Here is the rub that makes transverse interaction both so crucial to modern life and so difficult to analyze: it is interaction constituted by both conscious and nonconscious others; by both symbolic and physical processes, each with partial functional autonomy and no guarantee of harmony, indeed with growing evidence of conflict; and by centaurlike configurations of meaning that combine symbolic and physiconatural meanings.

As we learn to see symbolic-natural meanings with reference to particular environmental others like my lawn or the local landfill, the realization grows that the environment, writ large, is common to all of us. That is, we come to see a Generalized Environmental Other as the counterpart to the human species, indeed, to all living beings. We gain a more complete social self when we take the role of the organized responses of a community. Self knows a Generalized Social Other by anticipating the organized responses of collectivities or institutions, such as the responses of players on a "baseball nine" to a squeeze bunt. Transverse interaction reveals self in relation to a "Generalized Environmental Other," or GEO. Humans have long believed in holistic views of physical reality, that is, some form of a GEO. Within western history, there are religiously based GEOs from the vaulted cosmos of the ancient Hebrews to the divinely bounded spheres of Greek religions. Outside of western traditions, vivid cosmological myths picture the origins, design, and destiny of the universe precariously balanced on the back of a turtle, elephant, or Atlas himself. These views of the physical universe are now discarded as primitive, religious, mythic, erroneous, or in general, prescientific.

Even scientific worldviews change profoundly, however, as instruments for knowing and interacting with the earth change. Scientific views of the universe have changed from static concentric spheres to Ptolemaic wheels to exploding and imploding gases in an ever expanding spatial medium. Today, we see the earth simultaneously within different and often competing frames. A dominant frame is that of optimistic technological and scientific rationality summarized in the ideas of Progress and Control. Progress and Control are enlightenment beliefs about the universe according to which we increasingly intervene in nature and nature continuously supports this intervening species ever more comfortably—no matter what it does. Followers of

Progress and Control find support in their version of Darwinian evolutionism through "struggles for survival" and the resulting "survival of the fittest."

At first glance, moderns can congratulate themselves for being the fittest, since obviously they survived. Understanding evolutionary dynamics, however, includes ecological ways of seeing. The idea of Progress is limited in a powerful way, namely, the "fittest" are defined in terms of *dependency* on the precarious sustainability of environments. The realization dawned that in trying to control nature, humans may transform their environment in far-reaching ways that have unknown links to supporting human life. Breakdown in life-support systems of air, water, or soil would render humans "unfit." Such breakdowns, paradoxically, could result from our interventions into those life-support systems. Ecological biology carries a cautionary and perhaps pessimistic message for believers in unlimited intervention in pursuit of Progress and Control. For such believers, it is a "dismal science" (Worster, 1977).

In an ecological framework, the earth is known or believed in as a biosphere, that is, a functioning set of systems that support life, including human life. No one has direct sensory or empirical access to the biosphere; no one of us as an individual citizen directly knows the biosphere. It is not an object that we can hold in our hands or line of sight. The biosphere, like heaven or hell, is a faith object. But unlike heaven or hell, it is a faith object linked to us through chains of data and measuring instruments. We know it on the basis of our trust in systems of knowledge, networks of experts, and media that tell us about data generated by scientific communities. The recent development of ecological and environmental sciences (McIntosh, 1986; Miller, 1994) underwrites belief in the physical reality of a biosphere. Indeed, belief in the biosphere realizes a generalized physical other in relation to which we are developing a new sense of self (see chapter 7). A decisive moment for this new self is acceptance of a Generalized Environmental Other like a biosphere that supports the human species. In a word, we now have a new psychological and moral responsibility to choose whether to believe in a generalized environmental other that is adequate to our sense of who we are as moral environmental actors.

GEO is constructed through our internalized patterns of anticipated environmental reactions to individual and collective actions. GEO includes both humanly constructed symbolic meanings and naturally given environmental meanings. We define symbolic meanings however we want. Naturalistic meanings, however, are the objects of ceaseless searching. Our challenge is to construct symbolic meanings that adequately fit and grasp the ever-changing date on the environment. Rather than take a symbolic turn toward the constructed meanings of transverse interaction, I turn to the naturalistic meanings. Reactions by environmental others continually modify the symbolic meanings of what we do. Just as interaction implies one or more relevant others, so too, each interaction generates different kinds of meaning such as personal, generalized, or species meaning. The species meaning of millions of car exhaust systems goes beyond the personal meaning of each driver's intention. Meaning is not solely grounded in intentional or symbolic meanings, such as intended market profits for transnational corporations or the individual rationality of commuting to work. It also derives from the cumulative, even if unintended, impact of burned gas on atmospheric carbon levels. That is, our actions impact environmental others, known and unknown.

For a larger authentic self to emerge from transverse interaction, a modern person must take the role of the anticipated reactions of relevant natural systems, that is, self must know and respond to a GEO. The powerful consequences of human-environment interaction make it increasingly salient to, if not definitive of, social life. Walking across a natural meadow is a different social act than spraying pesticides on our lawn or, at the extreme, launching nuclear missiles from a command silo. What is similar is that each action, regardless of actors' intentions or knowledge, impacts on the world that is there. Social meanings inform individual actions and thus render them real and normal. Nature's reactions to us, on the other hand, are real in themselves through their effects on human life even before we impose social meanings to render them secondarily meaningful to us. The sum of all actions and reactions make up the physical world that we grasp as GEO. The key question is, Can actions rational within the social life process be irrational within the objective perspective of the world that is there? To the degree that the answer is "Yes" or "Maybe," the question points to a crisis, that is, a critical juncture of meaning. We need to relate symbolic and natural meanings to address this critical issue and choose how to act.

Scholars of the symbolic and affective meanings of built urban environments and of the "daydreams and nightmares" regarding the natural environment help us integrate transverse interaction within larger social actions (Firey, 1945; Burch, 1971). Newer perspectives such as "critical animism" and "topistics" show how subjective and emotional meanings are projected onto things and rooted in physical surroundings (Rochberg-Halton, 1986; Walter, 1988). We do find meanings in objects like furniture, photos, houses, cars, caves, trees, landscapes, and mountains. In such interactions, self embraces physical things within life's projects and bestows vital meaning on them. Our physical surroundings become a "furniture of the self" for living meaningfully (Erikson, 1976). Biologists argue that the long evolution of the human species formed genetically based affective ties between humans and natural others, that is, we have an inherited love of life's forms or "biophilia" (Wilson, 1984).

These new perspectives underline the significance of natural meanings for an adequate understanding of human life.

Understanding transverse interaction generalizes biologically selected environments such as the ox's grass-as-food to include symbolically selected human environments ranging from "thing-as-my-consumable-resource" to "thing-as-species-life-support-system." The biological *Umwelt* of natural meaning for animals is incorporated into the transformative power of the symbolic *Lebenswelt* of constructed meanings for human animals. There are no ironclad guarantees that symbolic worlds will sustain biological ones, or that our social life process will sustain the world that has been there for us.

Fitting Natural and Social Meanings Together: Irony and Image

The partial autonomy of physical versus symbolic interaction generates paradox. Rational and desired acts can cause negative physical reactions. In using, we destroy usable energy; in producing, we make toxic waste; in consuming, we destroy the consumed object; in living, we threaten life-support systems. Ironies follow the actions through which we give meaning to self and other. Institutional logics pursue actions that threaten the environments that support them and the communities that birth us. An interactional paradigm explicitly recognizes positive and negative outcomes; it builds understanding by making us aware of previously hidden physical outcomes.

✓ Environment-as-system is a constructed faith symbol that informs the selective perception of human knowers. In the currently dominant cultural paradigm, this cultural selectivity works toward legitimating lifestyles of production and consumption. The environmental challenge, on the other hand, focuses on sustainability. We need to locate both human responsive gestures and cumulative reactions of the natural environment in relevant temporal and causal frameworks. Environmental meanings are both within the time-action frames of individual intentions and social institutions and, more telling, within the time-reaction frames of natural physical processes. It may take generations, for example, to assess organic reactions to food additives or radioactive waste. The constructed times of symbolic interaction remain dependent on physical and geological times. The latter set the limits for human viability. Time frames are asymmetrical and potentially contradictory, like seeking freedom to consume now but facing the determinism of famine later, or desired nuclear energy now and undesired threat from radioactive waste for a foreseeable future.

We need to constantly remind ourselves that meaning is in nature both before and after it is in symbols. In taking the attitude—an imagined incipient or truncated response—of nature, we, like engineers, anticipate and participate in nature's reactions to our interventions. We grasp nature's reactions through vivid affective imagery or rationalized abstract constructs. Both are needed. Imagery carries emotional weight; constructs allow instrumental manipulation. Interaction is affective and cognitive, processual and emergent. Images and constructs function in all phases of the social act: impulse, perception, manipulation, and consummation.

A critical question is whether nature's responses to our interaction are "functional" for us. That is, will nature continue to sustain human life as we want it, no matter what we do? Are our images and constructs physically adaptive; do they bestow an evolutionary advantage; do they sustain our social life within nature? These are questions many scholars appear to beg or simply assume, perhaps because of optimistic evolutionary views. I believe that there is no evolutionary necessity that the images and constructs underlying human-environment interaction lead to adaptive or cooperative interaction with nature. Nor is there any assurance that the empirically most likely futures implicated in our actions are the same that inform our images and motives. Without our knowledge or intention, we are projecting some mythic, counterfactual, and destructive imagined futures in a "future perfect tense" so that they function as purposive motives guiding our action (Schutz, 1962). We may be forging a future that is not part of our intentions or images. Environmental science suggests alternative imagined futures to complement inherited images of Progress and Control.

Changing Frames for Seeing the Environment

Environmental scholars argue that the images of today's world point to new paradigms for what we see and how we act. Among sociologists, a "new environmental paradigm" posits the dependency of human life on the physical environment versus the "human exemptionalist paradigm" that analyzes society apart from its relationship to nature (Catton, 1994; Catton and Dunlap, 1978; Dunlap and Catton, 1983). In addition to scientific paradigms, cultural value systems need imagery adequate to symbolic and physical interaction. Transverse interaction is basic to the development of both new ecological paradigms for social science and new imagery for everyday motivation. Along with the socially constructed "facticities" of life, we need the physical "facts" of environmental responses as best these can be estimated. On this dual foundation rests our chances for "envisioning a sustainable society" (Milbrath, 1989).

Modern leaders, however, typically use counterfactual imagined futures built on mythic ideologies of unlimited material consumption, ever-rising standards of living, total free market functionality, increasing populations, and the assumed taken-for-granted viability of life-support systems. Inglehart

(1990) documents distinctions between traditional materialist and emergent postmaterialist value configurations that divide First-World cultural attitudes and the perceptions of older and younger generations. Older First-World political leaders tend to favor policies grounded in Progress and Control images of the future. Inglehart suggests that societies are approaching limits of physical sustainability faster than younger generations can move into leadership positions. There is a cultural and socialization lag in leadership during periods of rapid social and environmental change. As a result, nations are ruled by leaders who came of age "worlds" ago and who often do not adequately frame environmental issues. Leaders who grew up in an age of Progress and Control are not likely to see the world through an ecological framework.

Social action, especially technological intervention, is characterized by the historical irony of unintended or unforeseen outcomes. The future we build through collective action may not be willed by any individual, planned by any social agency, nor included in any institutional policies. No one explicitly intends climatic change, soil degradation, increasing toxicity, thinning ozone, growing garbage, or species extinction. Many ignore, others decry, these dawning images.

Empirically grounded, species-sustaining imagery challenges ideologically functionalist interpretations of human evolution or co-evolution as though human history were outside yet in tandem with biological evolution. Oppositional social movements generate different readings of environmental concerns. From highly bureaucratized environmental organizations with Washington offices alongside equally bureaucratized government and business offices to neighborhood groups protesting a toxic landfill, industrialized societies feature a range of environmental movements and organizations. Indeed, the patent irony of human exemptionalist thinking contradicts an overly literal reading of George H. Mead's comment that the human capacity to build environments spells "an end to the process of organic evolution" (1934: 252). Organic evolution does not end. It is not replaced by sociocultural or technological processes. It continues apace, even quickening, though not only along lines of natural physical processes, but also along channels of constructed technological intervention. Humans are speaking in more powerful engineering languages, and the natural environment is answering in more challenging systemic reactions.

Which Knowledge? The Imperative to Choose an Adequate Frame for Seeing the Environment

The bacteriological laboratory in an ox stomach is not my primary concern, though eating is an issue. Rather, I focus on the epistemological laboratory in collective and individual minds that fashions what we think we know. Today's frameworks for knowing are increasingly abstracted and mediated through technological channels. What urban moderns who rarely walk on soil take as the environment is derived from cultural and institutional versions of what is physically out there. Institutions increasingly do our thinking about, or at least framing of, what we take to be the natural world (Douglas, 1986). Institutionalized frames add great scope and power to merely individual perception, but they also "uncouple" or disengage thinking from the tacit knowledge carried by direct manipulation or instrumental contact with the physical world. The farmer spraying herbicides from a tank has different sensory contact with soil than one spreading cow manure from a barn.

Consider the kind of knowledge available to members of traditional cultures before the spread of transformative technologies. Members of traditional cultures grounded their world in tacit knowledge carried by the senses and assimilated without explicit attention to the constructed nature of what they took as known. Moderns and postmoderns, on the other hand, are deeply aware of the contingent knowledge we have of nature through its many mediations. Contrast the tacit knowledge carried to a blind person by the fingers, hand, arm, and bodily propriosensation via a responsive metal tipped cane with the virtual knowledge carried to a sighted modern with gloves and goggles mediating a world constructed with software images. In the latter case, there is *no* tacit knowledge of the physical world.

Virtual reality is a primary analog for technologically mediated links to environments, links that have broken tacit and sensory channels between the embodied knower and the physical world. Technology provides instruments for interacting with the environment and measuring the outcomes of such interaction. It both breaks the tacit knowledge link with nature and offers powerful instruments through which we indirectly role take nature to anticipate its likely responses to our interventions. Specialists feed growing bodies of data into models for depicting scenarios of future worlds we are fashioning through present actions. Burning fossil fuels is linked to buildup of carbon dioxide in the atmosphere causing rising temperatures and changing weather-precipitation patterns that may raise ocean levels and change agricultural zones. Such a scenario provides different potential meanings to the people of an island nation that will be o'erwashed by the ocean or prairie nations needing rain to feed its people.

Modern societies need more technology for data gathering and interpretation to make policy, and modern individuals need sufficient awareness of such knowledge to live a moral lifestyle. As environmental "laypersons," moderns depend on faith in specialists' knowledge and in the media through which knowledge becomes available. Once again, we as moderns depend on secular faith in those we decide to trust concerning the world in which we believe we live. The rupture between the signified world and the signifier transforms realistic representation into mere similitude. It introduces a crisis of authority in what we see as real and believe as moral (Baudrillard, 1981). This rupture deepens the "heretical" imperative mentioned earlier: moderns must choose which technological and institutional constructions of the real world they believe or even believe they actually see.

Environmental others are constructs, that is, mental groupings selected from nature and symbolically transformed into perceived objects toward which we act. There are three phases in the act that direct subsequent social acts: handling the constructed object, or manipulation; interpretively sensing the meaning of the object, or perception; and final disposition of the object, or consummation (Mead, 1934). The potential opposition between individually intended versus collectively caused outcomes of action generates a contradiction at the heart of consummation: an individual's aesthetic and rational consumption may contribute to destructive collective outcomes.

Our spontaneous impulses are well shod by the time we become adults. They are typically overlaid with a second nature for handling objects, namely, habits and customs that structure responses to others' expectations or provide accounts for seeing self as moral and normal. I emphasize perception, that phase of the social act so crucial for symbol-using persons and so dominated by symbol-making institutions. What we take to be normal everyday realities, both those we know as symbols and those we see as natural, are products of artful social practices that make up the object and make it appear typical (Garfinkel, 1967). By analogy with the ox's natural bacteriological laboratory that turns mere grass into food for organic hunger impulses, human interaction is a dramatic social laboratory that turns mere grass into lawns for status hunger impulses (chapter 5). The pathos of human-environment interaction shines through intended status-seeking that leads to unintended pollution through actions motivated by institutional advertising, cultural coding, and neighbors' evaluations of lawn manicure and color.

Everyday routines are based on taken-for-granted knowledge and shared frames that produce an apparently natural way of seeing and thinking. As Alfred Schutz put it, everyday activities follow "recipe" knowledge, a kind of cultural cookbook for acting out my identity through tactful interaction with artful others who play parts precariously intertwined with mine. The complex and increasing number of "trippers," that is, technological instruments for tripping environmental outcomes, show the power of recipe knowledge (chapter 3). There is no need to be an electrical engineer to turn on the kitchen light or start the car. The electrical engineer may know how to "talk" with nature, but all I need to know is the recipe for flipping the light switch on the kitchen wall. Flip the switch and light the light. Recipes tell us how to make the instrument work, even though we do not know why it works nor what the environmental outcomes are. Everyday frames and recipes put the rest of reality out of frame and thus out of mind.

A principle of social stratification is that recipe knowledge like all "stocks of knowledge" is functionally organized and unequally distributed in society (Berger and Luckmann, 1966). So too, definitions of self, our personal identities, are socially distributed and plausibly presented in recipes and stocks of knowledge (Weigert et al, 1986). Widely differentiated knowledge of self, society, and nature are characteristic of complex societies. Mutually untranslatable bodies of knowledge grow exponentially in differentiated "disciplines" with uncertain reference to physical contact with the environment. Modern occupational identities are fashioned, not primarily by what a person does physically, but by what that person knows and does symbolically. In a traditional or craft-based society, a shoemaker is different from a blacksmith by what he does based on what he knows how to do with leather or iron; his knowledge is more than head stuff, it is in habituated eyes that see and hands that turn physical things. It is based on tacit knowledge for manipulating the physical world.

In a postindustrial society, an activist environmental scholar and an international financial broker may both sit in front of video display terminals working the computer to make risky and hopefully profitable decisions. In a basic sense, both are doing the same thing with their fingers and eyes directed at similar tools, but each knows different head stuff. The shoemaker is clearly distinguished from the scholar by recipe and tacit knowledge of different things. The scholar, however, is better distinguished from the broker by different recipes of concepts that package what we take to be knowledge: paradigms, principles, rules of thumb, proverbial wisdom, ideologies, and arrays of empirical "facts," real only within the worlds of environmental policy or capital markets.

Today's world is postmodern in the sense that we are increasingly surrounded by "hyper" and virtual realities (Baudrillard, 1981; Rheingold, 1993). Symbols, signs, simulacra, or electronic images replace sensory or tacit contact with physical things. Modern warfare, for example, is played at computer screens and digital readouts for guiding smart bombs, just like computer games in the mall arcade. Contrast this with bloody bayonets or recoiling rifles that pierce bodies in full view. The greater the physical and symbolic distance between self and other, the more likely we will act violently toward the other (Milgram, 1975). This break between perception and the physical world indicates a profound change in knowledge of and action toward what we take to be the real world in which we walk, talk, eat, and breathe.

Specialized knowledge recipes exist in different languages, conversations, and thought. As a result, persons in the know live in different worlds with different universes of discourse through which they select their surroundings for constructing lives as they think they know them. Acting within their recipes of knowledge, they *realize* their lives in the dual sense of making them real and knowing them as real. Their taken-for-granted language and knowledge gives an unquestioned "accent of reality" to what they do and who they are, a warrant for believing themselves and their actions moral and normal. What is more normal than turning on a car or flipping on a light? What separate recipes leave out is the fact that individual acts are linked to collective problems. In spite of the growth in scientific knowledge, everyday knowledge and top-level policy decisions are still partially uninformed by ecological recipes for interacting with the world that is there.

Socially specialized and virtual head stuff deals in abstract knowledge. Such knowledge is not embedded in the body or in nature. Socially significant knowledge often says nothing of its empirical outcomes that could be fatal or fertile. Social significance is increasingly linked to technological means to intervene in the world that is there. Virtual analogues of the world leave knowers literally homeless and placeless, so they are likely to overlook environmental outcomes (Meyrowitz, 1985). Furthermore, specialized knowledge structures preclude knowing objects as total things. Through the prismed mosaic of specialized perspectives, we do not see the environmental other nor GEO. Ecological forms of knowledge, on the other hand, include a focus on the link between social significance and ever deeper interventions in the environment as a system.

The pragmatic axiom that meaning is in the responses of self and other applies to transverse interaction as well, and with wide implications. Humans anticipate natural responses through socially constructed interpretations of environmental others, not through first-hand knowledge of the brute physical others. Constructed environmental others are seen through socialized lenses and realized in normal behaviors. We anticipate environmental responses based on the processes we assume determine those responses. If faced with a stream punctuated by flat rocks, I assume that a rock is what a rock does so slowly that I anticipate its hardness as I step on it to cross the stream. Yet, rocks do crumble; the earth does quake; and rocklike plates move continents, though we never see them move. Clay, on the other hand, responds differently; and I must be aware of its interaction with rain to know that it can suddenly turn mercurial and slide me and my home down the mountainside.

Californians living atop mountainside clay or astride a geological fault transform anticipated natural movements into reasonable accounts to convince themselves and others that it is normal to go on living where they are. Transverse interaction acquires meaning through accounts that apply acceptable reasons to our responses in problematic situations. Rational accounts announce how problematic transverse interaction is transformed into normal and moral action. An interactionist paradigm focuses on the rationalities found in accounts of meaningful actions. Rational accounts underwrite normal attitudes toward environment others.

Accounts are verbal constructions that function as frames for perception (Lyman and Scott, 1970). We see the world the way we talk and thus think about it. The world *is* as we can *explain* it to self and others. Accounts, then, are verbal frames constructed *for* both self and other symbol users. In addition, accounts tell us *about* nonsymbol users and the brute physical world in our everyday interaction. Prayers *for* and *to* a deity assumed to be a symbol user like us may be *about* the deity, physical others, or other humans. We may pray *to* the deity *about* rain or sun *for* ourselves or others. Accounts are also *for* self and symbol-using others who may need protection, consoling, exhortation, or salvation. Magical rituals are meaningful actions to the shaman and clients for gaining a sense of control over life's risks. What is rational for the person in the situation is displayed in the accounts given in explanatory narratives. Of course, what is rational for self may be foolish to the other.

Each of us must ask of self, Which narratives do I accept as the best or most likely accounts for grasping natural meanings implicated in my life and the lives of others? In environmental discourse, for example, there are divergent accounts. "Cornucopians" argue the earth can support higher standards of living for ever-increasing populations of humans, so humans should continue increasing and conduct business as usual. "Doomsayers" argue that human intervention in life-support systems has already damaged them beyond their capability to regenerate, so that we are already short of clean energy, air, water, and soil, and thus faced with population "diebacks."

Accounts that we are willing to accept as rational typically contain justifications for continuing interaction until further notice. Accounts even become personal motives when approved by networks of confirming others, such as neighbors who share accounts for living in houses astride the geological fault, or fellow peasants fighting for subsistence by burning rainforests, or fellow executives arranging cute advertising for attracting youthful smokers, or sister travelers breathing the air downwind from Gary, Indiana, on Spaceship Earth. Yet, the social rationality of accounts may mask irrational outcomes, mythical historical genesis, and situationally limited applicability. Accounts change as historical contexts change. They are not always and everywhere useful. Interactional rationality is a contingent sociohistorical construction rebuilt in response to each epoch's challenges. Only through continual reconstruction do humans keep a sense of control over their lives. Today, that sense is unveiled as itself a social psychological construction with mixed chances of sustaining itself through uncertain links to environmental life-support systems.

A sense of meaning and control in our lives is a basic psychological function of culture realized in narratives about how we think the world works and how we relate to it. My life makes sense and my actions are meaningful because I believe what my culture tells me—or in a pluralistic society like ours, what my subculture tells me. On the other hand, technology is the instrument for making the physical world satisfy cultural needs over and above mere subsistence levels of calories, air, water, and shelter. Contemporary culture is dominated by accounts justifying technological intervention for Progress and Control for greater comfort and pleasure. Like all narratives, these are subject to re-sighting through frameworks that highlight new links between cultural and physical meanings. International surveys document the recent rise of environmental issues around the world in the mere blink of an historical eye. Environmental data flow rapidly along worldwide information highways. Real local problems like water shortages, famine, pollution, and crop or forest death arise ever more widely and quickly. Local problems linked with data about similar problems around the world fuel reconsideration of conventional cultural accounts for addressing energy, food, air, and water. Facts are integrated into patterns that are linked to values.

The contingency of what we take as rational accounts is hidden by their unquestioned normality as unexamined truth wrapped in statements such as, "Of course, that's the way it is." "Of course" statements have the massive efficacy of what every normal person believes (Berger, 1963). They are recipes for living because persons believe in them, even though we have no scientific understanding why. Social status recipes, for example, tell us that it is reasonable, indeed good, to buy a suburban house; surround it with that creation of the last thirty years, a chemically dependent "lawn"; and do a daily solo car-commute to work. Transverse interaction sensitizes us to question such recipes.

So What If We See Through a Transverse Interaction Frame?

A transverse interaction frame helps us re-sight the symbolic and physical outcomes of our actions. New accounts and their recipes motivate us to realign our actions based on recognition of environmental others (Stokes and Hewitt, 1976). In a word, we need new everyday accounts for transverse interaction. Such accounts lead to theoretical and empirical interrogation of environmental others with ideas such as self-other interaction, ecosystems, role-taking the natural world, and re-aligning our actions toward that world.

To these ends, I re-affirm the centrality of Mead's pragmatic lemma that meaning is *in nature*. This lemma starts with the fundamental given of living beings: life depends on support systems of water, food, temperature, energy, oxygen, carbon, nitrogen, etc. Natural meanings always, everywhere, and necessarily ground social and symbolic meanings. Social meanings exist, as it were, only within a spacesuit or spaceship, that is, within a narrow band of the tremendous range of physico-chemico-bio variations that exist in the cosmos. A few miles difference in the earth's distance from the sun or a small shift in the acidity of water would eliminate many life forms. Recognizing realist limits prevents analysts from a linguistic turn into the symbolic fallacy that reduces meaning to semiotic structures, contingent cultures, or virtual universes. Models for seeing must include and interpret the best available data—a never-ending dialectic (Wiman, 1991). Social life is indeed illuminated by thinking of it as text, and our understanding of action gains in depth and clarity if translated as a narrative. Text and narrative, however, are realized through actions with outcomes beyond merely symbolic communication. Dramaturgical and interactional analysts insist that action is primary and that interaction not only communicates but always does something to others.

A transverse interaction perspective underlines the importance of *grounding intentional and interactional meanings of the social life process in the natural meanings generated within the physical world.* Contemporary selves and societies need to see their actions within the natural meanings needed for existence. Social meanings must clarify and integrate natural meanings in sustainable ways. Competent moral selves know how to interpret their actions within the social life process as meaningful interaction, thus sustaining their normalcy. In addition, humans have usually but not always understood social meanings in ways that sustain the ecosystem supporting their society. The BaMbuti pygmies have lived over four thousand years in the Ituri rainforest. If long-term sustainability were the measure of a cultures's success, the pygmies would be running for first place. Sustaining the supportive ecosystem is an imperative for every society, including our own. Civilizations disappear when they destroy their supportive ecosystem.

For the first time in history, modern selves are self-consciously aware of the need to analyze their actions as transverse interaction within the world that is there for *all* humans. One of the outcomes of ever deepening technology, wider and faster communication highways, growing populations, and expanding markets is to make local ecosystem societies into worldwide *biospheric* societies. Global organization, accumulation of greater numbers of individual acts, and deeper technological interventions into the life-support systems make each of us a contributor to worldwide environmental changes. The accumulation of actions like starting my car, spraying my lawn with toxics, leaking chlorofluorocarbons (CFCs) from my air conditioner, or cutting my trees affects the conditions for human survival around the earth. Moderns are learning to think in terms of collective outcomes from cumulative actions of ever-growing numbers of individuals.

For just a moment, it is interesting to reflect on political and economic talk about one world governance for solving shared problems, a new world order based on negotiation and trade, and a world market with perhaps a world, or at least a European, currency. Environmental awareness and an ecological perspective suggests that there is a prior unity upon which institutions from nation-states to economic markets depend even as they change it. The human species, through the cumulative impact of billions of independent decisions and close to two hundred national policies and unknown numbers of entrepreneurial decisions, today affects the state of its own life-support systems. Humanly caused changes in global life-support systems, or "anthropogenic global environmental change," is now recognized as a major factor affecting the biosphere (Dunlap and Catton, 1994; Porter and Brown, 1996). The reality of a unified biosphere is that it makes each of us, no matter how small our causal impact, an intervener in the life chances of other living beings. How to construct new ways of intervening without threatening species sustainability, including our own, is one challenge of human-environment interaction today.

Fortunately, constructed shared meanings normally make it possible for most of us to interact in dramaturgically successful ways within the social life process. Less happily, humans collectively have sometimes been unable to live sustainably within their ecosystems, as may have been the case with the Maya, the Anasazi, Easter Island inhabitants, and the great migrations that shaped early Europe (Ponting, 1991). More recently, environmental degradation was a powerful factor in the social unrest that led to the breakup of the Soviet Union (Feshbach and Friendly, 1992). Analysts see environmental sustainability as a serious challenge to new nations in the developing world and to the politics of the First World.

The question of environmental sustainability is now raised not only for single societies, but for the human species itself. In other words, moderns face not only the crash of local ecosystems supporting a particular society, like the pygmies or the native tribes of the Amazon rain forests whose cultures will disappear if the forests are destroyed, but also the possible crash of biospheric systems that support societies everywhere. A contemporary global challenge is to recognize that there is as yet no one world order of social meanings guaranteeing that human-environment interaction will sustain human life.

An evolutionary truism is that significantly changed environments lead to species extinction. Evolution teaches that forms of life emerge and become extinct in relation to their environments. It does not teach that a form of life is guaranteed survival. Survival is a probabilistic population outcome, and the probabilities change with changes in the environment. A contrary cultural truism is that human history is continual Progress and Control. Paradigm blinders led many social thinkers away from the now obvious question whether humanly transformed environments might destroy the capacity of their ecosystems to support humans. This question leads us to assess the often competing claims about the outcomes of transverse interaction and translate our assessments into personal lifestyles and institutional policies. Understanding transverse interaction means understanding the production, distribution, and interpretation of specialized knowledge and believable narratives about our relationship with the physical world. New environmental sciences are emerging to fill in holistic understanding of nature by constructing an integrated frame for seeing environmental reactions to human intervention (Miller, 1994). The postmodern critique of what individuals believe about scientific knowledge puts responsibility for reasonable action beyond personal expertise. Yet, adequate empirical knowledge is crucial for defining right action with environmental others.

A third implication of systemic interactional meanings is *the necessity for relating to a Generalized Environmental Other (GEO) in order to act meaningfully as a total self in the modern world.* Just as Mead argued for the social psychological necessity of a Generalized Social Other, that is, internalization of organized community responses to form a moral and normal social self, so too, we posit the necessity of thinking in terms of a GEO: an integrated set of internalized expectations of the systemic reactions of the natural world to individual and collective action. Even cursory consideration of this issue raises profound questions. GEO presents us with an other that transcends the institutional logics, geographical boundaries, and life-support policies of dominant social organizations and conventional motives for acting. A systemic understanding of environmental dynamics rests on a paradox: specialized scientific paradigms for knowing the environment turn that physical reality into a faith object for most of us. Moderns may accept the reality of a biosphere or ecosystem through an act of faith in those scientists we are willing to believe. We are used to believing in scientific objects that we have never seen, like atoms, molecules, bacteria, viruses, and a host of incredibly *small* objects. In the case of the environment and life-support systems, we believe in scientific objects that are *too large* for us to see, like carbon cycles, ecosystems, radioactive clouds, a biosphere—a bit like our belief in an international money market. Once we believe in a biosphere or ecosystem, we see different meanings in everyday interactions with the physical environment. We reconstruct routine actions like spraying the lawn, turning on a light, or starting the car.

The reality of a Generalized Environmental Other calls for reconstruction of our actions as citizens of nation states, buyers and sellers in markets, consumers of products, producers of children, and in general, moral actors in today's world. Moral consciousness and our relationships to the physical environment are mutually involved in social reconstruction (Mead, 1964: 90). The challenge presented by transverse interaction as a sensitizing concept is that it enables us better to see what we are doing individually, organizationally, and collectively. With sharper insight, we can act with greater moral realism and work to reform institutional imperatives, motivational accounts, and interactional patterns to sustain earthly patterns that sustain us. Once we learn to see ourselves as transverse interactors, we see through issues like those in the following chapters. The next chapter, for example, takes us through ways of talking and thinking about what we mean when we say "environment," and what we think are the meanings of a governor of California's official proclamation, "The drought is over."

2

Which Natural Environment
Do We See?

The issue is simple: What does our social psychological perspective contribute to understanding contemporary human-natural environment relationships? The response is a complex and even incomplete examination of what passes for truth about the environment from individual and social sources. This chapter focuses on social meanings of transverse interaction and builds an analytic perspective on those meanings. The foundation of both the analytic perspective and the meanings is organism-environment interaction. Given our perspective, the focus shifts from organism-*natural* environment interaction to self-*symbolic* environment interaction. I think of persons as a tense dualism: the natural biologic individual and the social symbolic self. For human eyes, then, the natural environment, as known and acted upon, takes on the dualism of being socially constructed and physically given. Even what we take as the physical world includes both built and natural objects.

Humans have different meanings for the term *natural environment* as an object of knowledge and action. Differences call for analyses and syntheses; otherwise they generate fruitless struggle and mutual misunderstanding. For example, both a religious believer worried about eternal life and an ecologist analyzing hydrological cycles thinks about objects that they cannot see or point to, nor can they express them in a shared discourse. Yet, a religious ecologist who believes in both can try to synthesize them within one interpretive framework (Berry, 1988). Sociology of knowledge helps us understand how partial frameworks affect us and others who use them to interpret events differently. It clarifies how we came to know, talk about, and routinize what we take to be real, just as others do, but with different outcomes. Such clarification is a first step toward synthesis or at least shared understanding.

An interactionist perspective rests on a realist dimension: different kinds of interaction generate partial verbal accounts that grasp aspects of the natural environment. It is imperative that persons who claim to know accurately and to act morally take responsibility for stating whom and what they believe about the environment and how their beliefs inform their actions. Furthermore, interactional analysis focuses special attention on actions that are problematic and on the accounts persons give to explain problematic actions. Accounts point to identities and motives that give moral meaning to our lives.

The first section of this chapter explores meanings of the phrase *natural environment* and ways in which we make these meanings real by talking about them. In the next section, these distinctions are applied to authors who represent the natural environment as a whole or system. Such representations are crucial beliefs, since holistic knowledge of the environment is both needed today and in need of credible ideas. The environment as a totality forever remains a faith object. No one ever sees the total environment. No one manipulates, knows, or interacts with the environment as a whole. Immediate questions are, Says who? and Who benefits from what is said? Who constructs that holistic version of the environment I am willing to believe and act upon?

The constructionist angle highlights the social dimension of what we take to be real, and the pragmatic aspect highlights the imperative to act here and now. No empirical approach settles the truth and morality issues once and for all. Doable truth claims are always empirical, theoretical, contingent, and proclaimed by someone. Everyone's truth claim, furthermore, is socially located. We empirically investigate this location to evaluate the authority we ought reasonably give to that claim to truth. We then face the moral and pragmatic imperative to act. We are all earthlings and citizens; we are morally bound to choose a version of reality. We choose, or someone else chooses for us, a set of truths that we transform into our actions.

In the face of competing versions of constructed truth, we must still act. We cannot not act. Even if we are not self-consciously aware that we produce a real world through our actions, those actions cut a faith-derived path anyway. We cause as we do. We do as we believe, or others make us believe. We realize a reality in our actions, whether we intend it or not. That is "pragmatic pathos." Pragmatic pathos points out two empirical avenues for understanding a constructed natural environment: interpreting the way persons talk about it, their accounts; and analyzing the way they do it, their actions. The former locates us in myths, narratives, and symbolic worlds. The latter links us to behavior in the physical world. The distinction between accounts and actions helps us focus on the object of discussion, namely, natural environments as known through narratives and symbolic worlds. You and I, as self-conscious moral actors, must probe how we talk and think about what we take to be the natural environment and how we interact with it.

This chapter works toward clarifying our language. Clarifying language clarifies discussion, evaluates conflicting interpretations, and indicates the kinds of data needed to make sense of events. The discussion that follows is based on student comments and my responses in a number of undergraduate seminars. We unpack our thinking and understand our conversations by applying a theoretical framework that helps us analyze how we and others talk and think about natural environment. After introducing the theoretical framework, I briefly contrast selected traditional and contemporary worldviews; retell a spontaneous student-generated discussion about an official definition of "drought"; ask about the idea of societal sustainability; and tally current anomalies that fuel a new awareness of the ways we see and talk about human-environment relations.

Working through Definitions of Environment

Clarification begins with a nominal definition from the root metaphor of environment, namely, "that which lies around us," our surroundings, circumstances, milieu, or ambiance. Environment refers to persons, objects, and events that fill our social and physical lives. So far so good. Adding adjectival modifiers, we can, like listening to "Pictures at an Exhibition," move mentally through environments such as families, governments, schools, jobs, churches, parks, museums, beaches, and woods. These make up environments that are social, political, economic, religious, cultural, and physical. Finally, after briefly discussing these, we arrive at a more specific understanding of the general subject matter, the physical environment.

Our concern, however, is not the entire domain of physical objects surrounding us. Physical environments are both "built" and "natural." The first have a form and content that is designed and constructed by intentional human action. Built environments result from craft, artifice, or technology that applies science to the transformation of the physical world. They are, in that sense, artificial or intentional, though increasingly powerful and important for what concerns social analysts, namely, their unintended consequences. We build a house in which to dwell and simultaneously expel other animals and plants. Switching focus from built environments to natural environments brings us closer to the formal object we wish to understand: physical environments that originate in forces outside of human intentions, that is, in nature. Our focus is on interactional links among selves, societal realities, and the natural physical environment.

Now that we share a nominal definition of natural environment, we ask ourselves to apply it to things around us. Applications help discover whether we all place objects or processes into the same categories. Persons may agree on a nominal definition but not agree on which objects fit that definition. To further chances of agreement or at least of understanding how you and I see the world differently, we move to grounded or "indicative definitions" by asking everyone to point out instances of "a" natural environment.

Students made reference to things such as: woods that exist near their homes; an ocean, lake, or river in which they have swum, fished, or boated; or the mountains they have seen or hiked. In other words, students point to natural events as objects they perceive, interact with, or know about. Grasping complex natural events as though they were things or substantive objects is structured into the linguistic function of nouns, at least in English (Chawla, 1991; Whorf, 1956). One student asks whether houseplants are natural; another questions whether air in the house is natural. Finally, a philosophical student insists that all built environments are in some sense natural environments because even as transformed by human artifice, they exist as naturally occurring events. Built objects follow the same laws of the physical universe as natural objects.

These exchanges clarify ambiguities and help us agree on a domain of study: natural objects that lie around us without intentional human intervention; and in a more difficult grasp, those dimensions of physical things that are outside of human intentional intervention, such as the "laws of nature." This difficult latter issue reminds us that objects fashioned by human artifice continue doing what they do naturally. Asbestos intended to prevent fire continues affecting human lungs if a misguided drillbit spreads it into the circulation system of a university library and leads to an asbestos alert and emergency evacuation. Hence, we arrive at a momentary sense of agreement about a nominal definition and shared groupings of objects.

Eventually someone brings up the epistemological issues of truth, error, and ignorance about natural environments. At one level, the issue is as simple as remembering that humans used to think that all matter is fire; to believe that the earth is as flat as it appears; and to see the sun rise and set as it revolves around the earth. Furthermore, competent and elite members of society typically believed in a flat and cosmically central earth. The point is that socially accepted knowledge is culturally defined; cultural knowledge is created, carried, and taught within institutions. Normal citizens, like college students, succeed by believing what is taught as unquestioned knowledge here and now, even though it may later be seen as error. For centuries, scholars and citizens believed the heavenly bodies remained in concentric spheres, wheeled on wheels, or revolved around the earth. Not so today. What we take as reality is constructed, acquired, and validated through institutions and their framing of what we see and know. We see what and how we are taught to see what enables us to be perceived as normal, of course.

A further move in critical thinking arises. Students realize that socially legitimated statements about the world may some day be false—perhaps including truths they inherit from parents, teachers, or politicians. These realizations highlight the necessity of critically scrutinizing what we believe as truth, evidence, and plausibility. Everyone's statements are both socially constructed according to social location *and* make claims about how the world out there really works.

A Framework for Seeing and Talking about "Natural Environments"

To build a critical framework, I use theoretical distinctions concerning the ways we interact with others and with the natural environment. The first distinction sets up two ways "the world" is real. Using quotation marks looks like a linguistic confidence game, but their use points to a central feature of contemporary culture (Goffman, 1974). Framing the world tells us that humans do not live simply in a physical world; we exist also within a world of symbolic constructions like language, science, and religion. Yet we remain within the physical processes of the material environment that is never totally grasped by symbols. The self both is a physical organism by origin, behavior, and death, and lives a life realized through symbolic trans-formations into languages, motives, and social organizations. Selves are in two worlds simultaneously and are governed by two irreducible sets of forces. The *first* grounding distinction, then, is between the physical and symbolic worlds. These worlds remain in an order of dependency such that the first and last empirically decisive world is the physical cosmos; second and empirically dependent worlds are symbolic.

George H. Mead argued that, over evolutionary time, selves emerged from physically organized societies and now live in symbolically realized organizations. Symbolic worlds are not reducible to, yet they remain contin-gent on, the laws that govern the physical world. Each of us is both an organism, a biologic individual, and a self, a symbolic person. We live simultaneously in irreducible realities: the obdurate physical world that is there and the symbolic institutions of social life (Mead, 1934; 1964).

The *second* distinction is between organic and humanly constructed means by which environments are known as real and thus function as the worlds of individual experience (Schutz and Luckmann, 1989). The brute physical environment is known as the world for me as an organism. The importance of the perspective through which humans know derives from the fact that it puts us in contact with some but not all dimensions of that world and makes that world appear massively real to us, while simultaneously blinding us to other aspects of the natural worlds (Mead, 1964: 306–319). Animal worlds are made real through organically based knowledge mechanisms like the biological "laboratory" in the digestive system of the ox.

The emergence of symbolically organized societies gave human animals a paradoxically powerful and potentially alienating way of knowing that allows them to transcend the body's links to the physical environment here and now. Here rises the issue! As Berger and Luckmann (1966: 45) argue, different dogs have different visual perspectives depending on where they stand, but the different perspectives are always within the same dog world. There is, however, no "same" human world. Even within a single society, individuals both generate and know different worlds, like the village atheist in an otherwise all-believing village.

We live in multiple worlds in two senses: first, there are two kinds of real worlds, physical and symbolic; and second, we know these worlds through two knowledge channels, one bodily selected and the other symbolically constructed. Bodily mechanisms restrict all individuals in the species to one world, as in the dogs' world. In this sense, there is but one world for human organisms defined by the physiology of sensation and the ecological niches within which we animals survive and reproduce. Symbolically constructed mechanisms, on the other hand, can always be *re*constructed to select different social and physical worlds. Ancient forest peoples and modern city dwellers have the same bodily mechanisms for knowing the world, but the symbolically constructed instruments of language, ideas, institutions, and media have produced profoundly different worlds. Some moderns live in virtual worlds. Technology greatly enhances human worlds through ever-reconstructed artificial environments, but, like spaceships, these encapsulated worlds remain dependent on supportive natural environments. It is important to emphasize that, although such reconstructions are in part done by individuals, they are primarily social and institutional productions.

With these distinctions between the physical versus symbolic worlds and bodily versus constructed means of knowing, I identify five central meanings of the phrase *natural environment*. The first two referents are physical and organic: (1) the obdurate, brute, all-encompassing world that is there, that is, the "cosmic environment" of the material universe; (2) those aspects of the obdurate world selected by the organic cognitive mechanisms of biologic individuals in a single species, that is, the "species environment" (see Figure 2.1). The first referent grasps the meaning intended by the person who notes that it is false to claim humans are destroying the environment. Nature continues doing what it does even as humans interact with it, and it will go on doing it even if humans change it so much that they die out. In this sense, there is no "end of nature" as natural environment. The second referent fills out the universal claim that all humans as individual organisms of the same species share the same environment. If this shared environment were destroyed, it would mean the end of nature only in the sense of ecological systems that support human species. So far so good, but let us consider three more referents closer to our subject matter.

The next three meanings of natural environment are a mix of physical and symbolic, bodily and constructed elements. These natural environments are 3. the taken-for-granted, "relatively natural environment" in the grand narratives and dominant stories of traditional worldviews that enable us to see, believe, and talk about the physical environment, for example, as a divine being, a deterministic machine, or a dynamic system, that is, the "encultured environment"; 4. selected or constructed aspects of the world that are made into objects and rationalized by the logics of social institutions, that is, the "institutionalized environments" within which governments, churches, businesses, and other institutions operate; and 5. those aspects of the naturally occurring world that are realized in the perceptions of situated selves with experiential meanings, that is, the "personal environment" within which you and I live in personally seen and felt worlds. By contrast with the first two referents, the last three meanings are wholly or in part social, symbolic, and continually reconstructed natural environments.

The mixed make-up of the last three referents presents a central and endless task concerning what we mean when we say "natural environment": discriminating between the physical and organic given content versus the symbolic and interpretive constructed content. My aim here is to clarify socially constructed aspects of these three meanings by raising questions about encultured, institutionalized, and personal natural environments. An ironic aspect of human-environment interaction is that we never know the entire world as it is in itself, namely, the cosmic environment. We know it only selectively through organic and symbolic knowledge mechanisms. For humans, then, the natural environment is a five-layered complex of: the world that is there and that we know only in part; the world selectively grasped by species-specific organic mechanisms of knowing; and the three versions made up of natural and symbolic content continually reconstructed by culture, institutions, and self. The last three referents are socially constructed natural environments or "landscapes" (Greider and Garkovich, 1994; Klausner, 1971).

These five meanings clarify referents of the phrase *natural environment* and help us understand each other's comments. Clarification pinpoints the kinds of evidence needed to assess the truth claims of statements based on one definition with those based on another. We learn to relate seemingly contradictory statements, for example, the true assertions that all humans share the same species environment (meaning 2 in Figure 2.1) by noting that it is also true that members of different cultures live in differently defined and perceived environments (meanings 3 and 5); or that within one culture, institutions operate within different environments, as in the contrasting perspectives of a lumber company and a pharmaceutical firm on a tropical rain forest (meaning 4); or that individuals perceive different environments after embracing deep ecology or a critically injured son (Gore, 1992). Students go on to raise concerns about the implications of these definitions for understanding how we can sustain environments that support human life.

Figure 2.1 outlines a walk through the five referents of environment arranged in a "meaning tree" branching from nominal definitions through theoretically grounded distinctions and on to the five specific meanings numbered for our discussion. With this meaning tree, we can compare different ideas of natural environments in our reading and discussion. I will briefly discuss three illustrations: a comparative historical look at encultured definitions; a recent pronouncement that generated a wide-ranging student discussion; and some contemporary anomalies in personal environments. These illustrations preview the difficult task of acquiring environmental literacy.

A Comparative Historical Glance at Encultured Environments

I briefly sketch three contrasting examples of encultured environments: one ancient and barely surviving; one modern and dominant; and a currently emerging antithesis to the latter. Historian Max Oelschlaeger offers ideal types of natural environment as "wilderness" from paleolithic times to the present. Paleolithic believers in their culture's ideas of natural environment as wilderness typically understood it as follows. They "likely:

- believed that irrespective of place, nature was home
- regarded nature as intrinsically feminine
- thought of nature as alive
- assumed that the entire world of plants and animals, even the land itself, was sacred
- surmised that divinity could take many natural forms and that metaphor was the mode of divine access
- believed that time was synchronous, folded into an eternal mythical present

Figure 2.1. A Meaning Tree for Defining "Natural Environments"
(Follow the arrows to the five numbered definitions discussed in the text)

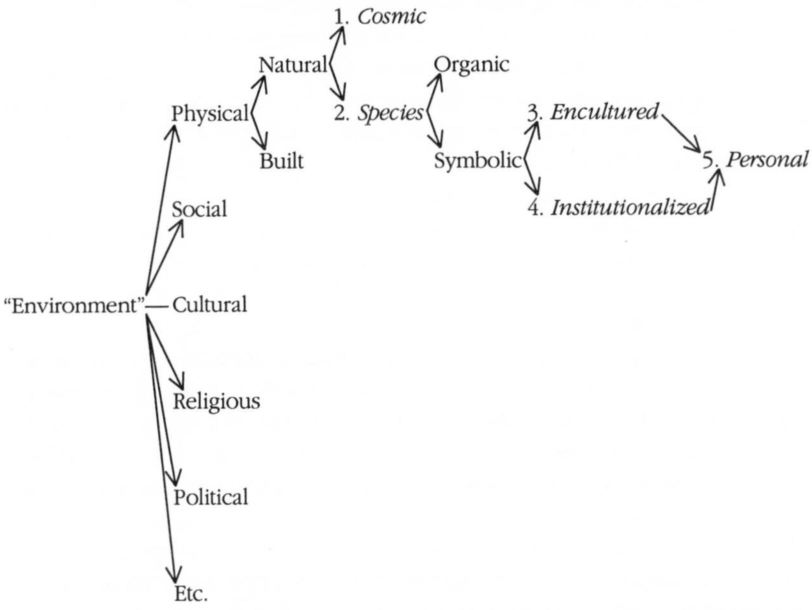

- supposed that ritual was essential to maintaining the natural and cyclical order of life and death." (1991: 12)

Anthropologist Colin Turnbull's story of his participation in the life of *The Forest People* (1962) puts flesh on this skeletal typology. The Forest People are pygmies. According to written references, the BaMbuti pygmies have apparently survived for over four thousand years in the Ituri rain forests of south-central Africa. They see the physical environment along lines that fit the Paleolithic typology. The rain forest is divine; it is placated and addressed through ritual; it is both mother and father; it is alive; it is home. The forest provides the BaMbuti with all they need to live physically, socially, and morally. The *molimo* rituals of music, singing, dancing, and feasting are key to their relationship to the forest. Time is primarily cyclic, following the hunting and foraging seasons such as the eagerly awaited search for honey. Individuals' personal environments are collectively shared and integrated into the encultured environment. There is virtually no institutional differentiation. Their life in the forest is highlighted by contrast with the somewhat more modern, market-oriented, and settled African "villagers" who live in dusty openings cut into the forest's edge. Indeed, the cultural distance between the BaMbuti and the villagers appears greater than that between the villagers and modern westerners.

Compared with the BaMbuti, the dominant worldview of the natural environment in which moderns live and believe is so different as to be contradictory. Building on a wide range of contemporary sources, Lester Milbrath characterizes today's "dominant social paradigm" of human-natural environment relations as follows:

- low evaluation of nature that is to be dominated and used;
- compassion only for those nearby at the expense of other peoples, future generations, and other species;
- acceptance of technological risk to maximize wealth;
- unlimited growth in resource use, population, and consumption;
- commitment to present societal organization emphasizing competitive markets, lifestyles, jobs, and efficiency;
- reliance on politics of experts with formal institutions, and featuring arguments over ownership of means of production. (1989: 119)

This dominant social paradigm defines the natural environment as a secular resource with no intrinsic value. Since it acquires value only when bought, sold, or used, humans rightly exploit it for ever-increasing consumption to satisfy their wants. Recalling that the BaMbuti have likely lived over four thousand years in the rain forest, students readily note that our society has existed only a few hundred years. The issue of sustainability as a crucial feature of human-environment relations is quickly put on the agenda.

Alternative world views now vie for attention even within the First World. By contrast with the dominant paradigm of "resourcism" defining the earth as exploitable stuff valued only for use, alternative paradigms range from a counter-cultural deep ecology or Gaia that sees earth as a living system with intrinsic moral standing independent of human use, to extended ethics of "rights" to include animal rights or even the rights of trees to counterbalance human rights. Other world views are based on preservationism, ecocentrism, or ecofeminism (Oelschlaeger, 1991: ch. 9). Indeed, to look at the earth from an ecological or feminist perspective is to see it inverted as we come to know it "from the ground up" compared to the human use and control point of view (Merchant, 1983: 42).

Survey evidence suggests that new sets of attitudes toward the natural environment are gaining strength worldwide. They are variously referred to as postmaterialist, postindustrial, ecological literacy, or new configurations of environmental attitudes (Dunlap and Mertig, 1992; Dunlap et al., 1993;

Inglehart, 1990; Milbrath, 1989; Morin, 1992; Orr, 1992). These emerging attitudes are consistent with alternative worldviews that contain components that contradict the dominant social paradigm of environment as mere resource. Central elements of the emerging alternative paradigm include the following:

- Humans are part of the earth's ecosystem and must live within nature.
- The natural environment is valuable in itself and must be *logical* protected at all costs.
- Natural resources are limited and must be preserved.
- World population has reached the earth's carrying capacity and must be controlled. (Olsen et al, 1992: 5)

As citizens at an environmentally crucial period, we are challenged to be sufficiently literate so that we choose and enact an adequate ecological worldview. Once literate, we can more reasonably assess encultured views of nature like those of the BaMbuti and conflicting groups in today's world. I suggest a synthesized Primer Paradigm for environmental literacy in chapter 6. Let us continue clarifying natural enviroment through student discussion of a political proclamation.

Unpacking Institutional Definitions: "The drought is over!"

Seminars have their surprises. One occurred the day a student started by reporting that the California drought has been declared officially over. This simple statement sparked a spontaneous discussion of institutional definitions that took us through many meanings of the natural environment. A first response was the basic sociology of knowledge question, Says who? The answer was that Pete Wilson, the Governor of California, proclaims that the drought is over. Interesting! After all, does he know meteorological or environmental science? We supposed that he did not base the proclamation on personal knowledge, but on the advice of advisors, hopefully scientifically expert advisors. If so, the statement is based, not on the governor's personal knowledge of the data nor on specialized scientists interpreting the data, but on his faith in these experts and advisors. The students' knowledge, then, is based on at least a triple layer of faith in the advisors, the governor, and the media. At any rate, there was no reason to doubt the governor's truthfulness; we believed that he was telling the truth—as he knew it.

A telling turn came with a student's insistence that the governor's truthfulness is not the point. The issue is the truth of the statement, "The drought is over." The governor may be totally truthful; yet the statement may be questionable, even false. Everyone agreed that if California reservoirs were now full and snowpack in the mountains was above normal, then the immediate shortage of water for human use was over. Several, however, remained uneasy about the sense of "over." After all, another drought may begin next year. Indeed, it may already have begun. The cosmic forces that produced this drought are still at work. Furthermore, it was readily noted that the idea of an "ending" depends on the time frame used to interpret events. A student aware of population pressures stated the likelihood that the water-using population will increase, so the demand for water will increase as well. The likelihood of drought, therefore, will increase.

A consensus seemed to emerge that it may be reasonable to say that "this" drought is over, but we recognize that drought-producing conditions are continuing or increasing. It is false to say that the causes or *context* of the drought is over. In a word, thinking of water in cosmic or other institutional frames led to different interpretations from that presented in the political perspective of the governor's proclamation. Students saw that the truth of the claim, The drought is over, depends on the definitional framework informing one's perspective. The claim may be seen as true in the official political institutional frame; of unknown validity in larger cosmic and alternative institutional frames; and conditionally and temporarily true in personal frames.

As the discussion continued, I pushed the social construction of meaning. I noted that discussants seemed to assume that there is a real drought in the cosmic environment. I insisted that, in the sense in which we use the term, there is no drought in the cosmic environment. Drought, as we understand it, is a totally social construction, not a cosmic event. To my surprise, these comments were met with what looked like bemused incredulity, almost as if I were talking in my sleep. Students quickly, almost dismissively, moved to *indicative* definitions, pointing, as it were, to the "facts" of empty reservoirs, low annual rainfall, little snow in the mountains, stressed or dying trees, and animals migrating in search of water. I tried to counter-indicate: insects living in dying trees, annual rainfall is a constructed statistic, likely spread of desert-like flora and fauna that thrive in dry conditions, and whatever else I could point to. The social constructionist viewpoint, I argued, is not based on things we point to or indicative definitions, but on theoretical definitions: drought is always drought from some perspective, so that indicated facts do not prove or disprove the existence of whatever phenomenon we intend by "drought." At the end of the discussion, I sensed that students were willing to grant this point nominally, but that they remained realists about drought in the cosmos.

A second point, however, gained more agreement, namely, drought has a "normative" aspect. Drought not only points out a condition of the natural environment, such as *dryness*. It also implicates the judgment that an area of the natural environment *lacks* an amount of water that *should* be there under normal circumstances. Furthermore, since drought is seen in the environment from the perspective of human use, there is a normative obligation implied for the way humans in that situation interact with water. In a drought, humans should conserve water by prioritizing use according to need. Cities or states may ban low priority activities such as watering lawns or washing cars. Saving water for drinking, cooking, flushing toilets, and bathing is far more important. Hospitals get water before car wash businesses. That normative realism refers to totally socially constructed meanings, institutional policies, and personal motives gained wide acceptance. Finally, it was thought that the governor's proclamation based the meaning of drought on a restricted institutional definition: official drought exists in the governmental definition that citizens' use of water will be regulated and violators punished. In fact, a new construct, "regulatory drought," has been coined to grasp this aspect of scarce water use. Regulatory drought explicitly points to the power of interest groups as the decisive force in defining whether there is a drought and choosing who will pay the price by restricted access to water, such as farmers, city dwellers, or hunters.

The discussion so highlighted definitional processes that I pursued the story. The opening line in the Los Angeles Times article captured two poles of the definitional clarification. Governor Pete Wilson is quoted as saying, "Thanks to God for ending the drought, and thanks to the people of California for enduring it" (Los Angeles Times, 1993: A1). In one sentence, he referred to a cosmic, though divinely governed, environment, and to both institutionalized and collective personal responses to the divinely guided natural conditions. All of these dynamics go into the total social and natural "fact" of a drought as he defined it.

I also came across a subsequent letter to the editor by Professor Norris Hundley, Jr., an historian of California water policy and use (1993; see 1992). He links cosmic and institutional environments by reference to: organic growth rings on trees; the idea of a ground-surface water hydrological cycle; and institutional and personal ways of thinking about water in terms of "average rain" or "normal use." He argues that evidence from tree rings suggests that it is "misleading" to think the drought is over or Californians can ever go back to recent practices of water use. He notes that California has had "droughts" of 61, 25, 20, and 11 years in the last 360 years, and the very idea of "abundant water" for human use is a myth dating from the turn of the last century.

The southern California waterscape seen through the eyes of a paleoclimatologist, furthermore, shows evidence of another meaning, "epic drought." Carbon dating and tree ring patterns from stumps exposed by low water levels in California and Argentina suggest two severe droughts in these regions lasting for "more than two centuries" and "more than 140 years" up to ca. 1112 A.D. and 1350 A.D., respectively (Stine, 1994: 546). These epic droughts coincided with an unusually warm period in Europe. Stine goes on to link warming with waterscape, and definitional meanings with possible future environmental patterns by asking whether warming caused by current human actions may lead to changes in precipitation like those of the medieval period, that is, an epic drought in California. Had a historian of California water use or a scholar of ancient climate made the proclamation, I doubt that either would have said the drought is over. We must ask, Says who, again.

Responses that deny the drought is over implicate other institutional meanings that may legitimate social planning and the imposition of regulations based on expected severe droughts, for example, restrictive water use, new cost policies, dry agricultural practices, re-aligning residential patterns, or formulating new water management assumptions (Stevens, 1994). Once we focus on institutional responses, we see that political negotiation and power struggles decide whose definition of drought prevails and who pays the price. Groups who profit from water use argue that the water shortage is best defined as an artificial drought, a regulatory drought, that is, a humanly constructed shortage caused by court rulings and government regulations (Los Angeles Times, 1993). Applying the definition, regulatory drought, stakeholders using the waterscape generate a "politics of drought" enacted in congressional hearings that feature definitional battles among conservationists, corporations, farmers, fishing interests, and local voters. Current politics of drought align the latest configuration of social interests in a two-hundred-year struggle for water among historical actors and different cultures from ancient native American groups to Spanish communitarian models and finally to Anglo-business and today's power politics (Hundley, 1992; New York Times, 1994). Mutual understanding in the midst of conflict requires definitional clarity. These conflicts show how hotly the issues are debated by officials, interest groups, and scholars. Definitional clarification and shared understanding, however, do not reduce the complexity of the issues, especially that of sustainability.

Question: Do All Definitions of Natural Environments Assume They Are Mutually Sustainable?

A final distinction addresses the question whether different beliefs about natural environments assume that they are mutually sustainable. Do we believe that the actions of institutions and individuals on natural environments sustain cosmic and species environments? Do we believe definitions that assume that the natural environment will sustain humans no matter what we do to it? The need for a coherent world view or at least peace of mind suggests that we tend to believe in a sustainable future. Such beliefs are subject to increasingly critical review. New environmental data and new understandings highlight personal responsibility for choosing to believe in a specific environmental definition. Our belief, then, calls forth a moral commitment to act accordingly. In new circumstances, individuals often, perhaps usually, lack decisive empirical or authoritative grounds for choosing among inherited definitions and for knowing how to act morally. Today, we know that we must choose whom and what to believe and how to act.

A social psychological perspective does not resolve these faith and moral issues. Nor does it supply the data, methods, or theory for understanding the environment in meanings 1 and 2 of Figure 2.1. They fall within cosmology and the physical sciences. Our question is whether we believe that social institutions and cultural beliefs are functional or dysfunctional for human life-support systems. This question raises a serious and paradoxical issue: do society and individual's interactions with the natural environment both temporarily sustain us *and* eventually threaten us?

Contemporaries are wary of unquestioning belief in Progress through Control and in vulgar functionalist understandings of "culture." Culture is no longer uncritically accepted as a fail-safe adaptive process of human viability. Historical research points to societies that disappeared as their environments were transformed. The functional-dysfunctional issue underlines a new understanding of consumption, population, waste disposal, global temperature, and change in atmospheric chemistry. We are coming to a deeper realization that self and society are *never* independent of the natural environment (Catton and Dunlap, 1980; Catton, 1980; Ophuls and Boyan, 1992). Indeed, contemporary life is characterized by increasing awareness of environmental anomalies generated from unintended outcomes of well-intentioned actions, for example, water pollution and degraded soil from modern farming, toxic air from manufacturing the good life, and piles of waste from an increasing consuming population.

Anomalies in Human-Environment Relationships

Anomalies, that is, significant threats from expected empirical patterns underlying contemporary society, lead us to question received definitions and search for new ones. Understanding how changes in definitions change our eye-sight shows why we did not typically expect anomalies and how it is that we see them now. Some anomalies arise from conflicts among previously separated definitions of natural environments. In his action-oriented psychological studies, Michael Edelstein (1988) coins the phrase "lifescape inversion" to refer to radical changes in persons' perception of their environment when they come face to face with a threatening anomaly.

It refers to a reversal in the interpretive and emotional meanings when one's environment is turned upside down. For example, the gradual changing taste of tap water leads to a reversal of household water from life-sustaining to life-threatening. It is not clear at what point a difference in taste or smell becomes an anomaly, that is, a newly known deviation from expectations that is strong enough to challenge the perceiver's worldview (Kuhn, 1970). When does a little "funny-tasting" safe tap water come to taste, look, or smell so different that it is redefined as "poison" water? Perhaps it happens the night a member of the county health department knocks on your front door to tell you not to drink the water. Once defined as poison, my tap water challenges prior encultured and institutionalized definitions that went into its meaning as safe. Tap water valued as life-sustaining is now repulsed as life-threatening. Simply put, toxic tap water exists in a different home, community, and world than safe tap water. Experience of lifescape inversion leads / victims to challenge even the authority of government and scientific experts.

Edelstein documents that persons living in homes with safe water believe in: personal control and security; the benevolence of community, business, and government; The American Dream of success; and a better life for one's children. Those in homes with toxic tap water, on the other hand, feel insecure, powerless, angry, and betrayed. They question beliefs in the goodness of institutions and even The American Dream. Like falling in love or into any deep emotion, the fearful drinker of toxic tap water lives in a different home in a different world. Inversion of household water's meaning challenges other official definitions of the natural environment. It may even threaten one's marriage. Edelstein's studies document conflicts among institutionalized environments as defined by realtors versus business versus governments versus communities, as they struggle to respond to the official announcement "not to use water for human consumption" (Edelstein, 1988: 29).

Rachel Carson's book, *Silent Spring*, framed a cultural lifescape inversion over thirty years ago (1962). She painted a nationwide picture that became an historical wake-up call for seeing the outcomes of then poorly understood official and institutional use of toxic chemicals in the environment. Her book built on the psychological and linguistic insight that the words we use to define situations can motivate actions whose destructive results are both masked and caused by those very definitions. The simple act of tossing a cigarette butt into barrels seen as safe because they are labeled "empty" of liquid results in an explosion—because they are really "full" of fumes (Whorf, 1956). Definitions and labels guide our motives and actions. Similar semantic masking labels toxins as "dusts" or "weed and feed" to be spread on our crops or lawns. Encultured values and institutionalized businesses turn toxic powders into safe dusts. In an ecological frame, such powders remain poisons that spread in water, along food chains, and accumulate in fatty tissue. We handle toxics differently from the way we handle dust. Battles over definitions lead to a battle of policies among institutional actors. Spokespersons for the chemical industry, for example, wrote misleading and dismissive reviews of Carson's book. Others used *ad hominem* arguments and attacked her personal life (Hynes, 1989). *Time* magazine at first labeled her "hysterical." Such oppositional responses underlined the social significance of her book. Their meanings became clearer when a presidential panel of experts concluded that Carson's scientific summaries and ecological arguments were correct.

Sociological analyses offer tools for understanding changes in and conflicts among holders of different definitions of environments. Grieving relatives and concerned neighbors, for example, may believe in "popular epidemologies" and struggle with official government and legal definitions of the facts, causes, and patterns of childhood cancers. Popular epidemiologies join encultured and institutional definitions with personal and community definitions (Brown, 1992). Whose definitions better grasp the cosmic and organic relationships between humans and their environments? Anomalies in perceptions of human-environment relationships make it clear that encultured, institutionalized, and personal definitions both change in themselves and conflict with one another. We need to step outside of received definitions to get a critical perspective as we try to decide where to put our faith and how to act rightly.

Personal Responses to Anomalies and Conflicting Definitions

One method for getting a grip on self-society-environment interrelationships is "reasoning to ground" (Milbrath, 1989: 67). In reasoning to ground, we weigh competing definitions of actions by linking them to alternatives in the light of our fundamental values. Milbrath suggests *sustaining the ecosystems that support human life* as a fundamental value that all of us can share because our descendents' lives depend on it. The next steps are to show how institutional goals and personal interests support or threaten that grounding value. Similar reasoning is called for by scholars reflecting on the moral implications of social policies, institutional logics, and personal lifestyles in building a "good society" (Bellah et al, 1991). After all, The American Way of Life, like any society's *summum bonum,* is built out of the same soil, water, and air all humans share.

Reasoning to ground sharpens a critical perspective. As suggested earlier, I use critical in two senses: recognizing that human-environment interaction is at a critical historical juncture for defining the quality and likelihood of human survival; and understanding that this juncture requires critical assessment of conventional truths to frame more adequate ways of seeing and reacting to the environment. In a classical sense, crisis refers to a situation requiring informed judgments that impact significantly on possible futures. Nuances I wish to avoid are crisis as a unique moment that can be disposed of once and for all or crisis as an occasion for panic and hopelessness.

Environment is an ever-present aspect of the human predicament; it is not a passing crisis. This realization locates fundamental choices as perennial issues rather than solvable problems, and sees personal troubles as indicators of society's perennial issues. This realization fosters "critical thinking" that puts issues into a larger context that requires more systemic and inclusive ways of thinking (Nelson, 1989). We can, for example, metaphorically reframe repeated discoveries of poisons dumped in neighborhoods as a pandemic "plague" of our times (Edelstein, 1988). Institutionally caused toxic tap water is not just a personal trouble or a local problem. Toxic tap water is a significant social outcome pointing to a defining set of contingencies in the contemporary world.

In addition to historical comparisons and value analyses suggested above, another method for thinking anew about the environment is "utopian analysis." To imagine human-environment relationships in a utopian context requires that we, as it were, turn the earth in our mind's hands and see it from many imagined perspectives. As we turn the world, we experience alternative cognitive and emotional responses. One way is to "image" a world or way of life based on literary creations that go beyond data-driven science (Boulding, 1990, for example, suggests imaging a world at peace). Utopian analysis is like a collective thought experiment that frees us from the controlling accents of what we were taught is real or believed was possible. From a utopian standpoint, we reinterpret and reevaluate the real world through the creative play of imagination.

Ernest Callenbach's book, *Ecotopia* (1977), describes an environmental utopia. *Ecotopia* depicts a novel response to the "What if . . .?" question in two senses: it is both new and fictional. This double novelty helps us imagine alternative ways of looking at and living in our environment. It allows us to pose a liberating challenge to ourselves: "Is it possible that the *empirical truth* of our environmental situation is stranger than the *literary fiction* of a novel utopia"? Once asked, this question takes on a haunting tone. Utopian analysis helps us shed the childlike blinders of inherited stories of reality. Environmental theologians or "ecologians" who present religious as well as cultural and historical perspectives for imaging worlds offer explicitly faith-based images of alternative worlds (Berry, 1988).

Our look at anomalies, historical comparisons, and utopian perspectives on human-environment relationships suggest two intermediate conclusions. First, basic facts about the environment cannot be known within the framework of personal experience. I refer to this as Darwin's dilemma, since he noted how difficult, if not impossible, it is for readers to accept his story of the evolution of species if no one lives long enough to see a new species emerge. So too, environmental scientists tell us that significant ecosystem changes are occurring and that they are beyond the range of individual perception. Evolutionary dynamics, atmospheric shifts, rising water tables, rising acidity levels, and other ecosystemic changes remain faith objects because they lie beyond the range of personal experience. Second, even scientific frameworks, we are reminded, lack sufficient historical comparative data and adequate theoretical understanding of the earth's ecological dynamics to translate brute happenings into definitive patterns and interpretations to guide collective action. Scientists are unsure of, and sometimes disagree about, short- and long-term outcomes of environmental policies and practices.

Using the five meanings of natural environment developed above, we see that different definitions have implications for what we take as facts and patterns and for what we believe is a right interpretation or efficient policy. Controversies within scientific communities and disagreements over national policies underscore the depth of our partial and inadequate understanding (e.g., National Academy of Sciences, 1990). How do we interpret the "fact" of a 90°F Indiana day in May? Is this day atypically warm in the temporal context of the last one hundred, one thousand, or ten thousand years? Even if we believe the answer is Yes, is this "fact" interpreted as: a random variation; an artifact of incomplete statistical history; a normal variation within cycles of temperature change; or a patterned sign of rapid warming of the earth from humanly produced greenhouse gases? The struggle is to know whether the warm day is a direct outcome of humanly caused global environmental change. If it is, then humans for the first time become knowingly responsible for changing weather patterns with unknown outcomes. Is the statement "Global temperature is rising" a mixed factual, definitional, and political statement like "The drought is over?"

A Definitional Formula: Natural Environments Are Given And Constructed

Today's citizen knows an unusually warm day in May as a complex "fact." The warmth is really experienced, but what does it mean? The experience is interpreted within faith-based frameworks for interpreting warm days. Until recently, such interpretations came from the random, folk, normal, or happily expected early summer frameworks. Today there is a new framework, humanly caused global warming or greenhouse effect, a framework that did not exist before. The realization that unusually warm days may indicate a process that no one ever knew about shows that the natural environment is in part a humanly constructed interpretation. To borrow a textual metaphor, environmental facts are not entirely exegetic, that is, simply read out of a perfectly clear text of natural events the way we read a recipe or a thermometer. Rather, facts are also and sometimes unwittingly "eisegetic"; that is, they are *read into* events, natural or otherwise, like a warm day as a sign of global warming from industrial pollution or a portent of apocalyptic fulfillment from the Book of Revelation.

The discussion leads to the following components in an inclusive definition of "natural environment"—what are taken as patterned facts within cosmic and organic processes; socio-cultural world views explaining and justifying such facts; institutional definitions of the factual aspects of experience; and personal experience of events interpreted as such facts.

Persons' experiences take on shared meaning through shared definitions. Just as science teaches us to redefine personal experiences of the world with a reconstructed vision based on faith in scientific accounts—as when we affirm, in spite of what our eyes see, that the sun does not rise in the morning sky or that, in spite of feeling at rest, we are moving in at least three directions at break-neck speeds rotating about the earth's wobbling axis, circling the sun, and speeding toward the edge of the universe—so environmental science tells us that an unusually hot sunny May day and sharper sunburn signal global warming, ozone depletion, and higher chances of cataracts or skin cancer. Science inverts an inherited definition of sunshine: from high status suntan to high risk cancerburn.

Clarification Is But a First Step

Meaning clarification raises questions concerning environmental literacy. The purpose of this introductory discussion is simply to see situations in which we begin to: unpack meanings of natural environment as central components of environmental issues; create a shared definitional framework over a range of content areas; and gain clarity within and among ourselves on the idea of natural environment, whether cosmic, species, encultured, institutionalized, or personal. Further inquiry asks about conflicts among believed definitions, interpretive frameworks, measurement issues, and policy implications. We find conflict among medical, business, religious, governmental, or neighborhood definitions and among personal, encultured, and institutional aspects of definitions. Regardless of one's commitments or objectives, clarification of meaning makes their attainment and our seeing more fruitful. Following chapters develop and apply environmental eye-sight. They begin with a look at the ways we trip and set off responses in the natural environment, often without seeing or intending what we are tripping.

3

Tripping the Natural Environment

Instruments, seen and unseen, surround citizens of technologically advanced societies. We constantly use instruments to intervene in the physical world and elicit responses from it. Modernity is built with sensitive, powerful, and high-energy tools that transform our interactions with the environment. High-energy tools characterize contemporary material culture, that is, the physical things people use to build the meaningful surroundings in which they seek their idea of the good life.

Material culture physically embodies the values, meanings, and motives that make up a society's good life. Reaching for the good life is why humans make material things. People's meanings and motives are in the way they build and use their physical surroundings. In this chapter, I talk about a category of things by which we express our values, sustain our life style, and physically interact with the environment. The Industrial Revolution greatly expanded this category of material things through new energy sources and technological inventions. Instruments of environmental intervention characterize industrialized societies.

I call these instruments of intervention "trippers," that is, socially distributed and valued technological objects that sustain our lifestyles and fulfil our desires by releasing natural forces and generating known or unknown, intended or unintended, outcomes. More trippers release more forces generating ever-wider patterns of short- and long-term outcomes. Part of these outcomes are anticipated by and acceptable to foresight and reason. Other outcomes lie beyond the knowledge or intention of those who use the trippers. Once we trip instruments, the responses are driven by natural processes outside of our control. Instruments have systemic causal effects in the world that is there, effects that pay no regard to human needs, excuses, and calls for sympathy or pardon. As we learn about the mixed outcomes of instrumental intervention, we see action pathos. We always trip more than we know or intend. Today, we know that this "more" is a mix of desirable and undesirable outcomes. Modern trippers and energy use make us more aware of action pathos. Earlier civilizations occasionally perished from action pathos as peoples pursued the good life in ways that led to their own disappearance.

A tripper, as an instrument that deepens action pathos, is a powerful social construction in two senses. It is a real physical thing or material process that sets off physical outcomes in the world that is there, like the stone that splashes in the middle of a pond. Second, it is, at the same time, a symbolic object in the social life process that displays the meanings of social and moral status. Some of these meanings are in opportunities, even demands, for acting in certain ways, like turning on the headlights when we drive at night. Trippers embody opportunities and demands literally built into physical circumstances, the way a handy gun invites us to fire it.

Recent wide-ranging scientific data show the growing power of trippers. Technology provides both more powerful instruments for intervening in the environment and more powerful instruments for tracking the outcomes. There is a risky time lag between the outcomes from new instruments of intervention and adequate data for evaluating them. Nevertheless, the growth of environmental data underwrites a new self-awareness and highlights the moral need to see the world through empirical lenses. With trippers as one lense, we see that everyday actions, like flipping a switch or starting a car, also initiate human-environment interactions.

"Primitive" peoples lived, and some still live, in environments with few and weak trippers. Before the Industrial and Energy Revolutions, humans had animals and simple mechanical instruments for interacting with the environment. Outcomes were locally limited by the energy and forces such trippers set off. Pre-industrial societies used animal power and natural forces like wind, water, and fire. Their effects were generally linked in space and time to short-term effects on the local ecosystem or bioregion. Limited effects can more easily be re-absorbed in the ecosystem dynamics within the time frames of local organisms and their life-support systems. It is as though primitive trippers were pebbles dropped into a big pond, such that the force of the splashes and ripples dissipates before damaging the shore. Primitive trippers leave the ecosystem sufficiently self-sustaining so that it can survive for thousands of years, as with the BaMbuti pygmies in African rain forests. Such primitive societies are "ecosystem" societies. Their tripped outcomes are spatially and temporally absorbed within their ecosystems. If such societies over exploit their niche so that the supportive ecosystem crashes, they may disappear; but their disappearance leaves societies in other ecosystems relatively unaffected.

Moderns, by contrast, use increasing numbers of trippers with technologies that unleash increasingly powerful forces with deeper outcomes.

Within the last two hundred years, industrialized societies have invented and turned on powerful instruments for doing work, transforming matter, moving things and people, and communicating. Modern societies are built on energy sources like the fossil fuels of coal, oil, natural gas, and now nuclear reactors. The energy is put to use through steam engines, electric motors, and internal combustion engines. These sources run the ships, railroads, airplanes, automobiles, trucks, buses, furnaces, appliances, electronics, computers, and air conditioners that make modern societies possible. They are turned on and off as desired. They are at the center of the comfort and convenience of the good life, yet most did not exist until about two hundred years ago. They have effects on the environment that we often do not or cannot see. As unseen, we rarely, if ever, think about them.

Some trippers, due to the tremendous forces unleashed or the millions of times humans trip them, activate outcomes in nature that transcend both the ecosystem in which the tripper exists and the time frames within which ecosystems sustain human life. Modern trippers drop huge boulders or millions of pebbles continuously into the pond of the natural world. The splashes and ripples of these stones reach the shores, bounce off, and continue interacting with further ripples coming long after the tripping organisms are dead. Think of the toxic lifetime of high-level radioactive wastes modern societies produce or the replacement time for water taken from relatively closed aquifers like the Ogallala stretching from South Dakota to Texas.

Constructing and spraying new chemicals; burning fossil fuels or city garbage; making chemical, biological, and nuclear weapons; and using transformed genetic material to grow or preserve food or human tissue illustrate ever-deeper tripping of the environment. Some radioactive wastes remain unsafe into the geologic time of thousands of years and some changes in air, water, and climate patterns continue long beyond individual lifetimes. Unlike primitives and their ecosystem trippers, moderns have their hands on *biospheric* trippers whose effects go around the world and touch everyone's ecosystems years beyond individual lifetimes.

One reason for thinking of our era as an "Environmental Revolution" brought on by the tripped effects of human intervention is this: modern trippers intervene into the *global* dynamics of the natural environment. Until rapidly growing numbers of humans began tripping forces of such power and scope, societies could rightly be thought of as local ecosystem forces affecting primarily their immediate physical environment in ways that it could regenerate itself, or at least not threaten societies in other ecosystems across the ocean. Environmental isolation is no longer true.

Modern industrial societies affect the life-support systems and environmental dynamics of everyone's life chances anywhere on Earth. The usual examples are acid rain, weather and climate changes, global warming, solar radiation through ozone "holes," and rising levels of chemical and radioactive toxicity in water, air, and the food chain. Only some of these outcomes are intended or regulated by social policy. Some outcomes are partially known. Others likely remain unknown. Some outcomes we know, intend, and prepare for, such as the car's increase in speed when we step on the accelerator. Others likely remain unknown or unintended, such as pollution from our car's exhaust.

Look around and note how everyday life is structured through the trippers we see and the large number we do not: switches; triggers; faucets; pull cords; laser beams; light, heat, pressure or sound sensors; valves; plungers; levers; buttons; keys; and so on. Each tripper is a physical thing that activates a technological intervention into environmental processes. It also elicits organized responses from experts who constructed and installed it and simple lifestyle responses from those who know only how to trip it for their convenience. A tripper is a meaningful social object made up not only of the physical stuff that locates it in the world of environmental forces, but also of the social stuff of relationships, values, and lifestyles among those in the know.

Trippers invite us to impulsive and habituated responses to satisfy our desires. They induce us to act. Recognizing, feeling motivated by, and manipulating trippers results from what Alfred Schutz (1970) calls "relevances" that structure our everyday experience, similar to a family home, circles of friends, traffic patterns, and the car waiting for us in the garage. These relevances allow us to act out what we take to be the good life. Recognizing trippers activates responses that are personally motivating, culturally meaningful, and instrumentally effective. They invite and sometimes impel us to intervene in the environment.

We know that activating trippers is a necessary and reasonable part of life. They guide us because they are linked with the appropriate talk and motives that make our world go. In a word, we moderns are native to trippers the way BaMbuti pygmies are native to the rain forest. Nativeness for us means specific knowledge to guide meaningful interaction with the physical world through trippers and provide personal fulfillment at the same time.

An example of a tripper-filled context is the cockpit of a jumbo jet bristling with switches. The array of instruments beckons pilots to perform actions that decide the survival or destruction of a massive plane gliding through the air toward a too narrow runway. Not only is the massive airplane in the balance; so also are the lives of passengers subject to the pilots' skills for tripping natural forces so that the 747 lands safely (see Zurcher, 1983, for understanding encapsulated persons, as we are on Earth). Pilots need specialized knowledge to handle the array of trippers so that the jumbo jet lands safely. Each tripper, like the bacteriological laboratory George H. Mead metaphorically attributes to the ox, relates passengers to the natural forces of air, gravity, thrust, and angles. Hopefully, each tripper elicits appropriate responses from pilots in the know. In their fatefulness, cockpit trippers offer a situation for thriller movies in which a layperson takes the place of dead pilots and works the trippers with verbal instructions from the control tower to land the jet safely. Some trippers, like rudders, realign a machine with forces of nature; others unleash additional forces to play out possibilities, like the plunger that dynamites the trestle as the train crosses. Trippers offer both new symbolic environments for social life and new instruments for intervening in the physical world.

Social and physical forces of trippers are in different but interacting domains. Social forces are motivated; physical forces are caused. Humans activate trippers to go to a store or turn on a light. We act intentionally and in some way freely. Natural processes then act back upon us in a deterministic or at least unintentional way to reset physical forces for the next sequence of action. Human survival is contingent on natural responses, so eventually trippers are fateful. The complete set of physical responses likely, and perhaps always, includes more than what is foreknown or intended by those who do the tripping, even by scientists and policymakers.

Even if the effects of trippers were unpredictably but immediately fatal, there would be no way to know what we were doing until nature's responses come within range of measuring instruments or personal perception. Outcomes appear at different time intervals following a tripper's activation. Sequences of tripped outcomes highlight a central axiom of interactionist thought: the meanings of an action continually unfold in the responses of others. Understanding human-environment interaction is based on distinctions between expectations and outcomes, and between symbolic representations and physical events. Adequate understanding challenges us to keep both realities within one framework—an essential characteristic of an ecological attitude. In addition, there are time lags between what we intend and what actually happens. Adequate understanding requires relevant time frames for interpreting trippers' effects.

A defining feature of today's world is that *the cumulative outcomes of modern tripped interventions exceed the effects we intend and know in our everyday actions.* Ecologists say that "we never do only one thing" (Milbrath, 1989). If we always do more than we intend, then we need to think more holistically about our actions. Holistic thinking challenges us to evaluate the two metaphors informing today's eye-sight: linear or cyclic views of the phys- ical world. Linear thinkers may nonchalantly believe that they throw things away. American culture has encoded this linear belief—witness the mounds piled high and holes filled deep with thrown-away garbage (Rathje and Murphy, 1993). In the United States, the daily waste thrown away by each person rose from 2.7 pounds in 1960 to 4.3 pounds in 1990, a more than 50 percent rise in thirty years, even as landfill space decreases (World Resources Institute, 1994: 90). Everything we throw away lands somewhere, or in some form comes back to us or our children. In the short run, poor peasants, wealthy ranchers, or large corporations may have a linear intention to grow more food or raise more beef as they trip fires to burn tropical rain forests. In the somewhat longer run, however, the impact on atmospheric carbon levels, global temperatures, rainfall patterns, and the short-lived fertility of the rain forest soil fail to sustain the linear goals that motivated the fires. Today the tripper may have the intended effect, but tomorrow is more difficult to figure, though essential for our children. Time frames are a crucial aspect for making sense of tripped outcomes.

Trippers in Everyday Life

Look around at trippers that make up our material culture and under- write both the doing and the meaning of the good life. The United States is sometimes called the "first modern nation." Part of the meaning is that the United States has grown as a nation along with the invention, application, and spread of technology and high-energy machines. These machines affect every aspect of society: how we transform material things into useful products; where and how we build houses; how often and far we travel to work; how and where we recreate; how and what we eat; and how and with what frequency we communicate.

Since the birth of the United States, inventions and applications of energy and machines patterned the warp and woof of American lifestyles. Consider household inventions around the eighteenth century: "water closet" (toilet), sewing machine, gas water heater, carpet sweeper, refriger- ator, lawn mower; and into the turn of the nineteenth century: electric motor and cooking stove, gas-oven thermostat, air conditioner, and microwave ovens. These inventions formed the material context in which an individualistic identity became the core cultural meaning of a person. A cleansed self nearer to godliness means something different to users of public baths and toilets compared to the private individual in one's own "bathroom," mirror and all.

In the last hundred or so years, use of electricity trips significant outcomes for the environment (see Table 3.1). In 1971 and 1990, approximately 40 percent of world electricity production came from coal. Over that same period, the percentage supplied by nuclear power rose from 2.1 percent to 17.0 percent. Air pollutants from coal-fired plants vary considerably but remain significant, especially for plants using older technology (Brown et al, 1994: 61ff.). Burning nonrenewable coal and oil fossil fuels still drives modern life. Analysts anticipate that China may fuel her modernization with vast coal reserves. Informed eye-sight sees *through* our everyday routines like flipping the light switch to the energy sources that light the lights. We now know some links between energy use and human-environment relations. One link is simple: burning fossil fuels has health-related outcomes in the environment. Table 3.1 offers one general schema for such throughsight. Throughsight helps us see the action pathos of everyday acts like switching on a light or starting a car—we never do only one thing, and we never know all the outcomes.

Thomas Edison started the world's first electric power company in 1880, and two years later turned on the first 158 electric light bulbs at the Pearl Street Station in New York City (Brown et al, 1994: 61). The light of these few bulbs soon spread over the nation and the world. They were joined by telephones, phonographs, radios, TVs, VCRs, fax machines, CD players, and now rapidly growing numbers of computers linked in electronic highways. The first computer was built in 1945. It weighed twenty-seven tons and had seventeen thousand vacuum tubes. By the beginning of the Computer Revolution in 1980, one hundred years after Edison's electric company, there were likely fewer than 2 million computers in the entire world. By 1994, there were an estimated 148 million, of which 135 million were personal computers. There is no sign of a slowdown in their exponential growth. The worldwide national average is approximately 27 computers per thousand population, with the United States far ahead with about 265 per thousand (Brown et al, 1994: 100–1). Some estimate that this electric- and battery-based technology uses about 5 percent of the United States' commercial electric load and is its fastest growing segment (p. 113).

This thumbnail sketch catches the rapid spread and depth of tripped interaction with the physical environment. Fill in the picture with trippers that are less understood or more out of sight, for example, chemical "tools" like propellants and sprays, and radioactive instruments for heat, energy, or cooking. Trippers reflect the growth of modern switchgears like levers, valves, circuits, laser beams, and sensors. Switchgears are instruments or forces for releasing, directing, and transforming energy and matter—the fundamental components of all ecological systems. The next and as yet incalculable frontier for tripper development is molecular. Applied scientists use molecules as switches that channel energy and molecular matter into new forms of matter and even life through biotechnology and genetic engineering.

Table 3.1. Selected Environmental Effects of the Nonrenewable Energy Sector

EFFECTS ON:	Air	Water (surface) underground, inland and marine	Land and soils	Wildlife	Risks	Others: wastes, human health, noise, visual impacts
ENERGY SOURCES	FOSSIL FUELS EXTRACTION, TREATMENT, TRANSPORT, WASTE DISPOSAL					
COAL	Particulates Various chemicals[1]	Acid and salted mine drainage Mine liquid waste disposal Water availability Wash water treatment Water pollution from storage heaps	Land subsidence Land use for mines and heaps Land reclamation of open cast mines	Natural habitat disturbed Exploitation of wilderness or natural areas for surface mining	Occupational risks	Noise of rail transport of coal Dust emission Visual impact of coal heaps
PETROLEUM PRODUCTS	Ammonia Particulates Trace elements Various chemicals	Oil spills Water availability	Land use for facilities and pipes	Natural habitat disturbed Pipeline impact on wildlife Wildlife polluted through leaks or spills	Blowouts, explosions and fires	Odor Pipeline leaks Spills (accidental and operational) Visual impacts of pipelines
GAS	Emissions Combustion emissions Various chemicals	Liquid residual disposal	Land use for facilities and pipes	Natural habitat disturbed Impacts of pipelines on wildlife	Blowouts High leak potential General safety	Spills and explosions Visual impacts of pipelines

ELECTRICITY GENERATION FROM FOSSIL FUELS (exluding nuclear energy)

	Water availability / Thermal releases	Land require-ment	Secondary effects on water, air, and land	Occupational risks	Visual impact of cooling towers and power lines / Solid wastes / Ash disposal / Noise
Trace elements, Particulates, Radionuclides, Long-range transport and deposition of pollutants, "Greenhouse effect"	Water availability, Thermal releases	Land requirement	Secondary effects on water, air, and land	Occupational risks	Visual impact of cooling towers and power lines, Solid wastes, Ash disposal, Noise

ENERGY SOURCES:

URANIUM FUEL CYCLE AND ELECTRICITY FROM NUCLEAR POWER PLANTS

	Mine drainage / Underground water contamination / etc.	Land subsidence (mine) / Land reclamation / Land use for mines	Secondary effects of impacts on water, land, and air	Occupational risks	Radioactive products / etc.
Radioactive dust, Gaseous effluent (radionuclides), Local climatic impact of cooling towers, Various chemicals	Mine drainage, Underground water contamination, Water availability, Thermal releases, Liquid radionuclide emission, Various isotopes	Land subsidence (mine), Land reclamation of open cast mines, Land use for mines	Secondary effects of impacts on water, land, and air	Occupational risks, Plant accidents, Disposal of high level radioactive wastes	Radioactive products, Mine water, Mill tailing water (toxic metal, liquid and solid chemical wastes, radiological wastes), Recycled fission products, Visual impact of cooling towers and power lines, Noise, Decontamination and decommissioning of nuclear power plants

Adapted from: OECD 1991a: 234-5. See also OECD, 1991.

[1] The original table lists various chemicals and isotopes such as sulfur and nitrogen oxides, cobalt and strontium, etc.

As use of molecular switches increases, we will trip environments, organisms, foods, and our children's genetic inheritance at ever-deeper levels. Such trippers spread the action pathos. The picture of modern society framed by a tripper perspective brings to light networks of interactional outcomes analogous to the visible objects we use in our household routines.

Over the 1970s and 1980s in the United States, the percentage of households with major appliances has increased significantly (see Table 3.2). Today virtually every household has a refrigirator and stove/oven, and in the last eighteen years, a microwave. Most households have powered cleaning machines such as vacuum cleaners or dust busters. Add to this a virtual 100 percent of households with furnaces in colder climates and increasing percentages with air conditioners in all parts of the country, especially in warmer climates, and we have four trippers serially activated in season or daily in the case of stoves and refrigerators. These trippers use energy sources almost entirely linked to coal, oil, gas, or nuclear reactors. One hundred years ago, few households had even one appliance. Most were invented or marketed in the later 1800s. Outside the house, we find urban settings with varieties of switches from traffic light buttons to sensors for opening doors; suburban homes surrounded by lawns tended with trippers from mowers to automated sprinkling systems; or rural settings with even larger trippers like tractors, combines, mechanical pickers, and sprayers for working farms, orchards, dairies, and meat producing enterprises.

No matter where we live, the likelihood increases that we are on the move, likely in an automobile. The number of passenger cars is growing rapidly in the United States and worldwide. From 1970 to 1988, the number of cars in use rose from 89.2 million to 137.3 million for a 54 percent increase in the United States, and from 193.5 million to 405.7 million for a 110 percent increase worldwide (OECD, 1991a: 214). At about the same time, the number of kilometers per household that vehicles are driven increased approximately from 20 thousand in 1969 to 24.3 thousand in 1990 for a 22 percent increase (Brown et al, 1994: 83). There are more cars and they are used more frequently. Growing numbers of auto ignitions in the world and the number of times they are tripped means increasing environmental impact.

There are paradoxes in this increase in cars and their use. From a luxury vehicle for play and status, cars have become as necessary as shoes. Because of work, shopping, and housing patterns, more driving is out of necessity, not pleasure or leisure. Although use in the U.S. increased 22 percent from 1969 to 1990, social and recreational driving *declined* 1 percent, while business and shopping use increased 137 percent and 88 percent respectively (Brown et al, 1994: 83)! Cars are no longer a pleasurable luxury but a demanding necessity—from Sunday drives to daily commutes. Paradoxically, larger numbers of cars on the road leads to

Table 3.2. Major Applicance Saturation Levels
(Percentage of U.S. households containing that appliance)

Appliance	1973	1991	Percentage Change
Dishwasher	34.3	47.7	39
Disposer	35.3	47.0	33
Freezer	31.0	33.0	6
Microwave oven	1.2	85.2	7000
Electric range	47.0	56.7	21
Gas range	52.0	45.7	-12
Refrigerator	99.9	99.9	0
Washer	67.8	73.0	8
Electric dryer	41.0	50.6	23

Source: Adapted from Standard and Poor's Industry Surveys, Vol. 2, May, 1993.

slower speeds and even gridlock. Urban travel averages 33 mph in Los Angeles, the city with the most highways, and much lower speeds in other city centers (Freund and Martin, 1993). Growing numbers of twentieth century urbanites in cars move at about the same speed as turn-of-the-century urbanites in horse-drawn carriages. The expectation is that urban and suburban automobile travel will slow significantly in the next ten years, even as roads are built, lengthened, and widened. Environmental effects will increase from both more driving and stop-start inefficiency that jammed traffic imposes. The tripping effect of cars on the environment will increase as long as fossil fuels are burned, even though single car miles per gallon and exhaust cleanliness increase.

Until cleaner energy sources like hydrogen are found and adopted, the oil-powered internal combustion engine will pollute the air at about the rate shown in Table 3.3 that presents some natural meanings of driving a car. On a typical ride, exhaust puts 19.8 lb of carbon dioxide and 1.1 lb of carbon monoxide into the atmosphere for each gallon of gasoline burned. These facts light up the action pathos in driving: turning on the ignition affects the atmosphere whether we know or intend it or not. The automobile is a mighty tripper, and it is multiplying and spreading. A news report suggests that in the next several decades, the average Chinese family is likely to afford a car, adding millions of cars to the worldwide fleet (China News Digest, April 8, 1994).

Suburbanites drive up to homes surrounded by lawns. Lawn caretakers drive motorized tools into view. An "industrial lawn" based on the aesthetic model of short, homogeneous, green, lush grasses requires constant chemical, mechanical, and water intervention (see chapter 5). The array of power tools is impressive: tractors, mowers, tillers, dethatchers, mulchers, shredders,

Table 3.3. Annual Emissions and Fuel Consumption for An "Average" Passenger Car Driven 10,000 Miles at Twenty Miles per Gallon of Gasoline

Parameter	Problem	Amount Per Mile	Pollution/Fuel Consumption
Hydrocarbons	Urban Ozone (smog) Air Toxics	3.5 grams per mile	77 pounds of hydrocarbons
Benzene	Carcinogen	0.09 grams per mile	2 pounds of benzene
Carbon Monoxide	Poison	25 grams per mile	550 pounds of carbon monoxide
Nitrogen Oxides	Urban Ozone (smog) Acid Rain	1.5 grams per mile	33 pounds of nitrogen oxides
Carbon Dioxide	Global Warming	0.99 pound per mile	9,900 pounds of carbon dioxide
Gasoline	Imported Oil	0.05 gallons per mile	500 gallons of gasoline

Notes:

1. The emission factors used here come from standard EPA emission models and assume an "average" properly maintained car on the road in the early 1990s;

2. Fuel consumption is based on today's average in-use fuel economy of 20 miles per gallon;

3. Average annual mileage source: "MVMA Facts & Figures '92."

Source: Adapted from U.S. Environmental Protection Agency. National Vehicle and Fuel Emissions Laboratory, Ann Arbor, MI, March 17, 1994.

**Table 3.4. Air Pollution Output in Hour's Use of
Selected Machines Compared to That of Passenger Car Miles**

Machine	Pollution Equivalent in Car Miles
Riding Mower	20
Garden Tiller	30
Shredder	30
Garden Tractor	30
Lawn Mower	50
String Trimmer	70
Leaf Blower	100
Chain Saw	200
Agricultural Tractor	500
Farm Combine	850
Crawler Tractor	900

Source: Adapted from U.S. Environmental Protection Agency as cited in World
Resources Institute, Environmental Almanac, 1994: 110.

trimmers, aerators, edgers, blowers, vacuums, sprayers, pumps, spreaders,
and sprinklers. Each tool is small, but the collective output of millions of
lawn trippers is environmentally significant. In addition, larger tools, tractors,
and combines work on millions of farms.

Comparing the air pollution per hour of use of lawn and farm trippers
with that from a car, we see surprising relative effects (Table 3.4). Part of the
surprise is the high pollution from two-cycle and other small engines. The
cumulative environmental effect of yard machines led to the introduction of
legal regulations governing their use in California and initiatives for national
regulations as well (Bormann et al, 1993). Even the fun of cooking over an
outdoor grill involves action pathos. Millions of barbecues started with
lighter fluid and burning charcoal add significant air pollution. These examples help us frame small trippers, like the pull cord on a lawn mower or the
starter fluid for charcoal, with millions of other pull cords and fluids that put
significant pollution into the air—like millions of pebbles constantly falling
into a shrinking pond.

Institutional Trippers

Grass-roots responses see many trippers as health-threatening.
Institutions need to place trippers somewhere, and that somewhere may be
near someone's home. Grass-roots "Not In My Back Yard" (NIMBY) movements are now characteristic of industrial societies. NIMBYism is a contro-
versial social phenomenon, seen either as ignorant luddite obstructionism

to progress or enlightened citizen empowerment against the threatening decisions of short-term profiteers, absentee bureaucrats, or military overlords. It refers to local movements resisting trippers imposed on communities by outside political or economic stakeholders.

Over the last few decades domestic patterns of toxic waste disposal and of siting dangerous production or incineration plants show a relationship to two social indicators: the poverty level and the ethnic makeup of the communities. In short, the production and/or disposal of toxics are located in communities that are poor or minority, and often both. Scholars see this pattern as environmental injustice based on class and race (Bullard, 1990). Furthermore, the international flow of toxics shows a parallel pattern: toxics originating in wealthy First World industrialized nations are sent to poor nations of the Third and Fourth World. There are both domestic and international environmental justice issues in the systematic flow of toxic trippers from the rich and powerful to the poor and weak.

In addition to intended trippers, there is the ever-possible accidental tripper. Given the realities of human or equipment failure, handling toxic materials carries a probability greater than zero of unintended but actuarially calculable accidents, or unpredictable and unavoidable natural forces like earthquakes or hurricanes. Training and quality control lessen human errors and material accidents, but never eliminate them. The last decades of the twentieth century are punctuated by major toxic events like pesticide accidents in Seveso, Italy; Bhopal, India; and Bern, Switzerland; and nuclear accidents at Three Mile Island, U.S.A; Chernobyl, Ukraine; and other former Soviet Union sites. Some occurred through human error in the predawn hours. These predictable "accidents" call for continual monitoring of the social organization, timing, and physical location of risky and dangerous trippers.

The stones and pebbles of environmental pollution alter human health patterns. Comparison of "causes of death" in less industrialized and more industrialized societies show patterns possibly linked to trippers. In advanced industrialized societies, for example, cancer causes approximately 20 percent of deaths; infectious and parasitic diseases cause less than 5 percent of deaths. In less industrialized countries, the causes of death are in the reverse order (Brown et al, 1994: 120). Although these numbers are difficult to interpret exactly, a preliminary message is clear. For whatever reasons, cancer is a characteristic threat to human health in industrialized nations. Data pointing to causal links between industrial pollution and human health are coming to light from heavily industrialized regions in the former Soviet Union and polluted locales in the Third World. The medical profession has a new category of "ecological medicine" that looks to patients' environments as well as their bodies for diagnoses. Indeed, "ecocide," that is, severe environmental degradation linked to visible health problems, was an important dynamic in the break-up of the Soviet Union (Edwards, 1994; Feshbach and Friendly, 1992).

Military Trippers

Highly rationalized and deliberately intended trippers could be the most consequential of all—military "ordinance," that is, explosives or chemical and biological poisons that trip the environment. Simply review the range of tripper ordinance: bullets, mines, torpedos, rockets, missiles, and bombs, both conventional and nuclear, as well as chemical poisons and deadly germs. Nations frame these weapons and their tripped outcomes as positive instruments for waging war or national defense. Through a military strategic frame, their use is seen as essential for national goals; to cost money; to be part of a balance of power; and to have antipersonnel and anti-object effects. As trippers, however, we see through them as having environmental effects both directly when they are exploded or used, and indirectly through their production, testing, and unavoidable though unintended accidents (Shulman, 1992). There is an "ecology of war" (Lanier-Graham, 1993) that studies environmental effects of warfare.

A modern military tripper multiplied so recently and rapidly that only now is partial data available. The historical instant of the 1980s marks a massive outbreak of "land mines." Although the manufacture and sale of land mines is partially secret for military and legal reasons, even modest estimates are sufficient to change our eye-sight. In the early 1990s, the U. S. State Department estimates the number of land mines deployed around the world at about *85 million in 56 nations*; the United Nations estimates that there are 105 million in 62 nations. Approximately 10 to 30 *million* land mines are produced annually by 48 nations. The secrecy of production and the laundering of sales makes it necessary to calculate these estimates indirectly from the profits of land mine manufacturers and from the number of casualties in mined countries (Webster, 1994).

Estimates put 7 million mines in Kuwait, 12 million in Afghanistan, 20 million in Angola, and uncounted more in Somalia, Mozambique, Cambodia, El Salvador, and other battlegrounds. Battlegrounds in the former Yugoslavia are now seeded with untold additional mines. Some mines are buried in known patterns and marked according to military conventions; others are indiscriminately sown anywhere people walk: in pathways, trails, fields, farms, and around water holes or market centers. Land mines are not targeted; they terrorize. Anyone may step on one. Victims are often children at play who stray afield; women seeking water, wood, or food; travelers; workers; and sometimes military, even peacekeeping soliders. The rapid explosion of victims has generated local cottage industries making artificial feet or legs and building wheelchairs from native materials and distributing them to the crippled. Land mines are trippers in an almost literal macabre sense: they forever mark the crippled lives of often innocent people who lived, walked, and tripped the forces housed in the mines by private profiteering businesses in market countries like the United States and Italy, or by state-owned manufacturers in China and Romania. Recently, there were reports of a new "breakthrough," namely, all-plastic mines that are undetectable by current "mine-sweeping" technology.

In addition to immediate damage to limbs and lives, long-term environmental effects are as yet uncalculated. The direct explosive effect is relatively minor, though the indirect effects of manufacturing add to the pollution flow. Finally, estimates for removal and disposal range toward the $200 to $300 *billion* level worldwide at a time when financing positive environmental projects is threatened. Ironically, it may cost between $300 and $1000 each to remove millions of about $3 plastic mines (Webster, 1994: 29). Aside from the economic effects that indirectly affect our relationship to the environment by diverting scarce monies, a common method for disposal is simply to detonate them in the open air, another tripped source of pollutants.

With land mines as an illustrative instance of military trippers, we learn to see through military expenses, research and development, training, target practice, and energy or fuel use to their environmental outcomes. We add an ecological frame to military eye-sight. What are the overall environmental effects of military technology, weapons, energy use, and waste disposal? The outcomes range from disposal of normal waste accompanying military production to the still unsolved disposal of nuclear waste and unused nuclear bombs.

Environmental outcomes spare no military power. They flow from military production within the domestic borders of the producing nation trying to protect itself from external enemies while paradoxically threatening its own citizens' air, water, and soil. An investigative journalist puts the issue as "the threat at home" of toxic domestic outcomes from military buildup, especially nuclear, biological, and chemical "weapons." Paradoxically, highly technological weapons for defense generate toxic wastes that threaten the lives of the nation's own citizens. Toxic weapons indirectly target ourselves—a variant of Pogo's dictum about looking in a mirror to see the enemy. After the breakup of the Soviet Union, toxic problems of military production became evident and remain unsolved, from nuclear waste in domestic and international waters to the cementing of a radioactive lake bed hopefully to entomb nuclear toxics for tens of thousands of years. Within the United States, plans and debates continue about cleanup and disposal of large amounts of ammunition, biological and chemical weapons, and nuclear materials in the form of waste and retired warheads. Environmental eye-sight provides a complementary perspective to military and patriotic frames for making rational decisions about weapon production and use.

A final framing of military outcomes asks about the environmental effects if certain categories of weapons are indeed tripped. Aside from the environmental damage of the war itself, we are learning additional lessens from the Gulf War. The direct and indirect environmental outcomes are still being counted and costed. What price do we put on the long-term health effects of persons whose lungs are slowly damaged by pollutants spread in the air by burning oil wells? Debate continues concerning health problems of the military who served in the Gulf War. These health issues help us re-sight military operations as linked to human life-support systems. In a word, we see preparing and fighting high technology conflicts through an ecological framework that illuminates health effects on military, citizens, and environment. The U.S. military is now re-sighting its official relationship to the environment as it faces the huge cleanup of past pollution and new policies for the future (Eyre, 1992).

A Metaphor and a Megatripper: "The Button"

As a primary exemplar of military trippers, I focus on a definitive instrument and symbol of transverse interaction, "the Button." The definite article, the, joined with the capitalized noun, communicates the proper object—so central is this thing in everyday talk. While there are piles of buttons in home button boxes, but there is only one Button. We all know to what it refers metaphorically, although we do not know where it, or more accurately, they are. We are talking about trippers for exploding and/or launching nuclear weapons, paradigmatically portrayed by that special Button in the attache case so saliently accompanying the U.S. president and USSR chairman during the Cold War. We are not sure where the Buttons are now or who is carrying them. In spite of the magnitude of its outcomes, it remains uncertain if military or criminal control systems can work as rational means for launching nuclear bombs (Ford, 1985: 25). Metaphorically, we speak of the Button, even though there are many Butt⸱⸱ many nuclear trippers. Nuclear proliferation means mor⸱ ⸱ They are contemporary trippers par excell⸱⸱⸱

Nuclear weapons have never b⸱ devastating and dramatic tripped effe⸱ dropped by the United States on Hir⸱ nuclear explosions produced what at⸱ destruction. In a virtual instant, they cr⸱ sands of persons and started thousands ⸱ and psychological trauma. The scale of t⸱

similar to the destructive power of but a single contemporary tactical warhead, that is, a "small" nuclear weapon designed for battlefield use. There is no test of modern nuclear forces to show for certain, nor can we imagine what would occur, if part of even one major nation's strategic or tactical nuclear arsenal were detonated.

We do know that a large-scale nuclear exchange would be far more devastating than the destruction wrought in Japan (e.g., Barash, 1987: 79; Kurtz, 1988: 43; Lifton and Falk, 1982: 45, 276). A report issued in 1983 depicted possible environmental climatic changes through computer simulations of long-term effects of a major nuclear exchange based on information from natural disasters, such as the Mount St. Helens eruption (Barash, 1987: 98; Kurtz, 1988: 27). Long-term radiation effects from over seven hundred atomic explosions at the Nevada test site on workers and observers provide additional hints of risks to human health. There are grotesque effects on Soviet citizens and military from radioactive exposure near the city of Semipalatinsk and its now sealed-in-cement radioactive lake (Edwards, 1994). Further evidence comes from the health problems of American "downwinders" exposed to fallout from nuclear testing in Utah. Through increasing knowledge of natural responses, we, like the engineer designing the bridge, learn to listen to the environment so we can better gauge the meanings of our interaction with it.

Interpreting Inanimate Responses: The Button as Metaphor

How do we symbol users project meaning and motivation on our tripping activities? How do we expect nature to respond and how do we interpret those responses and integrate them into our everyday world? What legitimating frameworks do we apply to expected environmental responses? Studying the extreme case of a major thermonuclear exchange, we document two frameworks that lead to opposite ways of thinking and feeling about it: a natural framework and a transcendent framework (cf. Johnson and Weigert, 1980). How would you react to the news that the Buttons are pushed and nuclear warheads launched? Such news can lead to anticipations as opposite as the celebration of sure human fulfillment through Divine salvation and new life, or the despair of horrible death and empirical devastation. The meanings can be as contradictory as transcendent life in God's Kingdom on a cleansed earth or widespread nuclear in a degraded physical environment.

ectations derive from the framework through which we imagine follow from a nuclear exchange. Persons can look through a nscendent frame (e.g., Lindsey, 1977). In a natural frame, antic-es are derived from empirically based inferences about natural forces that follow the same laws governing them until now. After an exchange of nuclear bombs, therefore, persons using natural symbols would anticipate destruction of life forms and devastating changes in the environment. The metaphorical descriptor is "holocaust," referring to a literal burning of large numbers of life forms and the freezing of others in the long winter expected after the first fires.

Believers looking through a transcendent frame, on the other hand, would anticipate responses derived from beliefs that events are subject to Divine power that govern natural outcomes at all times, and indeed at times and in ways that prophets already have told us. Transcendent framers may believe that a description of natural responses to a nuclear exchange are subject to Divine power and announced in ancient prophecies and by contemporary prophets (Weigert, 1988). An "armageddon theology" makes sense of great destruction by re-sighting it as a welcome and necessary step in God's plan for us (Kierulff, 1991). Proof is found in prophetically based interpretations of events as diverse as the organization of nations in the European Economic Community; the founding of Israel; rates of drug use and teenage pregnancy; or the spread of AIDS. Through a transcendent frame, believers see the Button not merely as launching nuclear missiles arching through the sky, but also as initiating the coming of Jesus and the Rapture of saved believers into that sky (Van Impe, 1984).

Rather than fear and apprehension at natural environmental outcomes, the Button may inspire joyful yearning for God's Kingdom (Ammerman, 1987: 44–46). These totally contradictory definitions of anticipated responses to a nuclear exchange derive from contradictory frameworks for seeing the situation. Frameworks and their eye-sights, in turn, are linked to the social contexts within which events are realized, that is, constructed as realities by the organized responses of members in the know, such as military officers, political or religious prophets, ethnic warloads, or terrorists. Furthermore, those with nuclear bombs in their possession can make their social frame- works physically real by pushing the Button or otherwise tripping nuclear bombs that affect all our lives, whether we have any say or not.

Some Contexts of Nuclear Trippers

The contexts in which we find trippers help define their social mean- ings. I consider five aspects of social contexts: who gets their hands on the tripper, or access; which organizations control them, or institutional embed- dedness; distance from everyday events, or spatial separateness; organiza- tional types of actors, or personages; and what I call "aura," the aesthetic and moral weighting of the tripper that our imagined meanings give it, especially an eschatalogical sense, or Endtime aura.

Access

In our everyday routines, we can ask, What trippers do I access on my own? A public tripper is available to anyone who knows where it is; what it is for; how to activate it; and is motivated to use it. Most city dwellers can read public signs; recognize the offset button in the traffic lightpost; know how to push it to gain the red for crossing the street; and have the moral presence to use it only as needed without making drivers stop needlessly. A traffic light button announces its access to any native of city streets.

At the other extreme of access are the garrison abodes of the wealthy and powerful; hideways of the criminal netherworld; guarded repositories of state, business, and religious secrets or sacred objects like gold at Fort Knox or silver at West Point; and stealthy arrays of "top secret" military weapons, above all, the Buttons themselves. Very few individuals are allowed to get their fingers close to the Buttons (Kurtz, 1988).

To keep the U.S. Button accessible to the commander in chief, a "black box," or metaphoric "Football," travels with the President. Presidential access, however, may have been only a show during part of the Football's history. As a former director of the White House Military Office remarked:

> Not one President . . . ever got an update on the contents of the Football, although material in it is changed constantly. Not one President could open the Football—only the warrant officers, the military aids, and the Director of the Military Office have the combination. If the guy with the Football had a heart attack or got shot on the way to the President, they'd have to blow the goddamn thing open. (quoted in Bracken, 1983: 226)

In days of U.S.-USSR summit meetings, a major with the lethal Football strapped to his wrist sat near the U.S. president, and the USSR president's bodyguard was said to be carrying the Soviets' own Football (NY Times, 1990). High-level national Buttons are mobile, apparently carefully guarded, and institutionally embedded in military hierarchies and rituals that supposedly gave instant access to the president, even though his access may have been doubtful.

Other Buttons, not under immediate control of the commander in chief, are accessible to a variety of military officers. Buttons or Keyholes for launching nuclear bombs exist in silos, submarines, and command posts, each with different command chains, and some with authorization to launch on their own in certain circumstances. Physical obstacles, specialized identities, requisite knowledge, and special keys or codes restrict access presumably to those whom we may legitimately trust to launch nuclear weapons or not—depending on our evaluation of the command and control systems for launching and of the morality of the weapons themselves.

Recent international developments and the breakup of the Soviet Union increased the number of command and control hierarchies. With even more uncertainty, the number of renegade, perhaps terrorist, fingers on Buttons may increase. Former members of the Soviet Union, now independent nation-states, gained access to nuclear weapons stationed in their territory. Other nations continue to develop nuclear weapons. Terrorists try to buy or steal them. As I write, nations with known on-line Buttons, or the capability to put nuclear weapons on line, number seven: United States, Great Britain, France, China, Russia, Ukraine, and Israel (Sivard, 1991). In addition, three other nations that had or were working toward nuclear capabilities have ceased these programs and accepted outside monitoring, namely, Argentina, Brazil, and South Africa (Sivard, 1993). Two other nations, Iraq and North Korea, were building nuclear weapons and possibly possess nuclear capability. Two others, India and Pakistan, are thought to have nuclear weapons, possibly aimed for each other. Some former Soviet Union members may have operational nuclear weapons, such as Khazakistan.

The seven nuclear and eight or so near nuclear nations have: different types of political and military governance; differently motivated and ambitious leaders; different reasons for developing nuclear weapons; different command, communication, and control linkages ranging from civilian to military to ideological strongmen; different groupings of friends and enemies; and different ideologies for using the weapons from apocalyptic holy wars to pragmatic bargaining chips. Consider that Israel likely has about. one hundred nuclear weapons; India and Pakistan may have on-line nuclear weapons facing each other; Iraq, Iran and North Korea are intermittently in the process of acquiring nuclear capability; and the Ukraine acquired already mounted and targeted nuclear weapons with the breakup of the Soviet Union. Of these nations, the first has a friendly relation to the United States; the second pair have ambiguous relations with the United States; the third group is hostile; and the last is in the process of working out its international relations, especially with Russia (Dunn, 1994).

This brief sketch of expanding nuclear weapon accessibility shows how complex are the social contexts of nuclear trippers around the world. The relations these nuclear nations have with the United States, their neighbors, and their enemies by no means exhaust the implications of nuclear weapons. "Friendly-hostile" descriptions simply highlight one dimension of the motives for use. To get a fuller flavor of the issue, imagine how complex are the relations among each nuclear power and the array of neighboring nations, that is, those within striking distance, for example, Israel and Iraq,

Syria or Iran; North Korea and Japan or South Korea; India and China and Bangladesh and Pakistan.

Over the last forty nine years, it is roughly estimated that nations have spent over *$4 trillion at 1993 value on nuclear weapons*, likely led by the *United States with over $1 trillion*. There are an estimated 26,700 active warheads in just the five largest nuclear nations representing "more than 1,600 times the destructive force of *all* firepower used in World War II" (Sivard, 1993: 11, italics added). If even one or two Buttons were pushed, the results would redefine human-environment relationships over wide reaches of the earth. Indeed, nations downsizing or retiring from the nuclear weapons' race have huge environmental cleanups in the range of $100 billion just for the United States over the next two decades (Sivard, 1993: 17). The manufacture of nuclear weapons is a very dirty toxic process. Disposal and cleanup, if possible at all, are both costly and risky. Nuclear bombs have been exploded in tests every year from 1945 to 1992. China and France exploded nuclear bombs in 1995 and France into 1996.

Aside from known nuclear nations, access includes the possibility that revolutionary, terrorist, apocalyptic, or secessionist groups may get nuclear weapons. This is a story line that Ernest Callenbach used twenty years ago in his environmental utopia novel, *Ecotopia*, to make plausible the scenario of Northern California, Oregon, and Washington successfully seceding from the United States (1977). Multiplication of the social contexts and accessibility of Buttons will arise if a terrorist group of any kind—political, revolutionary, ideological, apocalyptic, or profiteering blackmailers—steals, buys, or makes nuclear weapons. Some are already smuggling weapons-grade enriched uranium and plutonium on world markets (Time, 1994). Apparently, the initial motivation is profit. The question is, who has the use of nuclear weapons outside the control of the nation-state?

Access to nuclear bombs is increasingly open to any group with sufficient money and technical know how. These scenarios are grist for the literary mill of spy thrillers and spoofs, from movies like "Dr. Strangelove," James Bond novels, and the "Get Smart" TV sitcom of the 1960s that satirized the deadly serious real game of keeping track of black market nuclear weapons during that brief watershed period of the Cold War. At the time of writing, I know no instances of terrorist groups with nuclear weapons. If and when terrorists acquire nuclear capability, however, the Button's access changes significantly.

Institutional Embeddedness

A second aspect of a tripper's context is institutional embeddedness. The pedestrian traffic button is embedded in a network of public traffic controls and people's movements that ebb and flow in daily rhythms. Aggregates of individuals form transitory groups for short-term goals, such as crossing a busy street safely or rushing to work on time. The public pulse beats without formal organizational charts, contractual rights and duties, fixed territories, and hierarchical structures. The invisible hand of extended social organizations such as family or work coordinates the movements of large numbers of urbanites with open access to traffic lights.

The inaccessibility of the Button, on the other hand, forces us to rely on partial accounts of the often secret organization surrounding it. In general, there are highly formal hierarchical structures of entitled actors that embed the Button within restricted territories, although there may be operational gaps or breakdowns that threaten its efficient use (Ford, 1985). In the United States, the main structure is peopled by military commands crossed with civilian operatives topped by the president. The civilian commander in chief, however, is in a Catch-22 situation with the military who control access, knowledge, and means for launch. There are other launch command chains on land, in the air, and under the sea. Add structures built into the command chains of other nuclear nations or the fluid power lines of emerging groups.

Sometimes Buttons are surrounded by adversarial groupings such as protest demonstrations in the United States, or the women's encampment at a nuclear weapons site in Greenham Commons, England (Weigert, 1990). Such groups bring the formal structure of the political-military organization into ritualized conflict with the rather informal structure of antinuclear protesters. The conflict is aptly realized by the physical force used by the military to "defend" the Bomb against the symbolic threat of blood or red paint splashed by civilian protesters.

Spatial Separateness

A third dimension of trippers' contexts is spatial separateness. Some Buttons are geographically distant from population centers or protesters, as far away as submarines can get under the sea or airplanes up in the air. All are separated by built environments and hierarchies of guards and rules. The hierarchical chains parodoxically link Buttons to the lives of citizens by separating them spatially and interactionally.

Buttons are also separated by social psychological barriers. Persons close to the Bomb are screened for attitudes of obedience, nationalism, and war that are important to the command hierarchy. Does the screening process lean toward those who obey orders no matter what they are? Blind obedience is sometimes functional for warfare and football, but it may not be desirable in a thermonuclear exchange. Furthermore, behavioral and psychological routines of launch personnel must be constantly monitored:

upwards of twenty thousand U.S. service-personnel attending nuclear situations were removed for alcohol, drug abuse, or other problems in the years
1975–80 in what we assume was one of the world's safest nuclear commands
(Thompson, 1985: 58). How many were dismissed from other command
chains? The psychological separateness of Buttons facilitates "psychic
numbing" that may make it easier to obey a command to launch and to allay
anxiety from obeying the command (Lifton and Falk, 1982). Psychological
attitudes toward obedience in regular military command chains coupled with
apocalyptic groups' readiness to obey raise the devastating stakes even
higher.

Personages

The fourth contextual dimension focuses on socially constructed types
of organizational actors, or personages. Every one of us acting within
formal bureaucracies becomes a personage, that is, a type of person socialized into the ways of thinking, acting, and feeling needed to do the job day
after day without a self-conscious thought. In the nuclear silo, for example,
the personages with the launch key enact the Button's links with society
and are ready to initiate nuclear explosions. In the United States, at the top
of the main launch command chain is an elected civilian politician along
with other semi-independent chains of military personages who may push
the Button (Blair, 1985; Bracken, 1983).

Military personages are trained to fight "wars" with courage, obedience,
leadership, and perservance. In the ambiguity between the idea of war and
the actuality of nuclear exchange, however, there is no face-to-face
courage. In a highly technological and bureaucratic context, obedience
may lead to irrational and unintended outcomes; leadership may be elimi-
nated by breaks in computer links and failed electronic lines of command;
and enormous devastation can be visited within minutes either by human
decisions or built-in smart nuclear launching devices that virtually "know"
to launch if their sensors virtually "perceive" an incoming attack. We
moderns may now come face to face, not with an enemy, but with a smart
nuclear bomb launched and directed by preprogrammed electronic signals
precise enough to find military headquarters, perhaps.

Smart bombs with their own TV feeds lit up American screens during
the Gulf War, or so we were shown and told. Equally real issues of morality,
error, and outcomes are not preprogrammed into high-tech smartness. Even
at the supposedly alert heights of the Cold War, Paul Bracken summarizes
the cross-quilt of lines of authority for launching nuclear weapons as an
"ambiguous command" with no certainty of an efficient response to
perceived threat (1983: 224–232; Blair, 1985). To invoke a time-honored

cultural lag axiom, the technological means and environmental effects of nuclear weapons have increased far faster than the political, military, psychological, and moral abilities of responsible persons to evaluate them.

Since there has never been a thermonuclear *exchange*, there is no experiential learning or collective memory for assessing such an event. Hiroshima and Nagasaki are more misleading than predictive for understanding an exchange of modern nuclear weapons. *One* Minuteman silo houses Bombs with the power of one thousand or more Hiroshimas; there was no nuclear retaliation by Japan against the United States; and a relatively unscathed outside world was there eventually to assist Japanese survivors. It is as though the Enola Gay dropped nothing more than the firepower of one rifle shot compared to today's approximate twenty-six thousand nuclear bombs. In view of this enormous devastating power, how does a society: define the personages who can touch the Buttons; educate them to the deepest human values; and yet have them obey a command to launch? These imperatives involve contradictory ways of seeing and acting. Military authorities empirically resolve the issue. They do not want moral reservations in their "missileers," and perhaps as a result they prefer men to women (Maszak, 1988; Tobias, 1988).

Aura

The fifth aspect of the Button's context is aura. Aura refers to an experiential quality of an object traditionally linked with a religious attitude toward the sacred that elicits a sense of aweful otherness, alluring fascination, unique excitement, and unharnessed power. It is "totally other" in existence, power, space, and time (Otto, 1958). It is a numinous object in its holy place, its inner sanctum. Aura refers to the aesthetic and moral qualities that observers experience in the presence of power that so transcends their everyday sense of place and time that they believe it can absorb their lives and bring about their final destiny (Chilton, 1982). I understand a *numinous aura as a ratio of the sacred transcendent aspects to the profane empirical aspects of the powerful object in its place*. The ambivalent experience of the numinous ratio heightens our expectancy and alertness toward the believed power of the sacred object. It simultaneously excites and attracts us to embrace it even as it frightens and repels us into creaturely retreat (Van Der Leeuw, 1963; Weigert, 1991). The aura of nuclear weapons inherits the imagery of transmutation, belief in powers that transform life into death and perhaps death into life (Weart, 1988).

Robert Oppenheimer, co-creator of the atomic bomb, captured the numinous aura of its ambivalent power when he answered a reporter's question about the first nuclear explosion with the words from the

Bhagavad Gita, "I am become Death, the destroyer of worlds" (quoted in Weart, 1988: 101). Thus did a co-creator of the Bomb frame the first nuclear explosion that humans both exulted over and despaired about. Phenomenological analysis finds parallels between religious experience and the aura of the Button: sacred space such as temples and silos protected from profane feet; anointed personages who alone enter the inner sanctum; sacred language, titles, and identities separate from those of daily life; objects and relics toward which ritualistic deference is given and a person's demeanor is restrained lest a mistake unleash transforming power; a life of sacrifice, abstention, and asceticism for the attending personages; and the destiny of entire societies hanging on proper rituals toward, and touchings of, the sacred objects (Kurtz, 1988).

The place and status of these sacred objects are enveloped in secret rituals and priestly hierarchies that reinforce the ambivalent sense of mystery and awe that evoke both public interest and cultural numbing. In a word, the dramatic staging of the Button generates mysterious secrecy, a phenomenological mark of the sacred. The nuclear aura marks a profound historical transmutation. A secular weapon of deeply destructive interaction paradoxically recapitulates the phenomenology of sacred power. This paradox re-presents our newfound quasi-divine (if the word be allowed) human responsibility for our own existence, not by life's creation which still lies beyond our power, but by life's destruction which now lies behind our Buttons.

Salience of the Environment as a Tripped Other

Framing the Button as a tripper highlights the importance of the social organization of technology for environment interaction. Human organizations are complex systems of many modes of interaction: self-instrument; self-other; self-place; and what could not be clearly seen within western rationality until the emergence of ecological science in the nineteenth century: self-environment, and society-environment interaction (Blumer, 1969; Catton, 1994; Giddens, 1976; Milbrath, 1989; Miller, 1994; Schnaiberg and Gould, 1994). Who is positioned where in relation to which trippers tells us about hierarchical arrangements and the weighting of values through which we assess and activate anticipated environmental responses. Any urban pedestrian trips the traffic button. Power to trip the U.S. nuclear Button is denied to virtually everyone except a few politicians and mostly military men. Of course, international nuclear proliferation changes access and organization with every national decision or black-market deal. Who knows whose fingers touch the Button today?

Ritual chains of personages structure institutional and group interaction with the Button in the hierarchies that make up the launch command chains

of nation-states for military aggression or national defense. Apocalyptic ideo-
logues may have fingers on the Button. In both cases, military, ideological,
and political logics take precedence over environmental, aesthetic, or business concerns. Unlike social interaction in which persons change their minds
and redefine their deeds with disclaimers and excuses or redo their relationships through realigning actions, transverse interaction includes chains of
physical causality that determines environmental responses. Once begun,
transverse interaction plays out its environmental effects whether humans
change their minds or not.

In tripping the environment, symbolic meanings are translated into
physical responses. This is one root of action pathos. In symbolic interaction, others may pardon our actions and remake the social world as it was
before by accepting such accounts as, "He hurt me deeply, but I love him
anyway." The mix of nondetermined—determined responses in human-
environment relations means we cannot undo our actions by seeking
forgiveness or giving excuses. Once thermonuclear bombs devastate life-
support systems, environments cannot say, "Humans hurt us deeply, but
we'll support their lives anyway." The absurdity of this environmental
dialogue tells us about the potential danger in transverse interaction whenever persons accustomed to redoing social reality interact with inanimate
nature in ways that cannot be undone. Buttons once pushed are more
fateful than arrows once shot or words once uttered.

It appears that no empirically referenced version of the American myth
can absorb the nuclear Button to make it a legitimate instrument for
fulfilling that myth. Only transcendent religious myths that seek nonempir-
ical solutions, such as Christian other-worldly eschatologies or apocalyptic
escape by Rapture can transform the Button into a desired faith object
bringing God's Kingdom to a cleansed earth (cf. Weigert, 1988). Were
personages motivated by transcendent beliefs to push the Buttons,
however, the results absorb all earthdwellers into empirical devastation,
whether they believe in God's Kingdom or not.

We need to think critically about transverse interaction, trippers, and
environmental others. Today's trippers link self and environment to the
viability of life-support systems. We must learn to look for and listen to
nature's responses. The empirical future causally implicated in our actions
must become symbolically present in our intentions. Otherwise, we will not
learn to see through our actions to their environmental outcomes for us and
our children. One possibility is the cultivation of a "critical animism" for
interpreting self-environment interaction, that is, seeing ourselves as part of
an interrelated living system with the world that is there (Lovelock, 1987;
Rochberg-Halton, 1986). Moderns are coming to see the need for calcu-
lating the effects of trippers on our life-support systems and for re-sighting

their use in everyday life. The next chapter looks at powerful objects that are perennial symbols of life, but that are being re-sighted as threats to life as well.

4

Inversion: Environments Turned Upside Down

Seeing is a physical reception of stimuli and a perceptual imposition of meaning. It is a framing of events so that I experience them in a way that I can grasp them and go on with my life. My actions both modify the meanings of events and intervene in natural processes in the world. I am both physical and symbolic forces that play themselves out in the natural and social worlds. Because what is true of my interventions in nature is true for all, the processes of human-environment interaction involve collective social processes with systemic effects on the environment. Chapter 3 focused on often unseen trippers, physical means of intervening in the world, that have outcomes both intended or unintended and foreseen or unforeseen. Today, we are increasingly informed about unexpected or unintended outcomes that change the way we see our actions.

The expansion in scientific knowledge and measuring instruments make it possible to know more about the natural world, like the web of life that makes up soil, and to foresee more outcomes of our interaction, like the link between CFCs in air conditioners and thinning of atmospheric ozone. Anomalous facts like the discovery of toxics in tap water or poison in milk illuminate unforeseen and unintended outcomes of our actions. Data on patterns of illness, like cancer rates in Massachusetts, Louisiana, New Mexico, or Long Island, lead us to question industrial waste management or patterns of toxic dumping.

To be modern is to lose environmental innocence. Inherited ways of seeing and acting are no longer taken for granted. We rethink idealizations like, "We can go on with business as usual," "That's the way we've always done it," or "Gee, I didn't know that would happen too!" The accumulation of anomalous facts, unexpected patterns of illness, knowledge of ecological dynamics, and new perspectives on earthly events, such as pictures of the

Big Blue Marble rising and setting, challenges inherited frames for making sense of the natural environment and call forth new ways of seeing our relationships with it. This chapter looks at natural things and social objects that people are reframing through better knowledge of outcomes and new perspectives for seeing them.

Idealizations That Frame Our Seeing

An indicator of perceptual change is a sense that "the world is turned upside down." This sense of inversion refers to objects or images that take on meanings opposite to those that they typically have. In an upside down world, we define objects and events in ways that contradict inherited definitions; we interpret them in a new frame that changes their relationships with us and other objects; we reevaluate their moral worth; we experience feelings opposite to those that usually accompanied them; and we act differently toward them and ourselves. Changed perceptions re-do lived experience. Since we live in the public world, we discover that others also are perceiving these objects and images as turned upside down. The meanings move from objects in my personal sight to objects that exist within a collective eye. It is not only I, but also confirming others who sense that objects are turning upside down.

New perceptions indicate a socially constructed perspective that includes a personally meaningful way of seeing; a sense of objective reality that appears massively valid; and emerging groups or media that transform individual sights into collective sights, that is, individual perceptions are framed within cultural and institutional meanings (Douglas, 1986; Greider and Garkovich, 1994). Our everyday lives are grounded in underlying assumptions or idealizations about experience, sight, and action. I earlier mentioned two idealizations that Alfred Schutz used to grasp the experience of sameness and continuity. He refers to these idealizations as taken-for-granted beliefs that give us a sense of security and order. I typically believe that whatever I do, "I can do it again," in a world that will go on as it has "until further notice" (Schutz, 1962; Schutz and Luckmann, 1989; cf. Garfinkel, 1967). Without an unquestioned sense of personal and earthly continuity, life is unthinkable. Humans live, paradoxically, in anticipated futures.

I get up in the morning and drive to work in my car. And I can do it again and again. The world of roads, cars, and work will continue to exist; so these actions can be repeated until further notice, that is, until a major change in my life like illness or death, or in the world like an earthquake that closes the bridge or crumbles the roads. To appreciate the behavioral importance and personal consolation of these idealized assumptions, imagine what life would be if we or others so challenged them that we stopped believing in them. Yet, the assumptions are idealizations. They are human constructions that are ultimately dependent on empirical processes. Eventually, real events *will* render them false or inapplicable to my life and perhaps to the human species as well. Their truth and reality are contingent on natural forces that ultimately lie beyond individual or institutional control.

To understand how we interpret events is to recognize the social sources of the frameworks we use. For example, taking for granted that "I can do it again" in an environment that I assume will stay the same "until further notice," implies that others are acting from the same idealizations. We recognize that idealizations are *social* realities. The source of "I can do it again" is "*We* can do it again," and not just my, but *our* environment is assumed to remain the same "until further notice." Recognizing the collective sources of idealizations makes us face a paradox of social realism: we realize that idealizations informing my personal sense of a meaningful world are idealizations because others also believe them. The taken-for-granted convictions that I can live my life the way I want and that the environment will support my life by staying basically the same are now seen as social idealizations. An environmental perspective leads us to ask whether these idealizations are empirically feasible. Can everyone do whatever he or she wants "again and again," and will the environment remain the same?

Idealizations transform the flux of personal experience into social meanings that we assume remain stable for the time frame within which we act. They undergird the sense of secure and unquestioned reality that envelopes normal experience. In a word, the idealizations ground an "illusion of stasis," the sense that things will go on as they always have. The illusion of stasis supports our belief in everyday meanings and motivates us to repeat daily routines. At some point, however, we must reconcile the illusion of stasis with the awareness that things are not the same as they were yesterday, or ten years ago, not to mention in my grandmother's day, or in other parts of the world in which military, political, environmental, or economic changes contradict these idealizations.

The personal idealizations of "I can do that again" and "so on until further notice" imply, furthermore, that "I *want* to do it again" or that "It is *good* that it continue until further notice." The sense of a stable, dependable world implicates a *moral* sense that "It is good that I can do these things again and again, and that the social world continue as it is." We point to the universality of the idealization with the objective reference, "*It* is good." If it is good, then presumably it is good for everyone—my personal idealization leads to a moral universal. Yet, empirical outcomes may contradict this moral universality. Some ecologists, for example, argue that it is not good for everyone to have as many children as they want, if each wants more than the environment can reasonably sustain (Hardin, 1968).

Additionally, the idealization that events will go on "until further notice" or until a significant change occurs, expresses a shared belief in a dependable world that we must count on and that will change in orderly ways that we understand and can live with. This idealized world reduces our sense of time to the simple recurrence of what has happened before within the rather short term. Thinking about changes, however, implies an awareness of time passing on, not simply repeating itself. Time repeating itself is cyclic time, but there are linear and organic times. My lifetime is a linear, unstoppable process from birth to death. Lifetime is an arrow in flight. Each kind of time has its effect; we live in a world of cyclic and linear time (Young, 1988). Orderly changes happen in a world we define as good or bad, but either world is preferable to meaningless chaotic change. The two idealizations allow us to make sense of both the appearance of stability and the inevitability of change and to feel that both are meaningful aspects of our life and our community.

I suggest that notice is being served to the idealizations that underlay the taken-for-granted personal and collective sense of being at home in the natural world and of knowing how to interact with that world. We increasingly live in a fail-safe society with more known risks and a sense of even more that are unknown (Beck, 1995; Piller, 1991). The idealizations that generate the illusion of stasis are today challenged. The routinely unquestioned is now questioned. For example, many communities around the United States are challenging the previously unquestioned idealization that "I can drink this water again and again." Many are asking, "Is it OK to drink the water again and again?" Other routines are questioned. We are told to stop throwing out the garbage and to recycle it. The continuity is broken between actions and the goals we believe those actions reach. Action pathos is felt. We challenge previously unquestioned objects and motives, in part, because the idealizations that anchored those taken-for-granted beliefs are publicly debated. Environmental debates spark personal wonder that motivates a second look at the world that we believe is there for us.

Questioning can lead to a reversal of meaning. Reversals "de-realize" my immediate experience; that is, they change the accent of reality in my taken-for-granted ways of seeing things, and they disrupt my moral feelings about what I am doing. My questioning sense of what is real and good is no longer guaranteed, and perhaps opposite to what I thought it was. I refer to a reversal in the experienced world as "inversion," a sense that my world and my relationship to it is turned upside down.

Inversion indicates two levels of reversal. One concerns the object we see and the frame that defines it. The other refers to our experience informed by idealizations that give meaning and worth to what we do. At the first or object level, inversion is a redefinition of what we see and a reversal of its moral and motivational worth, for example, an action or object changes from good to bad, from attractive to repulsive. At the level of lived experience, inversion is based on new idealizations that contradict prior ones, namely, "I can *not* do it again," or "notice *has been* served." The taken-for-granted is denied; the OK is not OK. Reversals in the way we see the world change the way we evaluate our actions as well. In other words, we acquire a new idealization of action such as, "I do *not* want to do that again" and "It is *bad* to do that again." The main dimension for evaluating our experience, the "good-bad" axis, is reversed with respect to this object (Demerath, 1993; Osgood et al, 1957). Seeing the world differently involves a complex set of changes in the way we think, feel, and act. Changes in taken-for-granted idealizations change everyday experiences.

Look at a "natural" object, for example, a fiery sunset. Let us call it "Sunset A." As a sunset, it is a totally natural event in the western horizon. We see it as a natural object of beauty and inspiration. As a thing of beauty, we feel good about our aesthetic relationship to its color and grandeur. A religious believer may see in its beauty not just aesthetic reality, but inspiration for affirming the goodness and power of a designing Creator. Switch frames and look at the fiery sunset as a combination of natural processes and human interventions, or "Sunset B." We now see the fiery color as partly the result of burning coal or rain forests that add carbon and particulate pollution to the atmosphere. Burning rain forests, coal, oil, and other fossil fuels releases carbon into the atmosphere and reduces carbon-absorbing trees. Measurements recorded at Mauna Loa in Hawaii show exponentially increasing amounts of carbon in the atmosphere. Unburnt particles refract light waves and contribute to the fiery beauty that we see as a sunset. Framed in the latter way, beautiful Sunset A is inverted into a different object, polluted Sunset B. Sunset B elicits contradictory meanings, motives, and actions. It is a new object constructed in a new frame for seeing. Praise of Divine beauty changes into blame of human pollution.

Conflicting sightings of the same physical sunset exemplify inversion, a reversal in seeing. There are at least three mechanisms that make inversion possible today. First, new frames are available to contemporary viewers through better theoretical understanding of natural processes, such as the atmospheric chemistry of carbon cycles, CFCs, and a thinning ozone layer; second, new measuring instruments generate data that call for relevant interpretive frames, like satellite data on terrestrial hot spots or carbon buildup in the atmosphere; and third, new constructs and metaphors elicit conflicting interpretations of what our eyes see. For example, fiery sunsets evoke metaphoric panes of glass in an imagined "greenhouse" built from gases trapping warm air near the earth, like real panes of glass in a real greenhouse.

Reframing may transform an event from a natural physical process into one that is in part a human social process (Goffman, 1974). Social intervention becomes an intrinsic part of what we saw as natural processes. In a word, the Green Revolution in contemporary thinking points to a fundamental reframing: we now know that much of what we saw as natural is a complex outcome of natural processes *and* social interventions. Practical issues arise in our daily lives: how do we know which outcomes are natural and which are social; and what can or should be done about one or the other.

Environment responses are increasingly a mix of natural and social processes. Moderns who wish to see what is happening need to shift from a natural frame to a natural-social frame. Natural catastrophes like floods or violent storms, for example, are now seen as caused in part by human interventions. Hurricanes, excessive rains, unusual droughts, and extreme weather patterns are influenced by human activities. Think of temperature and precipitation changes across the United States; floods in low-lying regions such as Bangladesh; mountainside erosion from clear-cutting forests in the mountains of the Philippines; or the death of old forests in Europe, *Waldsterben*, and in the western United States caused in part by automobile exhaust and acid rain or snow. Inverting everyday events elicits meanings and emotions opposite to conventional ways of seeing.

Inversion of Everyday Natural Objects

Seeing natural objects and processes is a bedrock on which humans build their lives and institutions. The natural environment and the way we think we see it work is the context within which our lives make sense. These bedrock sights and assumptions typically did not change during a person's lifetime. Humans believed that nature abhors a vacuum; does not take leaps; is a sign of a loving Creator; evolves in an orderly, even purposive way; and reveals its workings to us so that we control it and make progress. This is a story of Progress and Control. We as individuals can count on nature throughout our lifetimes. The natural environment follows its own laws and will go on supporting us no matter what we do. These inherited beliefs inform dominant worldviews about us and the natural environment.

Inherited taken-for-granted ways of seeing natural objects no longer promise certitude, control, and progress. One question does not a revolution make, but patterns of inversions eventually challenge received worldviews. Patterned changes in natural meanings illustrate how taken-for-granted objects are being inverted. Shifts in "felt meanings," that is, feelings and motives related to the environment, are indicated by changes in how we use simple dichotomies such as: natural–social; good–bad; supportive–threatening; and active–passive. I will present selected aspects of the natural environment, the human organism, and technological instruments to illustrate this point. Each reader can reflect on objects undergoing inversion in his or her life.

The Natural Environment

Sun. For reasons as different as primitive religions or contemporary science, humans recognize the sun as the primary source of energy and life on Earth. People also know that too much sun kills. Weighing the life-giving versus life-threatening effects of the sun is shifting with recent awareness of a thinning ozone layer that filters harmful solar radiation. One danger is the rising risk of skin cancer. With less protective ozone in the atmosphere, rates of skin cancers have risen in parts of the world, for example, in Southern Chile or Australia. There are projections of rising cancer risks in other parts of the earth. Some observers estimate that the threat is likely to be irreversible during current lifetimes.

Among light-skinned peoples, interesting struggles in the apparent symbolism of tanned versus untanned skin continue. Segments of the youth culture and cosmetic advertisers value tanned skin, even as medical advisors speak of increased cancer risk, premature skin aging, and risks to the eyes. Advertisers targeting the young show skimpily clad bodies cavorting on the beach in full sun as symbols of fun, health, and the good life. Competing definitions, however, appear in "sun watches" and recommended "sun exposure time" in TV weather reports and local newspapers.

Another sun object is the colorful sky of a sunrise or sunset. Poets and theologians see radiantly colored sunrises or sunsets as bespeaking realities from aesthetic ecstasy to proof for the existence of a Divine artist who paints the sky for earthlings. A sunrise or sunset, as suggested earlier, can take on opposite meanings in frameworks derived from piety or from scientific knowledge of carbon buildup. We can see pinks and purples as indicators of atmospheric threats to our lungs, shifting rain patterns, and rising ocean levels. Seen through an ecological frame, sunlit colors are an oxymoron of beautiful pollution and possible global warming. The evening skies seen from a Caribbean isle are indeed beautiful, but data inverting that meaning continue to grow. Data from the Mauna Loa observatory show exponential increases in atmospheric carbon. Studies of Antarctic ice core samples suggest a positive correlation between levels of atmospheric carbon and warmer temperatures. I see a russet hue in the heavens during a contemplative drive through open spaces in southern Michigan. Its meaning is unclear, but possible interpretations add a disquieting tone to my choice of frame for seeing the sky.

Air. An undoubted source of life is the air we breathe. Older economics called air a "free" good, namely, a necessary utility in such abundant supply that its demand is met without cost; and thus it has no price or market for it. When I was young, air *was* free, in part because no one knew how we affected it, nor how to price it. Air no longer is free. Nor is it as clean. Indeed, politicians struggle over federal legislation such as the Clean Air Act. Is sustaining clean air a national priority? Policy debates over data showing clean air at risk face questions such as whether breathable air can be assured by governmental regulation and taxation or by economic markets for the right to pollute in the belief that pricing mechanisms will bring clean air by making it profitable for business and capitalist logic (Blinder, 1987). Others doubt whether an industrial civilization can ever have "clean" air. I am writing from northwest Indiana downwind from Gary and in a poor air category.

A happy person is figuratively "a breath of fresh air." Air is good, a medium of life. Everyday experience as well as scientific studies, however, verify a shift in the meaning of air inside and outside your windows. Homes sometimes pollute their own air. Modern building materials give off potentially threatening chemicals. Air in buildings has circulated legionnaire's disease; air across the United States carries carcinogens and other toxics. Communities like Los Angeles occasionally keep school children from recess play because of dangerous levels of air pollution. Awareness of air quality rises to new heights as events invert the taken-for-granted goodness of the air we breathe. Local weather announcers include an air quality index. "Is the air sustaining my life and also bringing on lung cancer?" This is a new and inverted question to frame how we see the air we need.

Water. Sun and air have great symbolic power. They link us to nature and evoke deep feelings, but they are not quite touchable. Water, however, is handled as a physical reality even as we feel its symbolic power. Water is an "up-close" and consciously swallowed source of life. It is a sensuous source that, in turn, can swallow us up in an oceanic experience from the amniotic sac to a Walt Whitman poetic immersion, even as we can pick up, pour, and swallow it in another turn. Sometimes it rains on us so hard that it floods our homes. Perspectives as distinct as evolutionary biology and religion agree that water is a source and symbol of life, both physical and spiritual. Christianity canonizes this theme in stories of Jesus giving living water to a Samaritan woman at a well or transforming water into wine at a wedding party. The symbolic realism lives in believers' baptism by water.

Contemporary life, on the other hand, brings the nether side of water into awareness. There has always been death by dehydration as well as drowning. Water is life only in proper proportions: too little or too much brings death. Water without alkaline becomes acid that burns and kills as it rains. Water is a medium for chemical combinations and biological organisms that kill. The polluted well and the liver fluke in the mountain stream threaten us with death and disease by poison or parasite. Scarce water brings conflict, even war. Civilizations build on water use, from the Tigris and Euphrates to the Mormon kingdom in the arid intermountain West. A Utah native recounted that local customs allowed killing a thief who stole your horse or your water. Both immediately support life; death could quickly follow their loss.

We face upward in a soft spring rain and warmly experience water. Indeed, the poetic imagination compares "a gentle rain from heaven" to mercy and forgiveness. Gerard Manley Hopkins saw it as the source of continued life in his cry to the "Lord of life" to send his "roots rain." Recently, however, a new scientific construct speaks of "acid rain." Acid rain gives the lie to metaphors of rain and life. In the earth's water cycle, rainfall is a key distributive process, as though it were Divine compassion that falls on the just and unjust alike. Today the cycle carries burnt waste so that rainwater moves toward the acidic end of the pH scale. It does not take much of an increase in acidity for water to threaten life. Around the North Temperate Zone, forms of life from forests of spruce and pine to fish in mountain lakes and crops in fields show the destructive effects of acid rain. Were it to become so acidic that we would have to protect our skin from a gentle spring rain, then we would have rain inverted from a source of life to a threat.

Humans are dependent on water. Yet, major bodies of fresh water are drying up, some likely beyond hope of reclamation, like the Aral Sea in Russia and some lakes in California. Two empirical dynamics call for a reframing of water: increasing pollution that is not practically reversible in a person's lifetime, and depletion of sources that are not renewable in a societal time frame, such as relatively closed underground streams or aquifers and large fresh water lakes. We must learn to "cost" water more realistically as a growing population's need for it grows.

Soil. As obvious as is the ground we walk on, it is difficult to see it adequately. Humans imagine the soil in many ways. Earth is terra firma. We know that it usually feels solid, but it is constantly in motion. It is spinning, quaking, circling, heaving, and tectonically sliding in ways that are normally beyond our senses. Earth, in some mythic worlds, is Mother Earth, the natural womb made fertile by rain. It is the tactile source of all life (Merchant, 1983). The earth is covered with negatively nuanced realities like dirt, muck, mud, swamp, hardpan, rock, and quicksand, or with positive resonances like sod, turf, ground, humus, prairie earth, and soil, or indeed, topsoil. Soil is alive (Berry, 1977). Soil is the medium for a complex living community in which grow the cereals and vegetables that support nonaquatic food sources. Topsoil is the source of most food. It is the lifeline from farmer to all of us.

Since humans became dependent on agriculture and large population centers grew up, the cultivation of the soil, agriculture, supports most human life. Stated baldly, the last statement seems like a truism, yet it is a truism that is violated as soil is actually lost in some modern food production. Some agribusiness practices do not cultivate soil in a sustainable way. Soil is: degraded by overuse; poisoned by chemical fertilizers and pesticides that weaken or kill the soil community; eroded by poor farming tactics combined with stronger wind and rain storms; salinized by irrigation techniques; or desertified through unwise use and changing climatic conditions partly brought by industrial wastes. Soil dies and is reborn on different timetables, but some degradation cannot be reversed in biographical or societal time. Topsoil is now lost faster than natural processes replace it. Lost soil is not naturally reborn in time to serve those who lost it.

As I grew up visiting my farming cousins, soil was a taken-for-granted ground of life. My uncles harvesting corn believed it was good, and they could do it again and again until further notice. Horse and cow manure was spread over the harvested fields. Soil could be counted on; it seemed ever fertile within our illusion of stasis. Soil is soil; it will always grow our food. Today, however, arable, live, and unpoisoned soil is an increasingly scarce resource. Paradoxically, modern farming may destroy soil rather than cultivate it. Wendell Berry (1977) captures the tension between agri*culture* versus agri*business* or agri*science*. These ideas are rooted in contradictory frameworks for seeing material life and health as well as in social conflict over human rationality, business logics, and cultural values. Rich Iowa topsoil is being lost. What do we think and feel as we see cornfields reaching the horizon without a weed in sight. Formerly framed as agriscience and progress, today endless cornfields reflect ambiguous outcomes and ambivalent feelings.

Trees. A life form that both physically links and signals the linkage between natural environment and humans is a tree. The symbolic power of trees resonates in the poet's rumination, "I think that I shall never see a poem lovely as a tree." Trees reach deeply beneath the surface of the earth and rise hundreds of feet into the skies. For some, they point to heaven. They breathe, as it were, both soil and air. They are black and green, deadwood and livewood. They are the largest and oldest living bridges between air and earth. The Book of Genesis tells of trees as symbols and sources of eternal life and the knowledge of good and evil. Indeed, Christianity sees a tree as a metaphor for its central symbol: Jesus, the god-human, hangs suspended between heaven and earth on the tree of the cross. It is an icon and an organism bridging soil and air, matter and spirit, mortality and divinity (Eliade, 1961). Human interventions raise the acid level of rain and snow. Trees with dying top branches and thinning leaves are inverted from signs of natural life and symbols of divine life into markers of acidity that threatens organic life.

The Human Organism

In this section, I frame the human body as both a natural physical thing and a constructed social object.

Food. Soil and water enter our bodies every time we eat. All food, even seafood, relates to the soil and its products. Food links us intimately and necessarily with nature. We eat nature and it becomes us. Food symbolizes life and physically sustains it. Shared eating is a dinner, banquet, symposium, party, indeed, a religious sacrament or eucharist. Table rituals reflect how we see and value shared life, or commensalism. The movie, "Babette's Feast," portrayed the graceful power of a shared meal to heal divisions, enrich physical life, and symbolize eternal happiness for all who partook. The ritual of eating reenacts our relationships to nature, self, and to each other (Tuan, 1982).

Successful food tastes, looks, and smells good. It is good for you. Until recently, "diet" was what was eaten for nutrition. Today, we invert the meaning of diet. Diet is what is not eaten or what is carefully selected to be eaten to avoid bad food. This negatively positive meaning is part of a pattern that inverts a typical, good-for-you American diet into a sight of too much sodium, fat, sugar, red flesh, bland or mulled foods in routines of unhealthy eating.

Pop culture notes this reversal in the meaning of food. Food becomes "fast food" that not only supports life but also threatens it. The oxymoron, "junk food," captures the risky balance between nutrition and threat. How widespread is the perception that scientifically and industrially produced foods are closer to the negative pole on the tastes better–is bad for you, or the nutrition-threat, scale. The combination of unbalanced diet and inactive lifestyle results in an American population increasingly overweight and suffering from illnesses derived from the way we eat and sit. Socially conventional food, a necessary source of life, is now seen also as a threat to health. This insight leads to a redundancy, "health foods," to answer the heavy advertising for junk foods. Commensalism and the family dinner is replaced by fast foods and individualized "diets" instantly and individually prepared in microwaves for each member of the household. An end point is reached in sufferers from anorexia or bulimia for whom food itself is a problem and diet is life-threatening.

The perception of threat is publically highlighted in debates over growth hormones and steroids for food animals like chickens and cows; chemical additives to produce cosmetic color and longer shelf life in fruits, cereals, and breads; polychlorinated biphenyls (PCBs) and other toxic residues in wildlife like rabbits or Great Lakes fish such that locals are warned against eating more than one lake trout a year; and the general application of genetic technology, radiation, or pesticides to fruits and vegetables with systemic effects, that is, the additives cannot be washed off because they enter the flesh of the fruit or vegetable.

Body Fluids. Food literally becomes part of self's body. Food becomes me. Earlier thinkers related ethnic identity to food and place, and suggested that we are what we eat and we think according to where we live: fish-eating coastal dwellers live in a different psychological world from cereal-eating plains people or meat-eating forest folk. An intimate food inversion is the technologically derived reversal of mother's milk from life-sustaining to possibly poisoned. Radioactive fallout and toxic residues accumulate in mammary glands. Breast-fed infants who are at the end of a toxic food chain—cereals → animals → mothers—suck milk with higher concentrations of poisonous chemicals. Such a chain began in the nuclear fire at Chernobyl, or Wormwood. Chernobyl infected milk in cows grazing as far away as Welsh hillsides and in Lapland reindeer. Thousands of milk-bearing cattle were destroyed lest the poison in their flesh and milk enter the human food chain. The primordial natural-divine symbolism of a mother suckling her child, as well as the simple cultural act of drinking milk as a symbol of good health, are inverted: is milk healthful or does it accumulate harmful radiation, antibiotics, or growth hormones?

The premier natural symbol among body fluids is blood. It is intuitively, experientially, and culturally a cause and symbol of life. Indeed, we speak of "life's blood" to indicate the core of life. Warriors drank the blood of defeated but honored enemies, even as they ritually tortured and killed them. Ancient fertility rites both spilled blood in sacrifices and drank blood in communal eucharists that gave birth to powerful collective identities. For nearly two thousand years, Christianity symbolizes transcendent divine life overcoming fleshly existence by eating and drinking the body and blood of Jesus Christ, the god-man.

Today we see blood inverted. It is known to carry the HIV virus related to AIDS. Blood, the central symbol of pulsing red-blue life, is now a source of a mysterious, spreading, and thus far incurable threat to life. Blood transfusions are a symbol and gift of life-sustaining solidarity. Freely given, they are vital altruistic gifts. We can give to anyone on Earth who shares our personal blood type. Indeed some of us are "universal donors" whose blood can support the life of any human being—a symbol of our common origins and shared biological life. In spite of the commercialization of blood-giving and the tragic poverty of those who sell even their blood to earn money, shared blood symbolizes human solidarity. No longer, however, can anyone receive blood or tissue from unknown donors without mixed perceptions that it may bring life or death.

The threat of AIDS-contaminated blood redefines interaction with doctors, dentists, medical technicians, and nurses. Those who deal in blood and body fluids become potential sources or victims of AIDS. Healers may become carriers of death or accidentally be exposed themselves. Doctors, dentists, and nurses have sometimes been infected, and they have at times infected others. These facts are firing fierce policy debates over mandatory testing of health professionals, publication of results, and safe therapist-patient procedures. Risks, of course, operate in both directions, so that health professionals are concerned to protect themselves against infected patients. The interaction of medical personnel and clients is evolving behaviorally, technologically, and perceptually—from plastic gloves and throw-away needles to careful screening procedures of donors.

HIV-positive athletes publically dramatize changing perceptions. Drops of blood interrupt basketball games; shirts and uniforms are changed; plastic gloves are everywhere. A drop of blood mobilizes protective responses to a possible deadly threat. As a result, blood now elicits two contradictory meanings: source and symbol of life versus cause and sign of death. Modern blood is a mixed medium of both physical and symbolic life and death. It is an inverted image mediating ambiguous meanings between healer and patient.

Mixed outcomes have long been part of the physical meanings of sexual intercourse. That sexual interaction both transmits diseases and creates new life is an old theme. The contemporary scene adds AIDS to previous sexually transmitted diseases. Intercourse that generates new life may simultaneously transmit death. The dilemma is starkly seen in the recommendation to use condoms. A partner who uses a condom to protect him or herself from the HIV virus also prevents new life. If moderns had to protect themselves from potential death in every act of intercourse, how can we remain open to new life? What if a partner or spouse wants new life? Then he or she must expose self to some probability of acquiring death. In a sexually mobile and experimental age, absolute certainty about a partner's sexual biography is impossible. The partner may not even know his or her HIV status—though he or she does know if there have been other partners, and today there typically are. In the place of certainty, we have only trust and a probability between new partners as well as between long-married couples that a dalliance not bring death. The moment of loving embrace becomes a moment of contradiction. Possibilities of life and death are both realized in sexual intercourse.

The possibility of sexual transmission of AIDS creates new social phenomena: known HIV-positive rapists can be accused of murder; HIV-positive parents give birth to infants who are innocent carriers; a tryst, new sexual partner, or marital infidelity can turn self into a carrier who puts lover, spouse, and potential children at risk; a scared teenager writes a letter to a newspaper pretending to be an HIV carrier who will deliberately infect as many partners as possible; or a vindictive carrier, whether lover or prostitute, can in fact do just that. AIDS inverts blood and sexual fluids, two symbols and sources of life, into signs and possible causes of death.

A Baby. Sexual intercourse can mean perpetuating the species and transcending personal death. Humans sometimes seek immortality, both symbolically and physically, by passing on their germ plasm, by "having a child." The innocent hope of a future symbolically embodied in the newborn is a perennial theme of art and reason. The Christian imagination encodes this hope in the Christmas birth of the Christ Child. Today's society transforms hope into a commercial holiday and the secular custom of exchanging gifts. For a religious imagination, Christmas is inverted when seen through a commercial frame.

We further reframe the meaning of a child in the context of an exponentially growing world population. In the mid 1990s, the estimated population is 5.5 billion and growing at the rate of just under 2 percent yearly. At such a rate, the doubling time for the world's population is about forty-five years. Some 11 billion people will need food, water, air, shelter, and warmth by the mid-twenty-first century when today's college students are in their mid-sixties. How much this growing population may consume over and above what it needs is the stuff of ecologists' concerns. As Emile Durkheim argued at the turn of the last century, demography is the morphology of society: population dynamics determine the fundamental possibilities of human life. Ecologists have physical images that make similar points: population irruption, ecosystem carrying capacity, consumption overshoot, species dieback, biological disequilibrium, environmental degradation, or species extinction. The paradox of growing populations and increasing consumption that destroys the sources of that which is consumed is the "tragedy of the commons" (Hardin, 1968). Ecologists teach that the earth is so interconnected that ultimately the globe is a "commons." Economics and ecology depend on accurate understandings of population and consumption patterns, though economics relies on abstract assumptions and ecology on biological patterns (Keyfitz, 1993).

If a newborn is seen, not as a symbol of my immortality nor as a gift from God, but as a sign of a growing "population problem," then the meaning of a baby is inverted from a symbol of hope to a portent of danger. This inversion carries profound implications for imagining the good society and valuing one's sexual self. Such a reversal is implicated in societal incentives or coercions to direct reproductive behavior and population policies. Unless one or more of the Four Horsemen gallop again in the form of death, war, diseases, or climatic driven famines, we can expect deeper cultural changes and/or state interventions to limit population growth. The worldwide population conference in Cairo, 1994, revolved around consensus on curbing population growth and debate on how to do it and on the value of individual life. The dialectic of consensus and debate highlights the tensions in different ways of seeing a populated earth. If population continues to grow exponentially, intervene technologically, and consume wastefully, the next generation may see the earth pushed toward outcomes no one can predict.

Some Technological Instruments

Cars. Historians note that the modern world was midwifed by harnessing natural potential energy and transforming it into working power. Futurists early saw the car as the symbol and motor of a new civilization. Energy translated through engines and gears drives moderns and their society. The residential, retail, occupational, and social structures of modern nation are based on personal and collective transportation dominated by internal combustion and jet engines over water, land, and air. Our focus here is on the car, the automobile, the "self-mover."

Cultural and psychological meanings of the car are many and deep. Given current residential patterns, the car is essential for commuting distances beyond the reach of human or animal feet. Suburban homes are driving distances from food, work, medicine, services, churches, and schools. Once a luxury, in the last fifty years, the car became a physical necessity for modern life. Paradoxically, in spite of the necessary dependency on a car, it remains a source of felt freedom, especially for adolescents. The car is a rite of passage and a vehicle of new experience, anonymity, or escape.

As a commodity, cars are sources of personal identity, peer-group standing, ideological announcement, and social status. A significant rite of passage for middle-class males and females is passing the drivers test and "getting" a driver's license. The privacy and mobility of the car provided the intimate space that facilitated profound changes in the dynamics of youthful love, sexual interaction, and choice of a first spouse. Although not necessarily agreeable to parents or neighbors, the car is a definitive physical and dramaturgical part of modern life. Indeed, financially able moderns use cars to announce and display that "I am what I drive." The announcement is made via exotic names and otherwise meaningless numbers and capital letters, usually a pulsing "X." I am a "Benz," "Beemer," "Vette," or "Jag" person. Self-definition is the message of car ads that love what they do for me, and those expensive high performance cars that advertise in exclusive print media. Car advertisements aimed at youth guarantee attracting a beautiful or handsome athletic passenger-partner with salient sexual features to match their cars. Cars are chariots to the good life.

Critics on a far lower frequency have noted negative features of car culture from the beginning. A new inversion, however, derives from recent car problems. As mentioned earlier, the exponential spread of cars results in gridlock that estimates traffic moving in London at about the rate of the mid-nineteenth century. Average urban speed varies from about 7 to 33 mph in some major world cities (Freund and Martin, 1993: 7). The realization is spreading that petroleum will run out in fifty or so years—given current rates of increasing use and known world reserves. Futurists extolling the arrival of the automobile civilization slid over the "how long," or sustainability, question. Civilization based on gas-driven cars may last no more than one hundred fifty years. Inversion is further fueled by knowledge that cars are poisonous chemical laboratories: exhaust puts particles, chemicals, and bioactive components into the atmosphere that threaten living beings from crops to trees to humans.

An inverted meaning of a car, a symbol and tool of modernity, puts contradiction at the heart of both the need to get to work or the store, and the need for validation of how we live who we are. The key in the ignition and the command, to paraphrase the Indy 500 call, "Gentlepersons, start your engines," are now signs of contradiction. To drive who we are is to threaten our environment.

Smoke. Smoke exiting chimneys and entering lungs suggests changing eyesight. From early lithographs to turn-of-the-century photographs and paintings to mid- and late-century advertisements, smoke bellowing from tall stacks bespoke the industrial might of Progress, Control, and the American way. Even nostalgic Christmas cards depict familial warmth and intimacy with thin spirals of smoke rising from snow-topped cottages on rolling hills traversed by horse-drawn sleighs. Grandma Moses knew well-curled smoke evokes warm fuzzy feelings. The single images complemented each other: tall-stack smoke says progress; curled chimney smoke says family values.

Smoke signaled economic health, even as public health officials worried about the physical threat to those living downwind. The barons of industry lived upwind, atop the hill, or out of town. Eventually, industrial coal-fueled cities like Pittsburgh were cleansed. "Stink industries" went overseas. Downtowns were razed and rebuilt as financial centers and franchised resting places for jet-set nomads. Perhaps Gary, Indiana, remains the last flaming, smoking, and partly boarded-up example of "cities" built to accommodate an industrial empire. U.S. Steel put Gary about midway between the iron ore of Minnesota and the coal of Pennsylvania. Ecologists from the University of Chicago noted that Gary lies in the midst of a rich and unique niche of glacial, and for some, singing and sacred sand dunes.

In environmentally awakened eyes, smoke is a beam. From a symbol of progress, it becomes a sign of pollution. It is waste that contributes to global warming and acid rain. The adult toy of a suburban fireplace is both inefficient and polluting. Smoke floats carcinogens into the air. Cheap sulphur-laden coal pollutes more than more expensive coals. Businesses and nonprofit universities find it difficult to install or turn on costly antipollution devices like smokestack scrubbers. The logic of our images is now dialectical: industrial smoke equals pollution as well as progress. What about individual smoke?

Smoking. We breathe smoke from individual cigarettes, cigars, and pipes. Pipes symbolize the reflective academic don who thinks wise thoughts as he tamps his smoldering pipebowl. A cigar, on the other hand, is an aggressive prop for the macho, cigar-chomping business go-getter; the basketball coach signaling another victory; the leader of a socialist island nation; or the father of psychoanalysis for whom the cigar was occasionally just a cigar.

The cigarette ranges widely across cultures, genders, and ages. It is a symbol of modern adulthood, sophistication, masculinity, and above all autonomy, including a new idea of femininity. In former times, young males oft held a secret rite of passage by sneaking smokes beyond parental eyesight and sniffing range. My first smoke was a drag on a home-drawn "cigarette" made by rural cousins out of dried corn silk and rolled newspaper. The meaning of the rite was magnified by my coughing fit. In my imagination, World War II movies announced the same male identifier, brought to a dramatic peak by Humphery Bogart's deft manipulation of the cigarette with talking lips and gesturing hands amidst swirling smoke that gave the scene a numinous aura. The quasi-religious sacramental meaning of the cigarette was portrayed in war movies in which the dying hero or hero's buddy is given a final gift of life: a cigarette lit between the lips of the living placed lovingly between the lips of the dying. "So Long, Pal!" The final gift of a cigarette becomes a living warrior's sacrament to a fallen fellow warrior.

Its power as a sophisticated identifier targets the fairer sex in recent decades. Cigarette manufacturers took aim at the liberated female as a new market. Indeed, ads such as, "You've come a long way, Baby," measured the cultural distance traveled by liberated female smokers. Of course, the repressive vocative, "Baby," supplies the ambivalent message that she has not yet left home to be on her own. She is still labeled diminutively by a powerful other. Nevertheless, the tripped outcomes of increasing lung cancer and related health problems among female smokers suggest that part of the target was hit. Similar marketing tactics are aimed at not yet fully tripped audiences such as younger smokers who like camels or horses, minority groups with their own billboards, and foreign markets.

Even as new gender, ethnic, age, and overseas markets are hit, the meaning of smoking is undergoing inversion. Redefining the long-standing sobriquet of a "coffin nail," cigarettes are acquiring empirically based definitions that link them statistically with diseases such as high blood pressure, lung cancer, and emphysema. In an outstanding institutional contradiction, the surgeon general of the United States insisted that the message, "Warning, smoking cigarettes may be hazardous to your health," be added to every pack of cigarettes, even as other government agencies subsidize the growing of tobacco. Indeed, the claim has been made that, of all cultural and legal personal habits, smoking is most strongly linked to increased probabilities of personal illness and loss of work time.

Growing evidence linking "secondary" smoke, that is, smoke inhaled by nonsmokers, to increased probabilities of illness generalizes the coffin nail metaphor. This generalization fuels debates over policies regulating where a person may rightfully smoke, for example, airplanes and other common carriers, classrooms, work sites, restaurants, jury rooms, waiting rooms, and prisons. These debates are akin to right-to-life arguments involving the state's right to protect a conflicting definition of human life from direct or indirect threats by others' free choices. Your smoking threatens my life, not just yours, when you exhale. The cigarette debate rolls on toward more complete inversion.

Risk. So what is to be done in inverted situations? A response is found in both pragmatic and traditional cultural imperatives: intelligence emerges to solve problems in living; and wisdom reconstructs inherited knowledge to address new problems. The imperatives address two defining characteristics of modern society: the increased reality of "risk" as an ever-present part of life and its social construction; and the inevitability of threats to life-support processes from personal and institutional actions (Beck, 1992; Giddens, 1991; Milbrath, 1989).

Inherited ideas of "natural" risks or "acts of God" are now seen as partial outcomes of human action. Climatologists project that electrical, rain, snow, and wind storms will increase partly as a result of increasing carbon in the atmosphere from burning fossil fuels and rain forest depletion. Measurements of atmospheric carbon levels suggest that continual burning of fossil fuels will generate increasingly severe weather. Furthermore, floods in Bangladesh, the Philippines, and elsewhere are worsened by deforestation higher up the mountains. Such floods are not simply "natural," nor, any longer, are changing rain and snow patterns that contribute to desertification in other regions. Patterns are partially tripped by transverse interaction.

Inverted Conditions: Illusion or Reality?

The "world turned upside down" is a world in two senses: it is systems of physical processes that make the world real in itself; and it is a socially constructed set of images and concepts that change with history and make the world real to us. These images and concepts motivate interaction with each other and the natural environment. Interaction maintains institutions and generates possibilities for living. The paradox is that institutionalized knowledge of the natural world comes to us through individual eye-sight and institutional logics that structure all our seeing. Misinterpretation, bias, ignorance, error, and incompleteness are built into our knowledge of the natural world. Inversions characteristic of our time are based on new data about the natural world. These shared data encode the natural world as an inverted image on the retina of our minds. Consider how the natural world looks if we "see" it framed by: limits on population or a consuming life-style that, if surpassed, lead to irreversible ecological changes; scarcities that make it uncertain that 11 billion persons will live well in 2040; more waste and toxicity than the natural world can re-absorb and continue functioning as a healthy environment for us; and continual interventions in the natural world that generate greater risks to species life.

Social analysts study conditions that lead to lifescape inversion. One source of inversion comes from an understanding of limits that show the possibility of transgressed limits and broken systems. Transgressions and breaks then elicit threatening natural reactions that may threaten previously supported life forms. A second condition is scarcity. Scarcity points to the foundational limit, the ratio between species need and natural resources. Although most humans have lived with scarcity sometimes overcome by the sweat of one's brow or social cooperation, only today are we aware of species scarcity, that is, scarcity within the earth's biosphere, not simply within an individual's situation or a community's ecological niche.

A world framed by scarcity belies the myth of progress. Change is no longer seen as necessarily leading to a bigger, better, happier, healthier world of ever-increasing populations living evermore consuming lives. Indeed change is inverted into an ironic process that has some probability of generating deeper problems than those resolved by the change. Progress is reframed as irony: action in pursuit of the good life that paradoxically generates risks in the systems sustaining species life. Ecologically speaking, it is impossible to do only one intended good thing when we intervene in natural processes. We always do more than we intend or know. This is an old lesson indeed. It is encoded in the contemporary imagination and portrayed in Michael Crichton's novel, *Jurassic Park*. My mother told me about the irony of the last straw that broke the camel's back. Freud told the story of the horse of Schilda that surprisingly died from the short-term cost-effective logic of feeding it one less stalk of oats every day.

The inverted images sketched above are instances of a larger paradigm shift, a change in the collective way of seeing that integrates experience in everyday life. I wish to reemphasize two ideas here. First, everyday life is grounded on phenomenological assumptions that create an illusion of stasis, namely, the belief that nature provides the massively stable world that is continuously and securely there for me. I assume that I can always do what I did over and over again until further notice. Life, however, is not rocklike stasis; it is systemic process. Second, the process of life is not progress in the mythic sense of the enlightenment project of rationality, science, and technology that brings ever greater control over nature to the benefit of all, including our children's children. Indeed, modern life is characterized by increased possibilities of greater numbers of people suffering from famine, newly recurring diseases, and poverty into the twenty-first century (Kennedy, 1993).

Inversions imply a shift in worldview from an inherited dominant social paradigm based on assumptions that business as usual and technological breakthroughs allow continual interventions into natural processes, and that they will solve the problems such interventions create. An ecological paradigm, on the other hand, offers an enlarged vision of human-environment relationships. Photographs from outerspace, for example, *The Home Planet*, support inverted eye-sight (Kelley, 1988). For the first time, humans look at photographs or "real" images showing our home sphere whirling through space, an *earthscape*. Sequences of photos show sights humans have never seen. Pictures of earthrise and earthset parallel daily experience erroneously interpreted as the sun's rise and fall. These realistic first-time photos invert inherited images and understandings that grounded our sense of the earth under our feet and the earth in our eye-sight. As the first generation to see photos of the earth as a single bright sphere in the darkness of space, we can never again see ourselves as nothing but hyperindividualistic spheres spinning in self-contained personal orbits. All of us share one sphere, one earth. Switching perspectives from the earth switches our perspectives on earth. To illustrate switching perspectives, the next chapter re-sights that small patch of earth many moderns see as their own when they look out the window. How do you frame a "lawn?"

5

Lawns of Weeds: The American Lawn as Status Struggling With Life

Even a lawn looks different seen through different frames. Everyday meanings derive from symbols that relate experience to the world that is there and to the logics of institutions, especially language. The dualistic perspective of this book focuses on the symbolic aspects of an object without ignoring the physical. Studying social status does not justify ignoring the natural environment. Critical issues concerning the social and the natural come together collectively as our life-support systems or particularly in objects like my front lawn.

The "lawn" realizes physical and social realms in a single object. Physical objects are also meanings constructed through our organized responses. A socially real object like second base exists only in a baseball game. It is not the physical cardboard or canvas sack ninety feet from "first base." It is made by the organized responses of all who play the game (McCall and Simmons, 1978: 50). Players, umpires, coaches, and fans construct second base through their actions in playing, regulating, assessing, and appreciating the game. Many of us touched, reached, stole, and doubled something real we knew as "second base." Whether it was a piece of cardboard or a square traced in the dirt is irrelevant to the game. So too, a lawn is a social and physical object, not merely the biomass of plants growing around a house. I refer to the brute biomass as a "sward." The lawn, by contrast, is socially constructed by the responses of all who transform sward into lawn. Lawn is a dual reality of status-generating physical and symbolic interaction between homeowners and swards. Transverse interaction requires us to understand the physical realities that make up the sward as well as the social definitions that are a lawn. We need to consider the lawn's physical being to "altercast" the other, the lawn, as total reality with which we interact.

111

The sward is part of the world that is there. The lawn is part of the social life process. Both are embedded in life and culture. The relationship between life and culture is continually reexamined. Although they are related in origin and dynamics, life and culture are irreducible to each other. In this understanding, we say that life is not culture and vice versa. A strong sense of their relationship recognizes opposition. Life as physically natural and culture as constructed form are in conflict: life breaks out of culture; culture constrains life. At the turn of the twentieth century, Georg Simmel stated the tension between form and life as the conflict and tragedy of culture. He characterized our time by noting that, "Although this chronic conflict between form and life has become acute in many historical epochs, *none but ours has revealed it so clearly as its basic theme*" (1968: 25, italics added). Our historical moment is in part defined by the contingent relationship of life and culture. We must reexamine assumptions that are mutually supportive, as in the strong functionalist interpretation of culture as positive adaptation or co-evolution. The mutual sustainability of life and culture is a precarious contingency, not an empirical given nor a theoretical certainty.

Against the Western myth of teleological evolution or progress, I adopt Simmel's lemma of cultural form in tension with life. Although such ideas seem "top heavy" for our mundane topic, I see the modern lawn as a telling instance of the lemma. I offer definitions and suggestions for understanding how the form of a modern lawn is constructed, announces high status, and generates strong motivation and moral demands. Next come empirical indicators of biological consequences from constructing contemporary lawns. At the least, this analysis shows the power that unquestioned definitions have on the way we see a physical reality like green grass and argues against teleological perspectives that see culture as only positive adaptation to ecological niches or progressive co-evolution toward better forms of life.

How Do Lawns Give Status?

Once a space is seen as lawn, a dialectic of opposites helps define its meaning. The dialectic applies the cultural analysis proposed by anthropologist Mary Douglas. In *Purity and Danger* (1970), she argues that simple dichotomies seem to be structural universals in moral codes. In everyday language, this dialectic generates perceptions of clean-dirty or pure-impure. These dichotomies are analogous to the central psycholinguistic practice of labeling objects as good-bad to weigh their aesthetic and moral worth.

If we assign the noun *grass* to plants with thin, green spike leaves that make up a good lawn, then the dialectic symbolically transforms such grasses, but not all, for example, "crabgrass" for reasons given below, into good objects in the lawn. Broad-leafed or nonconforming plants like dandelions are then transformed into bad objects, or "weeds" in the lawn (cf. Jackson, 1985; Jenkins, 1994). Such symbolic transformations are not physical processes that produce new physical things, but social processes that redefine physical things and thus produce new symbolic objects. Social transformations are ways of seeing the same physical things as new objects in a publicly certifiable way. Looking at a thin blade or broad leaf and seeing it as lawn grass or weed is a theoretical act made possible by the frame through which we see it. Sward is framed as natural; lawns are framed as social—the two foundational frames for seeing (Goffman, 1974). Perhaps unknowingly, we are quite theoretical in making sense of everyday objects.

Confronted with brute things that are thin, green blades and broad-leafed plants, the caretaker of a lawn is in a problematic situation. Deciding what to do demands a framework that enables him or her to categorize, evaluate, and act toward those things in a morally proper way (Hewitt, 1991). In a word, the caretaker symbolically transforms the physical blades and leaves into meaningful social objects and responds to them accordingly—nurturing one and poisoning the other. The caretaker accomplishes this transformation in part through a theoretical reconstruction of bladed grass and leafed weeds into indicators of high or low status in the community.

Consider how status is generated from nominally defined objects and a series of social relationships. Cecilia Ridgeway (1991) presents a social psychological argument that relates structural and situational elements to explain how the status value of a nominal category like gender is constructed in such a way as to rank men over women rather than making them equal or the reverse. I suggest similar theoretical steps that transform mere sward into high-status lawn and broad-leafed plants into weeds. First, a lawn and its good form are nominally designated: we know it when we see it; and we know how to label, discuss, and react to it. Exemplars of today's good lawns are found in wealthy suburbs and traditional towns. Historically, good lawns derive from lawns kept by the English-landed class. An original example in the United States is "The Lawn" established by Thomas Jefferson at the University of Virginia (Bormann, et al, 1993; Jackson, 1985). The vernacular front yard as lawn may have originated in the midwestern United States, perhaps spreading from Toledo, Ohio (Schroeder, 1993). Early lawns were associated with desirable qualities and resources such as wealth, Americanism, property values, traditional morality, gender roles, and the noble personal characteristics assumed to go with such qualities.

Situationally, homeowners hold high expectations about the moral worthiness of good neighbors who maintain good lawns. Routine encounters support these expectations both by interpreting neighbors' yards in accord with their good qualities and by eliciting favorable responses through friendly neighboring in return. Finally, links among good lawns, valued resources, and satisfying encounters lead us to generalize that all persons with good lawns are good neighbors and good persons who have good values. The high status of good lawns becomes a consensual belief, that is, a general shared truth, uncritically assumed, about your good qualities and mine.

A consensual belief aims cultural evaluations both at the other and at self. That is, if I have a good lawn, I know and feel good about myself, and about you if you have a good lawn. We both, then, know and feel good toward ourselves and each other, mutually enhancing our initial expectations (see Demerath, 1993, for positive feeling from a sense of shared certainties). In the end, you, I, and all suburbanites are highly motivated to have good lawns as both signs and enactments of my worth, your worthiness, and the collective goodness of our neighborhood.

Status is based on interpretations of signs, a semiotic of appearances (Stone, 1981), that is, on general symbols that announce my position in the status hierarchy, inform my value preferences, confirm my public morality, define my personal identity, elicit positive feelings toward myself and my neighbors, and link self to the collective identity of the community. Status is a dramaturgical effect of the expressions a person presents, grounded in the setting and scenery within which that person performs (Goffman, 1959). Setting and scenery are status expressions that support the situated identity of the lawn caretaker's self and, by extension, of the selves of family members who dwell in the house identified with that lawn.

As status symbols, lawns are constructed objects announcing caretakers' identities realized in the responses of those who interact with them. The responses also construct an evaluative hierarchy of lawn appearances through which interpreters rank the home and its inhabitants in terms of the rank of their lawn. Developers of American garden suburbs as early as the middle 1800s mentioned the positive merits of their landscape design (Jackson, 1985). A landscape guide in the 1930s declared that "if householders wished to be good Americans, they would maintain a respectable, open front yard with a grass lawn" (in Hecht, 1975). The lawn's appearance not only bestows status, thus rendering the lawn dweller a moral actor, but also ranks him or her, thus evaluating personal moral standing. Knowledgeable observers calculate the moral worth of the lawn through a series of seen dichotomies.

Dichotomies That Generate the Cultural Form of Today's Lawn

The first dichotomy concerns *origin*, introduced versus native. Introduced grasses are good; native grasses are bad. In early American lawns, introduced grasses replaced native grasses so rapidly that they are often assumed to be native (Bormann et al, 1993; Pollan, 1989). Currently, the builder of a new home who develops a new lawn clears local grasses and tries to prevent their return. Native soil may be scraped off and topsoil for the proper sward put down. The resulting lawn is a standardized artful ecological reality that does not occur naturally. It is sustained only with constant intervention. It is an artificial monoculture, a collection of identical introduced grasses that natural species would likely replace if left alone. To sustain a monocultured lawn, the caretaker overcomes soil, sun, moisture, climate, insects, diseases, and local plant competition. Human intervention transforms lawns across the United States into a facsimile of one kind of ecological niche in which only certain grass species are allowed to grow. The difficulty of this contrived ecological reality is manifest in the labor, capital, and resource-intensive means endlessly applied to the sward.

The second dichotomy refers to _tactility_, soft versus harsh. Silky soft and smooth grasses are good; tensely tough and toothed grasses are bad. Harsh grasses evoke what one neighbor referred to as a lawn of "hay." Besides, they may cut soft hands or bare feet. Seeds of imported or research-generated grasses with the valued tactility are introduced. There is an aesthetic preference for soft grasses; they look and feel better in the frame of suburban landscape aesthetics.

Next is _color_. It translates into a dichotomy of dark green versus other hues and colors, especially brown. An efficient spreading grass such as zoysia was a useful alternative until its habit of turning brown during dormant seasons in the Temperate Zones gave it a failing grade on the color criterion. The preference for a deep blue-green color makes "bluegrass" and similar varieties into high status blends, but they are difficult, indeed impossible, to grow in every situation. Ironically, they do not appear blue when they are constantly mowed short.

Once a lawn is started, there is a dichotomy of _density_: thick versus thin. A thick "lush" lawn is good; a thin "sickly" lawn is bad. Lushness is possible only with sufficient nutrients and moisture, akin to the precipitation of England where high-status lawns originated. Delivering adequate moisture to insure uninterrupted soft, green, and dense lawns is so difficult that suburbanites turn to an underground watering system that waters daily, automatically, at the same time, in the same amount, even in the rain. Ironically, brief daily watering creates a self-perpetuating watering necessity by generating lush grass with short root systems that go dormant more rapidly than infrequently watered grass, if the daily dose is lost. Nutrients, usually chemicals, must be added every season. Lushness springs from watered, nutrient-rich, frequently tended sward that marks a high-status lawn, especially amidst otherwise dry surroundings.

The thick-thin dichotomy points to the _production_ criterion: labor-, resource-, or capital-intensive versus light-labor, low-cost, or low-technology lawns. High technology and constant intervention produce lawns seen as good. Low technology and infrequent intervention produce lawns seen as bad. The good lawn is never brown, shaggy, variegated, tall, or thin, because it is watered, mowed, sprayed, and fertilized on daily, weekly, and seasonal schedules. Furthermore, constant intervention demands an array of hand, or better, power tools such as: tractor, mower, mulcher, thatcher, edger, weed eater, aerator, vacuum, blower, fertilizer, roller, sweeper, sprinkler, and sprayer. These tools join synthesized chemical fertilizers and pesticides to combat insects, weeds, moss, blight, fungus, grubs, and other threats to monocultured grasses. Partly because the good lawn has become so intensely capitalized, the final high-status move is for homeowners to drop the identity of caretaker and hand over lawn appearances to "professionals," just as bodies are attended by professional "beauticians" who know how to groom our "good" appearances. The lawn-care industry is growing, grossing about $2.8 billion in 1989, while the lawn and turf industry is an estimated $25-billion business (Bormann et al, 1993: 68; 83).

Since grasses grow continuously in season if fed and watered, there is a high-cost investment in the dichotomy of *height*: short versus long. Short, neat, well-manicured lawns are good; long, shaggy, poorly cut lawns are bad. Power mowers achieve the valued "crew-cut" look; mechanical push-reel mowers leave a "shaggy" look. Shortness is a key trigger that fuels intensive intervention. The shorter the lawn the faster it dries and the quicker it changes color; the more it must be watered; the more water will run off; if clippings are removed, the more it must be fertilized to keep it healthy enough to resist pests and weeds. Shortness speeds up the cycle of intervention. Because short lawns need to be watered and fertilized frequently, they grow more rapidly and thus require more frequent mowing.

Short lawns do not provide cover for insects that may keep each other in check. Shortness makes any illness immediately visible. The delicate condition of short lawns means that threatening invasions require rapid intervention, typically some kind of "cide," that is, the suffix from the Latin word "to kill" that we use to refer to toxics. Finally, short grasses never go to flower or seed. Thus, seeds must be purchased and spread. The end point on the shortness scale is a putting green on a golf course, a cultural form that cannot survive a single growing phase on its own, must be constantly nurtured, and requires protection from a wide range of threats. The shortness of the high-status lawn is a key feature that trips high investments of time, money, equipment, labor, and chemicals.

A general dichotomy is *consistency*, same versus mixed. Consistency cuts across previous dichotomies: consistent color, type, and height of grass are good; mixed colors, heights, and grasses are bad. A monocolored lawn is preferred to a mottled lawn. An acquaintance who had a new house landscaped, for example, asked the developer to replace dead spots in the lawn. Since the replacement grasses grew to a yellower shade of green, the developer then had to replace that healthy but overly yellow grass with a darker shade consistent with the rest of the lawn. Even a small yard likely has different ecological areas with different conditions of sun, water, soil, and use. Each area is likely to favor different grasses or plants. Lawns look alike only at a high cost.

A motivational vignette is occasionally enacted as I drive through the suburban neighborhood. A bespeckled executive-type middle-aged male with a pipe clamped in his mouth is kneeling and hand clipping deviantly tall blades of grass at the intersection of his driveway and the curb. I find it difficult to imagine any other motivational system, including slavery, that has the moral power to bring that type of actor willingly to his knees. The high-status lawn succeeds in getting high-status persons into deferential and humble poses.

The power of a high-status lawn is not a simple one-time effect; it is a ceaseless battle against natural processes. The high-status battle is summarized in *investment-derived* value criteria: difficult, scarce, and costly versus easy, abundant, and cheap. The cost of lawn care is exemplified in a 1986 survey in North Carolina that found an average of $407 spent annually on lawns averaging six-tenths of an acre (Bormann et al, 1993: 81). High investments fuel the conspicuous consumption of high-status appearances. Inexpensive and low-status lawns reflect biological diversity, cycles of growth and dormancy, and tangled vegetation. Preferred grasses grow from introduced seeds that display high status at high cost. Naturally abundant or invasive grasses like crabgrass are cost free, and consequently they are negative status markers for lawn cognoscenti.

A lawn that ranks high on the preferred feature of each dichotomy, that is, a short, lush, labor- and capital-intensive, monocultured, deeply green, soft, and consistent lawn requires constant intervention. In many regions of the United States, the caretaker is forced to: water regularly even daily lest the short blades dry out; apply pesticides four or five times yearly; and fertilize seasonally since the soil is likely to be either depleted or not appropriate for a grass monoculture, like the sands and soils of Long Island, New Mexico, South Dakota, or Southern California. I saw a high-status lawn boldly visible as the lush green surrounding a grand home on a trip through the arid Southwest. The dark green stood in stark contrast with the brown landscape punctuated by cacti. Lawns even play out the opposition of regional and cultural status in the ebb and flow of desert cacti versus grass, as in the yards of Tucson up to the mid-1970s. Cultural identities were presented with cacti as Southwestern or Mexican versus the grass lawns of Eastern and Anglo yards (Hecht, 1975). The standardized high-status grass lawn must be continually recreated through processes that may conflict with local ecological relationships.

The Contemporary Lawnscape: An "Industrial Lawn"

The typical high-status lawn takes the form of what a team of authors from environmental science and landscape design call an "industrial lawn." The industrial lawn "rests on four basic principles of design and management": composed of grass species only; free of weeds and pests; continuously green; and kept at a low, even height (Bormann et al, 1993: 62; passim). Adding its status dimensions, I see this lawn type, or *lawnscape*, as a system of appearances that announces the social and moral status of its caretakers and that forms self and community identity and motivation.

The American lawnscape is a cultural form developed from appearances of moral respectability from England and residential and technological changes (Jenkins, 1994). Increased transportation after the Civil War and the design of high-status suburbs of single-family houses set back from curving roads and surrounded by fenceless lawns attracted an expanding population to "garden cities" (Jackson, 1985; Schroeder, 1993). The lawnmower quickly evolved from its invention in 1830 to an efficient machine appropriate even for gentlemen and women. Suburban housing boomed after World War II. A growing lawn industry and a rapidly expanding chemical industry provided usable technology that put an industrial lawnscape within reach of all suburbanites. For those who hesitated, the reach was helped by neighborhood pressure.

A national survey of households reflects the motivational power of a lawnscape. Significantly more Americans, about 62 percent, spent time at lawn care in 1991–92 than at any other yard activities. Gardening was the next highest activity at about 42 percent (Bormann et al, 1993: 67). The endless physical demands of the industrial lawn forged decisions to pay for lawn care professionals. National companies entered the rapidly growing business. In 1988, a survey in Virginia found that approximately 17 percent of the households hired a lawn-care service compared to an estimated 11 percent nationally and growing (Halstead, et al, 1989; U.S. General Accounting Office, 1990: 8). By 1993, a Gallup survey reported that 17 million U.S. households spent $12.5 billion on professional landscaping and lawn-care services (Bradley, 1994). The industrial lawnscape motivates growing expenses. The dominance of the industrial lawn is part of a post–World War II growth of the turf industry and the spread of constructed golf courses.

The social power of a high status lawnscape is *realized*, that is, known and made real, in the moral norms internalized by both caretakers and neighbors. The norms, furthermore, are enforced by negative sanctions imposed informally by neighbors, and formally, sometimes coercively, by the law. Stories from aging professionals and defiant young couples show the power of "lawn norms" (Bormann, et al, 1993; Chicago Tribune, 1988;

French, 1989; Pollan, 1989). Legal, reputational, and even vigilante sanctions are directed at those who fail to mow their lawns or who grow swards of unacceptable plants. Such laggards or rebels feel the sanctions that support "the tyranny of the lawn" backed up by the power of lawn industry businesses that one observer likened to National Rifle Association pressure tactics (Schroeder, 1993: 124–132).

The public code governing suburbia is a "moral minimalism" (Baumgartner, 1988). Suburbanites want to get along with minimal moral involvement with each other. Suburbanites interact at a distance, avoid open conflict, and use weak indirect social controls. No one wishes to attract attention nor confront others who break the norms. Paradoxically, then, there is great pressure to act within the norms of suburbia. No one wishes either to confront or to break the tolerance limits. As a result, suburban moral minimalists avoid behavior that threaten your or my identity or cause you and me to engage in open conflict. A generalized moral pressure both pushes suburbanites and neighborhood yards toward socially acceptable lawns and deflects them from personally confronting the deviant whose lawn violates the aesthetic code. Disapproval, and even touches of violence, are done anonymously.

In one instance, a couple planted wildflowers in a small front yard in Kenmore, New York. Through the summer they received threats to burn their house, herbicides were put on their flowers, their cat was stoned, birds were shot and snakes released in their yard, and a local court fined *them* $50 a day for "creating conditions hazardous to health" (Chicago Tribune, 1988). Eventually, the young couple moved because of the "pressure cooker" atmosphere, since "It was all getting pretty tense and scary." An upscale version is the anonymous note received by owners of a half-million-dollar Maryland home to "*please cut your lawn.* It is a disgrace to the entire neighborhood" (Schroeder, 1993: 128, original emphasis). On a local scene, I overheard an everyday moral aesthetics of lawns and neighbors. In a small town cafeteria, an elderly woman speaking louder than conversational volume to her breakfast partner reported comments by a neighbor that the elderly woman's "lawn looked ragged." The elderly woman thought the problem was that you "got to mow it all one way" so it "looks nice." She went on to comment, "Let me tell how her lawn looks . . . " with a tellingly sarcastic tone of voice (June 22, 1993).

Many municipalities have ordinances against "noxious weeds," or stipulate that grasses must be cut below a certain height. A nearby city puts the limit at nine inches. A recent survey by its Department of Code Enforcement targeted "trash and tall grass" for stronger enforcement. Failure to observe local laws may bring fines, threat of jail, an unannounced visit from city mowers, and the dangerous disdain of neighbors. Sanctions show the reality of norms. The valued form of the lawn is outlined by deviant behavior that brings sanctions and in the responses that impose them, such as anonymous notes, extralegal physical force and legal police power. A woman in St. Louis who works, ironically, at the Missouri Botanical Garden was mightily surprised when she came home to find her yard mowed without her knowledge! Her yard was a "naturescape" that took *twenty-five years to grow* but one day to mow. The city told her "someone complained" (note the anonymity), so city officials ordered the mowing. The city forester, a proponent of naturescaping, said he was embarrassed. He underlined the eye-sight problem by noting, "what's nature scaping to one person are (sic) weeds to another" (South Bend Tribune, 1994).

A cultural move that strengthens the industrial lawn as a high-status lawnscape and motivates constant intervention is to construct ever-present symbolic enemies or "pests." Physical pests demand constant control. Pests give the caretaker endless challenges to moral status and opportunities to prove one's worth. Once seen, pests offer the lawn industry never-ending customer demand. I focus on one category of pests in the industrial lawn, the "weed."

Industrial Lawnscapes Make Weeds

The positive descriptors in the status dichotomies given above are the aesthetic features of a high-status lawn. Picture a manicured lawn of the latest introduced grasses, soft and silky, uniformly dark green, lush and thick, well edged, costly, so consistent that each blade is indistinguishable from the next, and so short that it stands at constant attention. The reality of our personal belief in the status theory outlined above is reinforced by the moral resonances these features elicit in us. Once the industrial frame of a beautiful lawn structures our eye-sight, we have internalized a shared experiential basis for recognizing a good lawn, the cultural basis for identifying that which is dirty or impure, and the moral basis for judging it as bad. A mere glance at a bad lawn arouses righteous emotions of anger or annoyance and motivates morally correct action in one's role as caretaker or caring neighbor. At its root, an industrial lawnscape is a frame for seeing a weed as a moral object. It makes a dandelion into a real negative invader within the cognitive and emotional moral order of an industrial lawn (cf. Harre et al, 1985).

The symbolic processes that construct a good lawn paradoxically create real weeds, that is, real plants seen as contradictions of lawn grasses. A weed is not a real physical thing. It is a plant wrapped in socially constructed meanings, like the piece of canvas stolen as second base. It is not a plant, grass, or any *thing* that grows. Rather, it is a social object constructed by overlapping institutional definitions, norms, motives, and actions that structure what we see, feel, and judge. Webster's dictionary definition captures this dialectic in the first meaning of "weed" as "any *undesired,* uncultivated plant that grows in profusion so as to crowd out a desired crop, *disfigure a lawn,* etc." (italics added). Our status theory of lawns would merely add that a commanding weed, like a dandelion, violates the moral meaning of a lawn.

The opening words of an Environmental Protection Agency pamphlet, "Lawn Care For Your Home," play out the moral dialectic of lawn and life. In the first place, "All of us want a *beautiful lawn free of weeds and pests* to provide an attractive *setting* for our home. In addition to its *eye appeal,* a lawn provides a *cleaner and healthier* environment for you and your family" (p. 2, italics added). On the pamphlet's cover is a sketch of grass and a flowering dandelion, and on the opposite page from the above quote is a robust dandelion wafting seeds from a threatening pose supported by a muscular taproot. The meaning dichotomy of lawn and weed is clear. The pamphlet goes on: "*Weeds,* destructive insects, and lawn diseases are the common *problems* you may encounter in establishing and maintaining a *good* lawn. You can *eliminate and control* them by using *pesticides . . . ."* (U.S. Environmental Protection Agency, 1988: 2, emphasis added). Contradicting these glowing words, the pamphlet later *warns* about use, misuse, and following instructions when applying toxic pesticides paradoxically needed for the "clean and *healthy*" lawn. The opposition between the so-defined healthy and attractive lawn maintained by applying poisons is my focus.

Seeing dandelions illuminates the frame that creates weeds. There was a time when the dandelion was akin to manna: a wide-ranging dietary gift accompanying European pioneers across western frontiers. Its young and tender leaves make an iron-rich salad, its flowers make wine, and its roots are dried and ground for coffee or cooked as potherbs (New York Times, 1965). In Vineland, the Dandelion Capital of America, they are a cash crop. How did they become weeds? A dandelion elicits no moral feelings on a walk through a meadow, but it is immediately seen as a weed once framed within a high-status lawn.

The frame provided by the industrial lawnscape reconfigures a dandelion as out of place, disfiguring, repulsive, threatening. The dandelion has the opposite qualities of lawn grass: its genesis is natural; it is broad leafed; it invades open areas at no cost; it becomes harsh as it ages; it blooms yellow; it lies flat; it requires no intervention; and it resists attempts to eradicate it, at least until constant poisons temporarily eliminate it from some lawns. Suburbanites need not invest in getting dandelions, only in getting rid of them. Thus, high status derives from the pricey absence of free dandelions, so much so that they are sprayed prophalactically or preemergently. Now, the highest status emanates from expanses of identical grasses without a dandelion in sight. No dandelions mark the triumph of the industrial lawn.

Poorer people with little extra money may have dandelions in *their* yards. Experientially, we infer which frame we use to see a lawnscape by the way we react to dandelions or other weeds. If the absence of dandelions evokes in us a pleasing feeling of moral approval, then the industrial lawn is the frame. If, on the other hand, the absence of dandelions evokes a morally disturbing feeling at the likely use of chemical poisons, then a natural lawn is the frame. The emotional response accompanying our eyesight signals the cognitive frame through which we see (Hochschild, 1983).

Shifts in the meaning of words mark historical shifts in seeing. The word "lawn" did not always refer to the modern form (Stein, 1993). According to the Oxford English Dictionary, "lawn" is derived from "launde." Both words had the same primary meaning, "an open space between woods; a glade." The first recorded use of lawn in 1548 refers to "a place voyde of trees, as a laune in a parke or forest." Today, by contrast, Webster's Dictionary gives its first meaning as "land covered with grass kept closely mown, especially in front of or around a house," not in a park or forest. The second archaic meaning is "an open space in a forest; a glade." Language use points to a four-hundred-fifty-year transformation of lawn from a naturally occurring object amidst other naturally occurring objects, a glade amidst woods, to a humanly constructed object surrounding other built objects, grass around a house.

Presumably, in the original sense, an observer would not see weeds in a lawn. No plant disfigures the naturally framed lawn or open glade amidst woods. In today's suburbia, however, culturally framed lawns make weeds immediately obvious, especially one so bold as a dandelion that flaunts its misplacement with a too tall dash of golden yellow. Now framed as cultural impurities, weeds motivate continuous expensive intervention to extirpate them from lawnscapes. Interventions in pursuit of symbolic status have physical outcomes as well. Applying Simmel's lemma of culture in opposition to life, we ask about empirical effects on life and health from interventions to sustain this cultural form. We look at the *material* conditions and outcomes of maintaining modern lawns.

A Weedless Lawn and Life

Modern lawnscapes sustain identity and status. They display community aesthetics and signal a sense of self-enhancement. Our dualist perspective leads us to ask about the *biological* and environmental outcomes that support or oppose life. Lawns are a dual reality of "socialised nature" (Giddens, 1991), that is, nature really transformed into symbolic meanings. They call for analysis both as social institutions of status and as material components of life.

I develop the "vital realist" claim that meanings are primarily in nature prior to their symbolic transformation in social actions (Lewis, et al, 1993; Mead, 1934; Weigert, 1991a). Simmel's lemma of culture in opposition to life focuses analysis on the physical consequences of maintaining a high-status lawnscape. To work this analysis, I reframe the modern lawn not merely as a status-producing form, but also as a biological reality affected by human interventions and responding to those interventions. The physical reality of industrial lawnscapes links them to our health and life.

Lawns are big business. In the United States, they cover over 25 million acres, an area slightly smaller than Pennsylvania (Bormann et al, 1993: 64). They cover acreage comparable to agricultural crops in the United States (p. 68). Mowing lawns, however, collects a huge useless crop, indeed one likely to have toxic residue and find its way into landfills. They receive pesticides at a higher rate than farmfields (U.S. Senate, 1990–1). Suburbanites spray "cides" to kill dandelions, weeds, fungus, and grubs. Today, unintended or previously unknown effects of pesticide use are documented for children, songbirds, house pets, and adults, especially if they are allergic or take daily medication (e.g., a poisonous interaction of Tagamet with a lawn chemical, Latimer, 1991; Time, 1991). A widely used active ingredient in broadleaf pesticides is 2, 4-D. It was one of the elements in Agent Orange used in Vietnam and is toxic to animal life, especially aquatic life. It is possibly linked to cancer in dogs and perhaps humans (Carson, 1962; Harte et al, 1991; New York Times, 1991). Yet, it is still used to kill broad-leafed plants. Awareness of physical outcomes suggests reframing lawnscapes from prideful symbols of good standing to poisoned signs of health threats. Lawn-care companies put little cardboard signs on short plastic holders in lawns after "treatment" to warn us that risks are greater than zero.

Over thirty years ago, Rachel Carson reframed chemical intervention in the natural environment by summarizing deadly effects on untargeted life forms. Still, a mid-western university recently sprayed American elm trees with methoxychlor to control disease and seasonally sprays lawns and playing fields with herbicides to kill broad leafed weeds, especially clover, crabgrass, and dandelions. The stated purpose is to save the trees and "kill the dandelions," especially before commencement ceremonies. Risks are justified by the negative status of dandelions. They pose no physical threat. Dandelions are a socially constructed aesthetic and status threat.

There are longer-term and more diffuse outcomes of high-status lawn care such as adding chemicals to the air from large numbers of two-cycle engines in lawn tools. One estimate is that Americans use 580 million gallons of gasoline annually with lawn mowers alone. Add other gasoline powered lawn tools, and the aggregate pollution is significant. California's Air Resources Board estimates that a power mower emits the same pollution in one hour as an average car driven 350 miles (in Bormann et al, 1993: 96). High-status lawn care with gasoline-powered motors affects our atmosphere. Millions of two-cycle lawn mowers generate less clean air and call for yet another solution to pollution.

The norms of short height and evergreen color require regular fertilization and watering in many parts of the United States. These two requirements increase the demand for water and the likelihood of chemical runoff. In water shortages of the 1980s and 1990s through the Northeast, the Northwest, and Southern California, local governments restrict or ban watering lawns as a low priority (e.g., Los Angeles Times, 1993). A study of groundwater pollution found that chemically fertilized lawns have nitrogen runoff two to three times greater than unfertilized lawns. Indeed, the latter may help purify water (Gold et al, 1990).

Aside from the pollution from exhaust or fertilizers, there are health effects from chemical use. Chemical applications are linked with outcomes as immediate as sudden death and as long term as poison accumulating in food chains. Since care of an industrial lawn requires repeated application of chemical fertilizers and pesticides four or more times a year (early spring—preemergence crabgrass treatment; early summer—broadleaf weed control; mid-summer—insect control; fall—weed treatment; see U.S. Environmental Protection Agency, n. d.), chemicals are a major factor in the health outcomes of lawn care. Once we support the lawn chemically, we must continue to do so to keep the same form.

Most (estimated 34 out of 36 in U.S. General Accounting Office, 1990) lawn chemicals have unknown links to human health, in addition to the cumulative impact on soil, organisms, birds, animals, and general toxic levels. U.S. pesticide consumption is increasing at about 2.5 to 3 percent annually. The United States produces about one-fourth of world market pesticides of which about three-fourths is used domestically; of that about 15 percent goes to lawns, gardens, and nonagriculture uses. Dollar value of pesticide production increased from $6.3 billion in 1987 to $7.76 billion in 1992 (U.S. Department of Commerce, 1993: 11-13). Part of the risk is that chemical use runs ahead of knowledge of long-term outcomes. Every time we spread chemicals whose long-term ecological or health effects are partially unknown—and long-term ignorance is unavoidably true of every "new" chemical—we engage in action pathos. Interventions have unknown effects that we accept because we trust in the institutional system that tells us to use chemicals.

"Expert" recommendations for a "perfect lawn" include one inch of water weekly during a twenty-four-week growing season (Stein, 1993). The temperate Midwest and West of the United States gets less than thirty-five inches annually and much of that in winter. The industrial lawn caretaker tries to grow grasses evolved from cooler and wetter English climes in drier and hotter niches. Introduced grasses replace native prairie, meadow grasses, and legumes that are better able to survive dry periods. Stein notes the necessary pattern of watering weekly; fertilizing four to five times seasonally; mowing frequently; and since the grasses grow so rapidly, bagging the clippings lest the lawn suffocate (pp. 136–7). She concludes that this perfect lawn is a "perfect antithesis of an ecological system" (138). A perfect lawn is "still" and "silent," whereas prairie or meadow hums with life (154–72). She reports an enlightening experience getting official permission for a triannual burning of her meadowed lawn.

Policy debates over pesticide and chemical use cannot be resolved by consensual public data. Either such data do not exist or people use contradictory frames to interpret whatever data there are. Unassailable experimental proof of single causes of complex environmental outcomes such as human health is impossible for many reasons, perhaps simply by the ethical impossibility of experimenting on humans with potentially dangerous chemicals. Those for and against trial-and-error chemical use divide on their first premise. Do we believe a chemical is safe until proven dangerous, or do we believe a chemical is dangerous until proven safe (see U.S. Senate, 1990–91; Edelstein, 1988, for such assumptions in pollution cases). Furthermore, professional experts and concerned laypersons typically use different inferential models to make sense of data (Brown, 1992). As long as persuasive proof, public consensus, and agreement on assumptions or inferential models are lacking, divisions in eye-sight persist and shared policy eludes us.

As noted above, some lawn chemicals are linked to health threats. A local study found that 80 percent of lawn caretakers used chemicals with some toxic potentiality (none were in the fourth, or "relatively non-toxic" category, Halstead et al, 1989). Only one in ten respondents who hired lawn-care companies asked what chemicals were applied to their lawns! Other studies found that lawn caretakers who apply chemicals themselves do not always understand or follow directions for use. In addition, some lawn care companies make questionable claims about the toxicity of materials they apply (U.S. General Accounting Office, 1990). These findings suggest excessive and poorly timed use of chemicals linked to toxicity and groundwater pollution. In addition, industrial lawns generate organic waste such as plastic bags of clippings that may carry toxic residues and become part of the garbage stream. Ironically, lighter clippings left on lawns are organic fertilizer (Stein, 1993).

Lawns writ large are golf courses, cultural forms analogous to lawns. They too started as, and some classic courses remain, rather natural areas. They evolved into a constructed cultural form requiring constant intervention with questionable environmental outcomes. Now managers are reframing their courses. Twenty-five golf courses in the Chicago area cut pesticides by 80 percent and planted native prairie grasses to replace bent grass in the roughs (Chicago Tribune, 1993). A course manager notes that this is a "different way of managing. It makes us an asset to wildlife . . . ." In 1989, the Audubon Cooperative Sanctuary System, a joint venture of the Audubon Society and U.S. Golf Association, organized to bring environmental practices to golf course management. The economic costs are so far about the same. Money saved from chemical applications and annual flowers goes to birdhouses and native perennials. Some golfers appreciate enhanced bird varieties. Others complain that certain areas "look neglected." The sense of a neglected look is an aesthetic response to sights seen through the framework of manicured golf courses on national TV tournaments. These courses are intensely prepped for months to acquire a look that even they cannot sustain. Although promoted via TV, the tournament look is but one version of how a challenging golf course should appear.

Golf courses continue to multiply, and depending on the form they take, so will their positive or negative environmental outcomes. Approximately two thousand new golf courses were planned in 1993 after almost a new course opening every day during 1991–92. Negative environmental effects follow from the dominant golf "coursescape" that requires large amounts of chemicals. Furthermore, new courses are often located in ecologically sensitive areas (Selcraig, 1993).

Besides their environmental outcomes, industrial lawnscapes and coursescapes support a narrow genetic presence. This restricted genetic presence is obvious in identical grass and in few spiders, birds, or small mammals. Monocultured lawns are restricted habitats that support fewer species than a variegated lawn or a yard with grasses, flowers, shrubs, and trees. Chemical use further threatens species that would survive even in a restricted lawnscape habitat. Maintaining the modern high-status lawnscape opposes genetic diversity. Genetic diversity is a long-term ecologically desirable condition intricately linked to life-support systems.

The Lawn as a Source of Individual and Collective Identities

In addition to tension between symbolic status and threatened health, the lawnscape plays out a social dialectic of individual and collective identities. This identity dialectic deepens the moral meaning of lawn appearances. The symbolic calculus of status puts a positive evaluation on lush, monocultural, short, green, weed-free lawns. Too much of a departure from this moral calculus makes one liable to legal and extra-legal sanctions from police citations to vigilante violence. Unkempt lawnscapes are suburban versions of dirt defiling clean areas. A defiled lawnscape displays a potentially immoral identity.

Lawnscape dialectics present individualistic Americans with an identity paradox. Creating and sustaining a lawn that communicates my personal identity as an apparently moral neighbor is realized only in my conformity to collective norms of good appearances. Suburban America confirms the sociological insight: personal moral selfhood is realized, that is, known and enacted, by conformity to collective rituals. Executive-type suburban neighbors display individuality and moral worth by conforming to imposed codes governing lawnscapes.

A final issue concerns subjective identification with lawn and home as my particular place. Social psychological analysis grounds a sense of local place in the particularity of this landscape. The widespread sameness of suburban lawnscapes, however, evokes abstracted space. Originally, "landscape" was a naturally occurring or local physical surrounding, often portrayed through the imagination of a painter (Jackson, 1984). A landscape used to be local and bonding, a "place" evoking a concrete sense of individual identity with where I am. "I live here, therefore I am." Scenery and setting announce my situated identity, as do personal appearances (Goffman, 1959; Weigert, 1983). A Berkeley-born friend refers with pride to her "golden hills of Berkeley" covered with grasses that appear brown, dead, and unattractive to my eye.

Today, landscape is a "landscaped" location made by imposing someone else's design on the local environment. A high-status lawnscape is a landscaped setting. It is literally utopian, or no place, because it is the same everywhere. Its sameness identifies nowhere in particular. As spaces lacking locality and particularity, lawnscapes also lack the power to elicit a sense of my particular place or announce who I am personally. Lawnscapes function like franchised strips of pizza parlors on roadways leading into and around modern urban locations—their sameness communicates an abstract standardized identity. They ground no individual sense concerning where or who, in particular, you are. Replicated franchise strips are paralleled by replicated lawns. Lawnscapes are nature socialized to present moral identities as minimal members of an abstracted collectivity.

These identity dialectics are socially and economically underwritten by the "lawn institution." This phrase refers to the widespread and functionally linked institutional arrangements producing lawnscapes, from transnational chemical companies and national lawn care businesses to community garden clubs and neighborhood associations. This institutional system does our lawnscape "thinking" for us. Though no individual intends to produce an industrial lawnscape as a cultural form that frames how we see moral standing announced by the setting for our homes, many think, feel, decide, and spray as a result of an unquestioned institutional creation, the industrial lawn. Institutions "think" by defining situations and constructing frames through which persons think they do their own thinking and produce their own lawns (Douglas, 1986).

From fleets of lawn equipment and piles of toxic chemicals in suburban garages and on to patterns of seeing, feeling, and neighboring, the lawn institution links suburban Americans into a physically risky status-producing system. The system induces us to want lawnscapes announcing moral identities that in some of its physical outcomes threatens our own health. Furthermore, the system gets us to like doing the lawn, or, if that fails, to fear not doing it. The dialectic of individuality-conformity deepens to that of symbolic status life versus physical biological life.

From Industrial Lawns to Ecological Yards

Analysis of lawns as cultural forms with outcomes that threaten life illustrates the power of a dualistic perspective. Instead of reducing lawns to status forms seen through a dominant social paradigm based on ideas of expanding frontiers, limitless resources, and technological interventions that have only positive effects, we see through a framework based on scarcity and toxics with risky effects. This chapter adds a social psychology of status to the process of envisioning a sustainable lawn. The broad question, "Why do wealthy and privileged strata of society surround themselves with toxic risk and use scarce resources in pursuit of a particular cultural form, an industrial lawn?" is partially answered by symbols of moral appearances. Good lawns realize good neighborhoods, acceptable moral standing, and your upright identity as well as mine and ours.

Sociological analysis combined with data from the natural sciences, however, offer throughsight enabling us to see often hidden outcomes of modern status seeking. Such throughsight suggests realist avenues both for understanding what we are doing and perhaps to change. Is it possible that an industrial lawn could be seen as an object of a "not-in-my-backyard" movement? Local issues constantly challenge previously unquestioned perceptions. Critical environmental attitudes are no longer limited to an expert elite; they are global phenomena. Critical attitudes suggest that the sights and motives that relate us to the little pieces of earth that are our yards are changing significantly.

The argument of this chapter is not that any open grassy area is in opposition to life. The object is not any sward seen as a lawn. Rather, the object is a historically recent, industrially constructed, and culturally hegemonic *form* of a lawn, the high-status industrial lawnscape and its physical outcomes. Moderns could reframe lawn into physical forms more adapted to local conditions that uses the diversity found in any 30 ft. by 50 ft. lot. Framing a lawn as a biologically diverse array of flowers, grasses, broadleaf plants, ferns, shrubs, and trees requires a different aesthetic of appearances that reframes self and other within a different world from that of the conforming caretaker of a high-status lawnscape that appears the same as every other.

Genetically diverse and flowering lawns, mowed periodically with no synthetic chemicals or added water, is a reframing that values ecologically sustainable and less toxic yards. Ecological conditions differ across the United States and even within one's yard. To produce the same lawn over every square foot is to impose a form against the life that would grow there without constant intervention. Breaking free from the dominant frame empowers us to see a variety of lawnscapes as aesthetically pleasing and morally good.

Even a local rather conservative Midwestern newspaper editorialized that Americans need a "new way of thinking about lawns" as it recommended environmentally harmonious ideas for one's yard (South Bend Tribune, 1993). A Canadian newspaper editorialized that lawns have as limited a meaning as a "polyester leisure suit" and called for home caretakers to plant gardens (The Globe and Mail, 1994). We can free our yards from the tyranny of chemical lawnscapes. Such "freedom lawns" (Bormann et al, 1993) would be seen as "lawns of weeds" if framed by today's norms. Freedom lawns are life breaking out of form. They reawaken the dialectic in Simmel's lemma of form in opposition to life, and life breaking through form. The next chapter offers a more general set of lenses for seeing through human environment relationships.

6

A Primer Paradigm for Seeing the Challenges of Environmental Citizenship

We live in the world we see and talk about. Authoritative others and dominant institutions validate our sights and conversations so they have the unquestioned ring of normalcy and legitimacy as real and true (Berger and Luckmann, 1966). In this chapter, I suggest a general set of lenses and a vocabulary for seeing and talking about environmental issues. The hope is to work toward a framework for shared understanding within which we can clarify differences in ideology or values. I invite readers to construct their own "primer" lists of concepts and words, their own glossary of eco-talk, so that they can see and talk about earth matters more realistically with self and others. Primers are beginnings, not endings. Lenses offer focus, not final visions. Moderns need to bridge differences by sharing ideas and sights on their journey.

The scope of the natural environment as an object of knowledge demands vocabularies from various disciplines, each with its own perspectives, inferential logics, and methods of inquiry. Disciplinary differences are simplified here in the spirit of a primer. Other scholars would pack and unpack these constructs into different frameworks. Whatever frames we use, we all seek better understanding. In this chapter, I try to think about them as a citizen seeking to understand more of today's world and to share understanding with others, just as you wish if you have read this far. The common goal is shared eye-sight for informed citizens.

The lenses allow us to re-sight ourselves from the point of view of the environmental other. Look at self from an earthly perspective. Seeing self or objects from the standpoint of the other is *role taking*, that is, putting oneself in the place of the other, in the other's shoes as it were, and seeing

131

objects as the other does. This process is fundamental to George H. Mead's social psychology (Cook, 1993; Blumer, 1969). As we saw earlier, Mead suggests that engineers take the role of the physical other to analyze the forces and responses that determine whether the bridge will stay suspended between the two cliffs as we walk over it. Role taking is fundamental to shared understanding, starting from the developmental process through which a child learns to leave its ego-centered perspective and see the world from the perspectives of significant others such as parents, teachers, peers, generalized others, and for an ecological self, the earth.

Taking the role of the other is a cognitive and emotional process: we come to see and feel about ourselves and objects the way others see and feel toward them, or in general, we respond to ourselves the way others do. Obviously, the earth does not know or feel anything toward us. Nor does the earth make excuses or switch frameworks to allow us and our environment to go on as before, no matter how much we intervene. It is important to reflect on these trite statements. We know the earth responds in naturalistically meaningful ways. Thus, moderns need a new kind of role taking to become aware of our new environmental selves, namely, role taking an other that makes no emotional responses nor action realignments through etiquette, charity, justice, or excuses. Nature responds to us, but its responses are unsympathetically naturalistic and physically causal. We need to learn a new mode of role taking to interpret our relationship with the earth.

For the first time, instruments provide visuals of the earth as other. Shuttle or satellite measurements and photographs enable us to view earth from space and to link that view with everyday eye-sights from where we stand here and now. Viewing the Big Blue Marble gives us a global perspective on personal experience. We can role take the environment by seeing our responses to earth as though we were on the receiving end of what we do. Just as new self understanding emerged when humans made microscopes to see the tiny worlds within their blood and skin, and telescopes to see distant celestial worlds ever beyond, so too, new selves emerge as we "see" ourselves related to the earth in pictures taken from outer space; in bubbles found trapped in Antarctic ice; and in DNA recovered from human ancestors, dinosaur bones, or mosquitos preserved in amber.

Holistic understanding of ecosystems and the biosphere enables us to respond imaginatively to our actions in a way that relates natural processes with personal experiences. As we eat a fast food hamburger, we remember satellite photos of burning rain forests and imagine: burning trees; new grass growing; beef cattle grazing; thin rain forest soil giving its last nutrients to grass and cattle; and more carbon in the air.

Moderns need to know about food production. Cultivating "agricultural literacy" means knowing the history and possible futures of food availability (Douglass, 1985). Food literacy is a corollary of environmental literacy. Recall images from space pictures you know, and imagine how the earth is responding. Graphs link acid rain to dying spruce forests and fewer fish in Adirondack lakes. By role taking the earth or one of its life-supporting dynamics, we see self anew—as an interactor within the biosphere. We re-ask what we are doing when we put "weed and feed" toxics on the lawn. Role taking the earth brings us closer to the more adequate self George H. Mead urged as a citizen's ideal over sixty years ago (1934). What paradigm, or set of cognitive constructs, do we use to frame our role taking of the earth? As yet, there is no single authoritative paradigm. Indeed, none is possible, since no single discipline or paradigm is adequate to the task. A tentative and ever reformable multidisciplinary Primer Paradigm is the best I can offer. Hopefully, its validity will be measured by better paradigms that replace it.

Toward a Primer Paradigm for Seeing Through Human-Environment Relationships

I suggest the following seven constructs for a Primer Paradigm: holistic system; biosphere; ecosystem; carrying capacity; dominant cultural subparadigm; institutional logics; and personal eye-sights. These constructs and supportive vocabularies come from philosophy, physical and biological sciences, engineering, demography, psychology, sociology, and aesthetic and value analysis. Together they are necessary but hardly sufficient for thinking in conceptually self-conscious and empirically grounded ways about sustainable human life as we know it now.

Holistic and System Thinking

Thinking adequately about the sustainability of human relations with the earth starts with seeing the earth as a kind of functioning whole, as in some sense, *one* thing. Functioning oneness underlies the Gaia Hypothesis of the British chemist and cybernetic scientist, James Lovelock (1987). He argues that we are better off thinking of the earth as alive, *as a living organism*. Although he stretches the idea of "living," this way of thinking calls us to a gestalt switch, that is, a new way of seeing and thinking about the natural environment. Seeing the earth as a living organism transforms thinking about it. Earth is not clusters of discrete elements linked in linear causal and separate relationships. The earth is not like a pile of rocks. Rather, it is a single interacting totality that emerges, transforms itself, and is only contingently controllable.

The integrating idea of oneness underlies the picture of earth as the Big Blue Marble. The primary analogue of oneness is a living organism. Each of us, for example, normally has a sense of self as a single being, a continuous living entity. Nonliving things we see as though they can be separated into smaller units without losing their way of being: a brick taken from a house is still a brick in a strong sense in which a finger taken from a human body is not. To think of the earth as a living organism enables us to think of it as a stronger unity than a stack of bricks seen as a house. Picture earth as a single functioning entity. Once the earth is seen as a singularity, a living whole, we can transform it into the abstract language of dynamic systems. We now see the earth, including its gaseous atmospheric envelopes, as a single functioning whole within which every part is strongly interrelated with every other in a somewhat self-regulating dynamic system. Earth is a working oneness, akin to the oneness of our bodies.

Seeing earth-as-single-system frames ecological thinking as an integrative discipline. Partial, discrete, and linear models of knowing and inferring are integrated into cyclic models. As a result, we see that interventions in nature never have only one outcome; it is never possible to do only one thing when interacting with the environment; nor can we ever predict all the outcomes of our actions. We learn to integrate specialized partial knowledge with generalized ways of thinking. There is no guarantee that future responses of earth-as-system to human interventions will sustain human life. Earth-as-system may well continue as a mutually adjusting system of living and nonliving components. It is not a single system of fixed harmony (Botkin, 1990).

A key assumption in discussing human-environment relationships is: do you believe—no one can *know* for certain—that, no matter how much humans intervene in the earth's dynamics, the life-support systems will always respond in ways that support human life? An adequate answer must respect the unfolding empirical and evolutionary record: all species live within the limits of geo-chemo-biological buffers, and changes in the environment that break down these buffers cause the death of life forms dependent on such limits. Too much acid in the water kills plants, trees, fish, and eventually humans. We live within a buffered zone of acid and alkaline. The evolutionary record is a story of the death and birth of species based on changing environmental conditions within a single biosphere. Such is one lesson of Darwin's famous "tree diagram" showing the divergence of living forms and emergence of new species alongside many that become extinct (Darwin, 1975:66).

Biosphere

Biosphere refers to the largest system that both supports the survival of human life and is directly affected by human interaction. It refers to biogeophysical realms within which nonliving and living forms supportive of human life, and human life itself, exist. Biosphere includes the reaches of outer space and the oceanic or earthly depths that support life. In this "life-sphere," all known life exists supported by complex systems of water, soil, and air; the cycles of carbon, hydrogen, nitrogen, etc.; and the physico-chemical atomic and molecular structures that make up living beings.

Picture the biosphere in the 1968 NASA photo of earth as the Big Blue Marble spinning, wobbling, rotating, and moving into space. Life as far as we know exists only within the layers of space around the earth: the atmosphere, stratosphere, and troposphere that reach a few miles spaceward, like concentric spheres. On the surface, most life appears within about a mile of the surfaces of oceans, lakes, ponds, and rivers, or rooted in the relatively shallow, usually a few inches, of living crust of soil. Within these cosmically thin zones, natural systems sustain the zone of the living, the lifesphere.

The astro-physico-bio sciences provide primary data on the workings of the biosphere. These primary data are synthesized and integrated with that of other sciences in environmental science (e.g., Miller, 1994). Environmental science grounds environmental literacy in: vocabulary; interrelated sets of concepts; knowledge of natural systems; and general knowledge of the sizes, directions, and rates of change in systems for human sustainability (Orr, 1992). Debates over biospheric processes such as ozone depletion, greenhouse effect, global warming, acid rain, toxics in the food chains, ultraviolet rays causing skin cancer, global climate change, genetic changes, or genetic loss through species extinction require understanding of measurement problems, data accumulation, and interpretive ambiguities of data that all accept.

Ecosystem and Energetics

Ecosystems are based on two foundations: the transformation or movement of matter as when big fish eat little fish in a pond; and the more basic process of energy flow and change. Energy budgets, or energetics, record energy sources, flows, transformations, and degradation. It focuses on the foundational physical processes of the material world. Cosmologists argue that energy is the first and indispensable source of reality, including living reality. Furthermore, all energy available to earth dwellers ultimately comes from the sun. Some of the sun's energy is stored in the earth as fossils: coal, oil, or gas. Other energy is held within atomic structures that can be unlocked by fission or fusion. Other kinds of energy can be tapped by transforming the power of moving water or air. Finally, there is the daily radiation from the sun itself, at least until further notice.

Energetics also asks about the net energy outcomes of human attempts to find and use energy sources to support life. A new and defining question asks about the net energy gain or loss from society's production, consumption, housing, and agriculture. Do profitable practices of American agribusiness, for example, lead to a net energy gain or loss? Is more energy put into food production than comes out in produced food? Do we put more energy into locating, purifying, using, and cleaning up atomic, oil, or coal sources than these sources supply for human use? An ecosystem lens sees human activities in a simple equation: energy output minus energy input equals net energy outcome. Is the net outcome a gain or loss? If it is a net loss of energy, as analysts say of American agribusiness, is this activity sustainable without reducing the ecosystem's capacity to feed its life forms? In general, do modern societies add, subtract, or retain the same amount of usable energy available on earth? Ecosystem analysis asks these questions and frames our interpretation of human populations as consumers and transformers of energy. As users of energy, we are ever in search of new sources to support growing numbers of humans at higher levels of production and consumption. The key is to build society on renewable or sustainable energy sources so that our ecosystems can continue supporting us, especially if population continues to grow.

Carrying Capacity and Exponential Population Growth

The decisive dynamic linking systems of organisms and environments is population growth and change. Population biology and human demography study the rates, patterns, and causal dynamics of population change. A key finding is that populations grow at an exponential rate until they run into some limit or barrier. Exponential growth reflects the fact of "nature's fecundity," namely, organisms produce far more offspring than the earth could ever support into adulthood, a fact known from antiquity (Darwin, 1975; Dillard, 1985). The "Four Horsemen" of war, death, famine, and pestilence were thought to hold down population growth.

Today's empirical dilemma is that human population is growing exponentially, *and* no population can *continue* to grow exponentially! An exponential curve grows slowly until it reaches a stage of "take off," after which it grows increasingly rapidly as population doubles ever more quickly. Visualize a simple letter *L* lying on its back. No individual can ever see the exponential increase in human population. Indeed, the concept is just that to us, a concept or idea. No one sees the empirical reality of population growth as it occurs. If we had ten fruit flies in a jar of food, however, we would see the results of exponential growth in a few months.

Human population growth is unseeable for at least two reasons. First, exponential increase is a collective empirical pattern generated by populations, not by an individual. If we lived on a lake that was host to water lilies that grew unchecked, we may see the effect of exponential growth, namely, a lake totally covered by lily pads. We cannot see human population patterns unless we have a godlike vantage point and see populations growing within ecosystems we also see holistically, like fishbowls. During early stages and close to the last observations, exponential increase is hard to see, unless we carefully counted lily pads every day. The abruptness of exponential increase is suggested by the question: if water lilies grow exponentially and double every day so that they cover the entire pond in thirty days, on which day is the pond half-covered? Unless schooled in exponential growth time, we may think the pond is half-covered somewhere around the fifteenth day. The answer is: the pond is half-covered on the next to last day, the twenty-ninth day. Exponential rates generate population increases that are gradual at first, but which irrupt in larger numbers after the takeoff point is passed.

The exponential curve fits the history of human population increase. It took *millions* of years for the human population to reach one billion around 1810. Today it takes about *nine years* to add another billion people. After millennia of slow increase, in the last three centuries the *rate* of worldwide population increase has a doubling time of about forty to fifty years. With a population of about 5.5 billion in the mid 1990s and an approximate 1.7 percent annual worldwide rate of increase, the earth will hold about 11 billion humans around the year 2040, assuming current population dynamics continue. If these rates keep going, the earth's human population would be about 22 billion around 2085, 44 billion around 2130, 88 billion around 2175, and so on. That is how exponential growth works. In 180 years, population could go from about 5.5 billion to 88 billion! The earth would have over seventeen times as many humans unless some causes both slow growth rates and lower the absolute numbers. No analyst I have read believes that the earth can support such population growth over the next 100 or more years. Either humans freely lower birth rates or natural and imposed causes, such as war or famine, may do the job.

By analogy with the water lilies covering the pond, we can ask how many years before the earth is so "covered" with humans that growth stabilizes or drops? The answer is not a simple extrapolation of the current population curve. Indeed, populations never continue at high rates of increase or shorter doubling times. There are many reasons why populations stop expanding exponentially. Ecologists use the concept of saturation point or carrying capacity to refer to natural limits on the number of specific organisms an ecosystem can support or "carry" without itself undergoing a significant and perhaps irreversible lowering of its capability to sustain its populations. Two central controls on exponential increase are food supplies and predators, either large animals or small microbes or viruses.

The metaphor of a single species like humans covering the earth the way water lilies cover a pond is not too helpful, though it is vivid. Ecologists who study the interrelationships of organisms with each other and the environment find upper limits to species' population that an ecosystem can support without "crashing" so radically that populations die back, that is, their numbers are forcibly reduced by changes in the ecosystem. If we do not reduce growth rates humanely, violent and painful causes will. Today's context requires us to look at population issues through an ecological framework and not simply through the business-as-usual dominant subparadigm.

Dominant Cultural Subparadigm:
A Frame for Seeing and Designing

Architects, landscape designers, engineers, and scientists do different things, but all are in the business of specialized seeing. They also teach us how to see as members of the society they help shape. These specialized seers look through perceptual frames they share with members of their group. The powerful twist in our story is that the frame dominating an entire culture's way of seeing is typically invisible to its members, even as it eliminates some and points to other interpretations of nature and preferred ways of acting on it. The cultural frame through which we see the world so informs what we think is really out there that we do not routinely distinguish the world that is naturally there from the cultural content we impose on that world. The cultural frame is the dominant lens that accents what we see as totally natural and immediately real.

I grew up in the dominant subparadigm of Control and Exploitation of the earth for never-ending material Progress and Growth. Contemporaries, however, are questioning that subparadigm so deeply that it no longer supplies taken-for-granted assumptions that produce personal certainty, shared "of course" motives, and confident social and economic policies. Control, Progress, Exploitation, and Growth within the culture of technological capitalism are now unanswered questions rather than unquestioned answers. Moderns see them as empirical questions to be calculated and evaluated, that is, measured in terms of true costs and benefits and weighed in terms of human and ecosystem sustainability. As a result of these empirical retranslations of Control, Progress, Exploitation, and Growth, we can begin to judge whether the dominant cultural subparadigm of industrial technological capitalism is running into physical limits, interpretive challenges, and policy contradictions. Critical questions, health threats, environmental risks, cognitive anomalies, value conflicts, and new data are motors driving environmental movements and thinking about the future. We sense change when we think about society and environment in an "age of ecology" (Oelschlaeger, 1991; Sale, 1993). It is an age that presents us with "wicked" problems in designing new ways of living that are sustainable (Buchanan, 1992).

Environmental movements often include two ancient but newly realized ideas for seeing the human-environment relationship: Harmony and Sustainability. These two ideas inform the somewhat misleadingly labeled "New Environmental Paradigm" (see Catton and Dunlap, 1978). Moderns are rediscovering these old ideas as we try to become "recovering moderns," that is, to free ourselves from a culture of unquestioned assumptions about environmental interaction based on a consuming view of the world. Some liken modern consuming interaction toward the environment to an "addiction": compulsive patterns of destructive actions beyond the control of personal will and knowledge (Gore, 1992). The new environmental paradigm, on the other hand, invites us to unpack the dominant cultural subparadigm and see sustainable human-environment relations. The new environmental paradigm incorporates a vital realism that grounds knowledge, values, and life-styles in an understanding of the interrelationships of organisms and environments needed to sustain life.

Institutional Logics

Within the overarching cultural paradigm are institutional logics. Logics are ways of defining, interpreting, and evaluating nature that guide the activities of institutions driving our culture. The logics of three institutional domains that dominate society's relationships with the environment are sketched here: the economic, political, and social. Each institutional domain teaches us to see the natural environment through different lenses that shape what we see: as resources for profit, as territory for sovereignty, and as consumption for status.

Resources and/versus Sustenance. Economic logic within a technological capitalist market system teaches that the physical environment is a resource. As a resource, the earth is seen as material to be transformed to satisfy our desires and generate profit for those who exploit it. The earth as profit-generating resource contrasts with ecological or religious views of earth as life-support system or sacred creation. Seen solely as a means to consumption and profit, natural realities have no intrinsic value. They acquire extrinsic exchange value only when they are bought and sold in a market and use value only when they are consumed.

A stand of old-growth evergreens in the Northwest, for example, has no economic value as long as it stands there, except as potential logs to be sold. Once the trees are cut and sold, they acquire exchange value in the market, and this value is measured by the price they bring. Seeing nature-as-resource is realized in the accounting practice that does not calculate the destruction of the old-growth forest as a cost to be subtracted from the sale price. Nor are ecological outcomes included in the market cost/price. Habitat destruction is a zero cost. In a word, harvesting a forest is pure profit measured by sale price minus incurred costs of cutting and shipping, such as labor, machines, and fuel. The fact that the forest is now gone and that it would take hundreds of years to regrow, if at all, is ignored in the cost accounting, as are ancillary outcomes affecting wildlife habitat; soil erosion; air quality; water, oxygen and carbon cycles; and weather patterns.

Reckoning zero costs for long-term natural objects extracted from the environment is a logical fiction built into calculations of the ruling yet partial measure of an economy's well being, namely, the gross national product. Seeing natural objects that are formed over hundreds or thousands of years like forests, trees, coal, and oil, as nothing but profitable resources minus handling costs is institutionalized in measurements of economic activity. Scholars today question the truncated logic of this price/cost system as inadequate for seeing environmental outcomes (Daly and Cobb, 1990).

Calculations of true costs that include outcomes external to market logic but real to environments can be applied to air, water, soil, and the food chain. An accurate cost of farming the dry land of the Nebraska plains, for example, includes the cost of lowering the world's largest known aquifer, the Ogallala. It supplies water necessary for irrigation at a rate eight times faster than its renewal rate (Miller, 1994: 262). Lowering an aquifer at a faster rate than it can replenish itself in human time is a true environmental cost for future generations who will not have that water available. An accurate price system needs to put a price on such one-time resources if we are to see long-term outcomes of farming practices and make reasonable policy. Once relevant costs are included in pricing such practices as emptying acquifers, the economic interpreter has a truer picture of the net value of dry farming. Current accounting practices measure short-term profits that such economic activity produces. We fail to see total costs if we ignore long-term outcomes that affect sustainability, such as the cost of handling waste (Dowd, 1989).

Sovereignty and/versus Security. Political logic in an international system of nation-states defines the environment as territory subject to national sovereignty in pursuit of national goals. Nations are founded on the principle of sovereignty. Nations may dispose of natural resources and transform environment at will. As a mere means to national goals in the exercise of their sovereignty, the natural environment has no independent political-legal standing. A nation-state, therefore, uses the environment however it wishes to further its goals. A salient example is the cutting of temperate forests by the nations of Europe and the United States in previous centuries, and now of rain forests by nations in Central and South America, Indonesia, Philippines, New Guinea, parts of Africa, and the Amazon region most notably. The logic of absolute sovereignty—if a nation decides to cut, burn, or transform forests to other use, then it may legally, morally, and politically do as it decides—puts no limits on the right of nations to dispose of its natural environment. At least, this is the logic that nation states use to justify their actions. If a nations' actions impact on other nations, however, the logic is called into question by neighboring nations. Ironically, nations of the First World who already felled their temperate forests appeal to Third World nations not to cut their rain forests lest the oxygen and carbon cycles threaten everyone's well being.

The use of river water is an ancient issue that cuts into national sovereignty, regional survival, and personal rights to the present day. The history of river use exemplifies how limits on sovereign rights over a natural resource can arise. Within a society's lifetime, rivers: remain relatively permanent; are identified as a single waterway from source to mouth; often flow through or between nations; and are necessary for the life of the peoples who live in their watersheds. In addition, rivers flow in one direction. The directionality of rivers determines that actions by upstream nations have outcomes on downstream nations. Ancient conflicts over river use continue and worsen to this day: the Tigris-Euphrates since the birth of civilization; the Jordan between Arabs and Jews; the Rhine and Danube throughout European history; and the Colorado among midwestern states and between the United States and Mexico as the oft-dammed river virtually dries up before reaching Mexico and Baja California Bay. Histories of the American West, especially Utah and California, record constant battles for water, including the use, diversion, damming, and depletion of rivers (Hundley, 1992; Reisner, 1993; Walton, 1992). Wars have been and will be fought over river use as nations claim sovereignty over a natural resource; recognize that the river's continued existence depends on power or cooperation; and eventually face the logic of limits imposed by wider regional interests on absolute national sovereignty.

Use-and-depletion conflicts over regional resources; the pollution of shared life-supports like air, water, and soil; and climate changes that cross borders lead to further empirical and moral limits on absolute sovereignty. Examples are acid rain and atmospheric carbon increases from burning fossil fuels and rain forests; the transportation, burning, or dumping of chemical toxics and radioactive wastes into common resources like rivers and oceans; nuclear accidents and testing; and release of chlorofluorocarbons and other gases that thin the protective ozone in the atmosphere. Increasingly, national policies and activities have health and survival outcomes on people anywhere on earth. Within an ecological framework, the logic of absolute sovereignty is an abstraction that is empirically and morally inadequate for framing contemporary social-environmental policy. Scholars who study the reality and conditions of international peace focus attention on links between ecological security and real peace (International Peace Research Association, 1989).

Status and/versus Consumption. Belief in the logic of the absolute right of individuals to consume whatever they want is at the heart of identity and status in Western capitalist culture. The logic of status stratification ranks individuals according to their wealth or income and the display and consumption of status. The status dynamics of society create expectations, behaviors, and comparisons of conspicuous consumption that are both enacted by self and evaluated by others. Conspicuous consumption displays status, a central motivational force that is intense and widespread (Veblen, 1979).

Members of society experience status dynamics partly as resentment and envy generated by their perceived relative disadvantage compared to others with higher-ranked possessions and thus higher status. We display enviable high status by consuming luxury products like a Mercedes Benz in a four-car garage, or a five-bath three-fireplace trophy house. Such displays fuel the consumption dynamic by generating resentment and envy in others. Feelings of inferior social status fuel desire and action by inferiors to buy and consume the same status items or less costly imitations.

The logic of status consumption also drives political dynamics in our democracy. Contending party lines define their leaders and constituencies as privileged success stories or losers in an unfair contest within the mythic understanding Americans have of their society. Winning voters who desire to consume high-status politics requires candidates marketed similar to the way business advertizes products for sale as both a sign of, and a means to, success and emulation. Politics, at least at the national level, becomes a contest of marketing images evoking the cultural myths that motivate political consumers to vote for a candidate who embodies the status voters wish to realize. Consider the positive marketing of one's candidate (McGuiness, 1970) or negative marketing of the other party's candidate as in the 1988 and 1992 presidential campaigns with Willie Horton as a threatening racist image. The status logic of social, economic, and political envy and resentment transform institutional definitions into personal motivation.

Personal Eye-sights: Experience and Motives

The logic of comparative status perception socially frames personal experience. It informs how we as individuals see our situation and how we translate what we see into motives for responding here and now. Cultural frameworks become individual frames that shape the personal picture we think our eyes see.

As mentioned in the introduction, the eye is a brute organ of individual seeing; the frame is the shared structure of cultural sight; the combination is each individual's perception, that is, the personal picture of the situation seen through my internalized version of the cultural framework. Eye-sight has something particular and individual—the perspective of each individual's organic eye and physical location, and something shared and collective—the cultural framework of our time and place, our history and society. The two together make up my gestalt, the meaningful whole that each of us sees—with my own eyes! There is truth in the saying that each sees the world differently and occasionally sees a different world, but there is a prior truth in the statement that we share a cultural way of looking and we live in the same perceptual world. The same moon is up there orbiting the earth for all of us, even though it means something different to the love-struck and the lunatic.

Each perception adds a temporal frame that orients our seeing. If we see situations and plan actions within present-oriented short-term time frames, then we live for immediate outcomes and evaluate them for quick payoff. A culture of individualistic profit-taking uses a present-oriented, quick payoff time frame. The cultural power of short-term profit-taking is accepted as unquestioned rationality. Short-term, interest-based actions are effective means to achieve immediate individual goals. We experience them as satisfying and legitimate within current cultural accounts of what is rational action.

Ecological seeing, however, raises again the issue of short-term versus long-term rationality in motives and actions. An ecopsychologist finds that short-term motivation is so powerful that, even if buying more expensive light bulbs saves money within a somewhat longer pay-back time, individuals find it difficult to spend extra money at the moment of purchasing the bulbs. Administrators of a medium-sized university have a similar difficulty overcoming short-term rationality as do individual homeowners, plus a university has the added obstacle of bureaucratic inertia against change (Howard et al, 1993). Result: both homeowners and universities end up spending more money for light bulbs and electricity than they would if they were to see and act in terms of longer-term rationality. These studies in the short-run psychology of rational action support arguments of environmentalists and economists that today's seeing and decision making needs a longer-term rationality framework even to use resources more efficiently. The Iroquois nation evaluates outcomes according to their effects on the seventh generation. As holistic thinkers insist, we must always ask what happens next. A longer time frame and new lenses change the world each of us sees.

Figure 6.1. Seven Lenses of a Primer Paradigm For Environmental Seeing

Concept:	Holistic System	Biosphere	Ecosystem	Carrying Capacity and Population	Dominant Cultural Subparadigm	Institutional Logics	Personal Eye-sights
Disciplinary-Domains:	Philosophy; Theology	Geo-Physical Sciences	Ecology	Population and Biology	Design and Aesthetic Disciplines	Social Sciences	Psychological Sciences
Images:	Circle	Earth from Space Big Blue Marble	Energy in-Energy out & Moving Matter, A Pond	Exponential-Curve with Upper Limit	Humans Seeing Earth Through a Screen	Earth Divided by Nations Boundaries	Earth as Field of Vision & Action
Issues:	Worldview, view, Ideology	Data, Measurement; Macro Life-Support Systems	Life Matter Interactions; Energetics	Life & Ecosystem Thresholds; Irreversibility	Aesthetics, Architecture, Engineering	Nations, Markets, Status Systems	Seeing, Motives, Decisions, Actions
Suggested Sources:	Leopold 1970	Miller 1994	Hagen 1992	Hardin 1968	Simmons 1993	Milbrath 1989	Bandura 1986

For attitudinal changes: see Inglehart, 1990; Olson et al, 1992; Dunlap & Mertig, 1992; Dunlap et al, 1993.

Synopsis: A Primer Paradigm

New lenses that sharpen our focus on the world raise a cultural issue, namely, the need for a synthesis. Redefining what and how we assume we know about our environmental situation requires a new worldview incorporating new ways of seeing and acting. Business as usual will not do. The inherited dominant subparadigm for making sense of environmental issues is now measured against new and more inclusive environmental paradigms emerging in scholarly and public discourse. Figure 6.1 is a synoptic presentation of seven concepts as lenses in a Primer Paradigm for environmental seeing.

The environment is a holistic reality, but our knowledge remains partial. After learning all we can about the parts, we need to think about them holistically. Part of human pathos is that adequate holistic thinking is beyond the reach of individuals, perhaps beyond our species capability. The best hope is teams and shared multidisciplinary perspectives to pursue ecological understanding of the human place in the world. Once we have multiple perspectives on the same object, then we come to think *integratively*. In a sense, we normally look at an object with two eyes, sometimes with the "three eyes" or "four eyes" of microscopes, telescopes, glasses, or contact lenses; and yet our brain integrates the results of binocular or "multi-ocular" seeing into a single object. Can we learn to see with seven "eyes" or seven corrective lenses like those in the Primer Paradigm and still see one object, the earth? I believe that we can focus each of the lenses separately *and* learn to see through all seven simultaneously. Then, we integrate what we see into the vision of a single object, as the brain makes a single orange out of the plural inputs from our two eyes, nose, skin, and hands, as we hold the orange. The rest of this chapter looks integratively at lawns, selves, and everyday things as both natural objects and human constructions. The aim is enhanced environmental literacy.

After Seeing Anew, What Next?

Comparisons of historical and cultural definitions of human-nature relationships liberate our thinking. Analyses of competing environmental worldviews both show how they contrast and suggest shared lines of action (Norton, 1991). Americans with different perspectives nevertheless share strong support for addressing environmental issues. Different environmental subparadigms exist in collectivities as different as local grass-roots NIMBY (Not In My Back Yard) groups, national aggregates of concerned citizens, and bureaucratized professional organizations with offices in Washington, D.C. (Sale, 1993). The subparadigms of these groupings justify responses from near violent "ecotage" to bureacratic compromise and collaborative law making (Dunlap and Mertig, 1992). Significant shifts in citizens' values and attitudes justify speaking of changing worldviews. Changes, as we saw above, are supported by surveys of worldwide attitudinal and value realignments toward the environment.

To imagine differently constructed social worlds requires that we turn the earth like a globe in our mind's hand. New thinking and emotional appreciation turn the globe. Such imaging is further facilitated by literary fictions that are grounded in practical plausibility. This genre of literary constructions allows "utopia analysis" to supplement data-based analyses of policies and worldviews. Utopia analysis helps us imagine alternative worlds of human-environment relationships. It frees our minds from the constraints of inherited ways of thinking. Seen from a utopian perspective, the received and supposedly real world reappears in new outline. Utopia analysis gains support from environmental theologians who offer alternative moral and religious as well as fictional, institutional, and historical perspectives for imagining our worlds (Berry, 1988; Cross Currents, 1994). They invite us to a thoughtful moral journey through new personal gestalts, social paradigms, and cultural worldviews.

If environmental problems are real and alternative worlds are imagined, what can be done next? Concern for What can be done? is part of a pragmatic understanding of social change. Whenever a new problem is seen, inherited and unquestioned rational action is blocked; received ways of moral thinking and feeling no longer motivate. Blocked action, ambiguous morality, ambivalent feelings, and inadequate knowledge generate a sense of crisis. This personal sense realizes the social crisis that I now experience as real in my life and foresee for my children's lives.

A crisis impacts more deeply than a problem or issue. Problem assumes an answer or a solution; issue implies a difficulty that recurs periodically and is resolved for the time being. Neither problem nor issue denotes a significant and perhaps irreversible historical turning point. Crisis bespeaks significant change, that is, potential historical ruptures that have no precedent and may be irreversible. In this classical sense, crisis refers to combinations of conditions within which a person and society must make judgments fraught with deep and long-term outcomes in the face of ignorance, uncertainty, and conflict. Crisis is an ever-ironic possibility of human action, because all actions have unintended or unknown outcomes that may negate what we intend. Critical decisions alter the course of events with reference to key physical processes or personal and social values, such as sustaining a biosphere in which our children can live. The expected outcome of crisis is another kind of faith object, that is, a projected future constructed according to the projector's worldview and warranted by a limited understanding of how the world works.

As we gain critical awareness, we need to look at conventional models for understanding social change. Simply and briefly put, analysts explain social change by: 1. the power of a charismatic leader who synthesizes a new worldly vision to resolve issues arising from inherited but altered social and physical circumstances that present new challenges, like environmental changes linked to the disappearance of ancient civilizations; 2. the self-adjustment of a social system that functionally re-forms itself in response to internal and external pressures and maintains a working equilibrium with its social and physical environment; 3. the evolution of either genetically programmed or rationally intended institutions that continually adjust to circumstances as immediate problems are resolved and new ones are born; or 4. the emergence of social movements that coalesce into collective forces for restructuring institutional values and policies in the face of threats and tensions that may or may not have permanent solutions. One or another of these kinds of change occur in historical crises. In a complex moment like the present, each model has some relevance across the spectrum of social and environmental issues.

The social psychological perspective of this book suggests social movements as forces for change. Today's society is crosscut with social movements concerned with human-environment relationships. What are current developments in, and the effects of, environmental movements for understanding my experience and society's priorities? Analysts distinguish two levels and organizational types of environmental social movements: large and elite policy organizations on the one hand, and small grass roots activist groups of concerned citizens or victims of environmental outcomes on the other hand. The latter are sometimes new forms of community, *basic contaminated communities* that are defined territorially by their exposure to environmental threats to health, homes, or jobs (Edelstein, 1988). Furthermore, it appears that current institutional dynamics lead to continual environmental problems and anomalies that generate grass-roots perceptions of threats and injustices. Local anomalies, in turn, stimulate personal gestalt switches, fuel paradigm changes within organizations, and render alternative worldviews more plausible. Since environmental problems are typically distributed along established lines of power and wealth, they also contribute to racial or class inequity and conflict (Bullard, 1990).

The literature on social movements is vast; that on environmental movements is young and growing. Recent analyses highlight the importance of what we think we know about the environment and the practical consequences of the way we act on it, that is, "cognitive praxis" (Eyerman and Jamison, 1991; Melucci, 1989). Will cognitive changes with new environmental awareness and education lead to deep changes in motives, actions, institutions, and culture? Will environmental change lead moderns to a new *summum bonum* of biographical and institutional self-understanding that will produce significant social change? Can moderns fashion new institutional planning and acting adequate for environmental conditions? The move from interpretation of self-society-environment relationships to understanding how such interpretations tie into social change is important both intellectually and morally. Thinking about our cognitive praxis bridges the gap between what-we-think-we-see and what-we-actually-do. It points to action implications of world views. Analysis of action also requires utopian and policy dimensions. Each dimension includes desirable social arrangements projected into a future time. Projections are faith objects known in the "future perfect tense" (Schutz, 1962). Constructing believable futures that are also empirically viable demands responsible action. Learning to act in terms of a long-term sustainable environment is a contemporary version of civic rationality for the common and future good.

Toward Environmental Citizenship

Even well-meant cognitive praxis, that is, action informed by right knowledge, may not sustain our life together. Contemporaries are increasingly aware of the contingency of individual and social life. We must seek cognitive praxis that leads to plausible individual identities within overarching collective identities based on responsible life-styles. Today, both levels of identity need a realistic grasp of human-environment relationships. A contemporary self includes an environmental identity (see chapter 7).

Environmental identity responds to a defining identity question of our time: Who am I in relation to the natural environment? History and anthropology provide previous answers that are profound and complex. Indeed, the answers lie at the heart of the action dynamics of earlier cultures that guided human responses to the natural environment. Some cultural responses sustained social life, others changed it or eventually ended it. Contemporaries are coming to realize that they must take the natural environment as a major source of self-identification.

Social movements and organizations anchor various types of environmental citizenship. Citizens' responses range from radical ecotage by Earth-Firsters or Monkey Wrench Gangs to research groups working for mainstream political parties or transnational corporations. The types cover the gamut of responses with the possible exception of organized violent revolution. Environmental movements offer collective symbols, cognitive praxis, and social opportunities for generating both formal participation in mainstream institutions and informal protests through grass-roots coalitions. Recurrent environmental problems and attendant social ferment spawn demands that may underwrite another period of progressive politics beyond the platforms of traditional political parties (Orr, 1992; Paehlke, 1989). Re-sighting the environment brings a new look at old political parties. European countries show that a full-blown political party is a possibility as the German Greens and various ecological parties translate environmental issues into political platforms. The publication of *Earth in the Balance* by Al Gore and similar messages from other political leaders speak to environmental issues at a high level of frequency in American politics.

The necessity for a contemporary environmental identity derives from the crisis of perception. As I argue, the crisis follows from two aspects of self-environment interaction. First, basic facts about the environment often cannot be known or seen within individual experience, that is, I cannot indicate them to myself as my experience. This is Darwin's dilemma. He recognized how difficult it would be for readers to accept a story of the evolution of species that depends on facts and processes beyond individual experience. No one is likely to live long enough to see a species emerge. So too, ecological processes that environmental citizens need to see lie forever outside their perceptual fields. The small gradual changes occurring beyond our sensory apparatus put many environmental dynamics into the shadow land of unseen forces that nevertheless power the chances of survival.

Human evolutionary dynamics, biospheric changes, and ecosystemic transformations remain faith objects that transcend everyday experience. These are environmental variants of the psychological phenomenon of a "least noticeable difference," or unseen gradualism that eventually changes the object (Graumann and Kruse, 1990). We see a big picture without noticing the small changes that signal a system at a critical juncture. Our ancestors never wondered if the rather chilly morning signaled the coming of an ice age with glaciers moving ever closer to destroy their way of life. It is, as it were, the reverse process from that which enables us to "see" the real dots of paint in a Seurat scene by getting closer and closer to the painting. What looks like a painted seascape is nothing more than an array of dots, or "points" of paint. The dots are "really" there on the canvas but we normally do not see them. We see the sea, beach, and bathers that our eye-sight "constructs." They are not "really" painted on the canvas, only the dots of paint are there.

In addition to unseen facts underlying an evolutionary or ecological story about the world, observers cannot assess competing interpretations of those facts they do see to transform them into certain events. For example, is this October day in fact significantly warm within some relevant time period, say the last one thousand years? Is last year's rain and snow shortfall an isolated event, or are we entering a period of severe drought? Furthermore, even if one were to accept a warm day or dry year as a signifi-cant change within a statistical framework, there is no definitive method to validate one causal story about these facts beyond the shadow of a doubt. They could be interpreted as a rare and meaningless random variation; an artifact of inadequate statistical history; a normal occurrence within cycles of climatic variation like an annual skunk cabbage rising in the snow; or atypical events signaling rapid warming of the earth's atmosphere caused by human greenhouse gases that bring disruptive changes in temperature and weather patterns.

A modern person experiences such events by accepting scientific facts and applying an interpretation grounded in faith-based inferences about experience and the frames for interpreting it. In a word, any environment is in part a social construction. The environment as known is always a form of landscape, an interpreted physical whole (Greider and Garkovich, 1994). The realization is startling. It is an oxymoron pointing to the clay foundations of the human condition: we stand on an *interpreted physical* reality. We too have feet of clay. The facts of the environment and its meanings are "eisegetic" not exegetic. They are read into the world on the basis of institutional logics through which the perceiver transforms brute phenomena into interpretable facts. Thus, as stated in chapter 2:

> "Natural Environment" = what are taken as patterned facts within cosmic and organic processes; socio-cultural worldviews explaining and justifying such facts; institutional definitions of the factual aspects of experience; and personal experience of events interpreted as such facts.

Personal experience typically frames the natural environment with only one of the meanings given in the earlier discussion of Which environment? Just as science teaches us to reframe our experience by denying the truth of what we think we see and to believe in reconstructed versions of experience—as when science tells us that, in spite of what our eyes see, the sun does not rise in the morning sky; in spite of the resistence we feel, the desk is more space than matter; and in spite of feeling completely at rest, we are moving at break-neck speeds on an earth wobbling on its axis, rotating about its axis, circling the sun, and speeding toward the edge of the universe—so too, environmental science is teaching us that an unusually warm, sunny day may indicate depleted ozone likely combined with global warming with a higher chance of skin cancer and changing weather patterns. Science suggests a lifescape inversion turning the received meaning of sunny experience from high-status suntan to high-risk cancer-burn. The world that is there is continuously translated into an environment, a scientific faith object, to which moderns learn to respond according to stories that contradict personal experience and that are based on natural sciences mediated through politically influenced logics and communication channels.

Media and electronic channels, combined with the inescapable mix of truth and error, knowledge and ignorance, or adequate and inadequate interpretations, present a complex nest of often conflicting stories about the world that is there. Add the postmodern cleansing that must be applied to all social constructions to burn through conventional perspectives on the world, especially static, rational, gendered, and class-based ones, and the task to understand self-society-environment relationships becomes staggering.

We moderns, therefore, must commit to one of the worlds of faith and its ways of seeing. We need to relate personal experience to socially adequate knowledge. We seek personal motives for socially responsible action in accord with real conditions. As the lemma has it, moderns must learn to "think globally and act locally," or even "think globally and act globally." Religious leaps of faith take on empirical meaning to the extent that they refer to the world that is there. Different Christian worldviews are significantly related both positively and negatively to environmental attitudes and behavior (Eckberg and Blocker, 1989; Greeley, 1993; Guth et al, 1993). For example, Christians who believe literally in the Bible and have punishing images of God are likely to undervalue environmental issues. Furthermore, analogous types of fundamentalist religiosity are growing worldwide (Marty and Appleby, 1992).

I reemphasize that a key aspect of social change is shifts in cognitive frameworks. Discovering poisoned tap water leads to an individual gestalt switch that transforms home from secure haven to a risky threat; knowledge of agricultural chemical sprayings leads to a change from unquestioned faith in year-round supermarket fruits and vegetables to preference for organic vegetables in season; widespread attitude changes challenge conventional worldviews and the *summum bonum* of ever-consuming life-styles based on waste-generating production. We experience gestalt switches in our own perception; we realize paradigm changes by decisions to participate in specific reference groups; and we expose unquestioned assumptions of how the world works by evaluating inherited worldviews critically. In these senses, an environmental self participates in cultural shifts of consciousness grounded in ideas of nature as a totality, a consciousness that is contrary to the fragmented selfhood characteristic of postmodern life.

Moderns face the empirical truth and moral dilemma of the "law of large numbers" versus the small good that happens to me as an individual. Today's challenges include seeing through what is good for me to what is good for all of us. Consider individual versus collective paradoxes like the profit a cheater makes as long as others follow the rules; the death of the town commons when too many individuals use it for personal gain; indi-

vidual life versus community sustainability; or more generally, the individualistic fallacy that choosing and consuming what is good for me is the best
way to achieve the good for all. This individualistic fallacy is a generalized
application of Adam Smith's axiom that I see as the most powerful and
overapplied cultural equation of individual and society relations. Smith's
axiom links individual utility with the aggregate good and individual action
with collective outcomes within the single logic of an unrestricted market. It
asserts that each person acting to maximize individual utility inevitably
advances the collective good, even though this outcome is not intended or
even known. An invisible hand guides everyone's pursuit of individual gain
so that the common good is most efficiently reached. This reconciliation of
individual interests and collective good assumes, however, a sustainable
relationship with the environment. Challenges to this unstated assumption
are voiced by commentators who locate market actions in realistic contexts
defined by environmental outcomes, finite material resources, expanding
human desires, increasing population, degradation of available energy, and
carrying capacities of ecological systems.

A misleading corollary of the individualistic fallacy in the context of
large human populations sounds like this: my single act of turning on the
engine is trivial, and, indeed, so tiny that it does not register on any
measuring instrument anywhere in the world. Therefore, in a real but inadequate sense, my polluting act makes no difference to any individual's or
species' life chances. Yet, paradoxically, as increasing numbers of persons
act thus, the aggregate outcome *does* affect ecosystem survival as well as our
species' viability. What is rational, pleasurable, or good for the individual
becomes irrational, painful, or bad for the collectivity. The paradox is biting:
will moderns apply a collective environmental ethic to define the moral
worth of individual acts, and will we act for a long-term common good
rather than maximize short-term personal consumption? As Emile Durkheim
taught, social mores inevitably leads to morals, and morality matters because
human desires are unlimited. Such is the ethical turf we enter from a social
constructionist perspective on self-society-environment relationships that
focuses on an emerging self interacting with a Generalized Environmental
Other. In this see and act, give and take with the environment as other, a link
is forged between what we think we see and how we think we ought to act
here and now—our cognitive praxis.

Seeing Real Paradoxes

If we give a probability greater than zero to the likelihood that my
actions impact on a projected future in which desirable human life would
not be sustainable, then the "Great Naturalistic Paradox" takes on interpre-

tive power. In a simplified understanding of Darwinian evolution, species survival is a function of its adjustment to a sustaining environment such that genetically varied individuals pass on their survival advantages to succeeding generations. As George H. Mead noted, however, the emergence of symbolically organized human society means the "end" of this type of evolution for two reasons: symbolic transformations provide humans with a nonphysically based mechanism for selecting new environments that may or may not support them; and the technological power of symbol-based knowledge enables humans to transform and build new environments. Paradoxically, evolution now means that humans' survival increasingly depends on their ability to adjust to environments they themselves build or cause. The pathos of such power is that adjustment to self-made environments both frees humans from the constraints of naturalistic environments and introduces new risks to survival. Increased use of chemicals for everything from lemon meringue pie to synthesized wood and air sweeteners produces a chemical mix that our bodies may not accept, as in controversies over multiple chemicals syndrome illustrated by the "bubble child" who is protected from "normal air."

What ideologists of free rational individuals pursuing self-interests in an unrestricted universal market overlook is the possibility that adjustments to symbolically selected and technologically reconstructed environments may fail to sustain life. What is the likelihood that one or another system of human-environment interaction will rapidly, perhaps exponentially, reach the limit of a life-support system like air, soil, food, or water. In building symbolic environments, we may produce both more life-supporting goods and more life-threatening waste. The growth of life-threatening wastes leads us to see through culturally functional production to biologically dysfunctional results. The documented and relevant exponential phenomenon is human population increase. If the exponential increase continues and we link it to the idea of carrying capacity, that is, an upper limit of a life-supporting system, we see that the limit will be approached. Once a carrying capacity limit is approached or surpassed, the system is likely to suffer unknown outcomes. Outcomes may include large population dieback or negative changes in the life-support systems that do not recover in the time needed for species survival.

Ecological thinking relates populations to their environments and suggests reimagining expected futures. The carrying capacity of an ecosystem, for example, raises questions about buffer conditions and threshold levels. Examples are the acidity in water that kills trees or fish; the thinness of ozone in the atmosphere that raises rates of skin cancer or mutations in ocean plankton and field crops; or multiple chemical exposures from human products that may cause immune deficiencies, falling sperm counts, or rising cancer rates.

The higher the plausibility we attribute to the Great Naturalistic Paradox, the lower plausibility we give to ideological formulae such as human evolution as unending progress to higher forms of life or human culture as functional adaptation so that dominant institutional logics carry the best likelihood for sustaining life. The Great Naturalistic Paradox is reflected in Darwin's tree of species descent that shows many species evolve toward extinction. The current human situation resembles a fork in the road that is in part a crisis of social perception. Is it possible to see or experience the Great Naturalistic Paradox? If not, how can we know whether to take it seriously?

This question leads to a companion paradox, the Social Psychological Paradox. This paradox refers to the condition of human selves as a population of biological emergents that, through exponential growth, symbolic needs, and social motives, eventually produce outcomes that threaten their own supporting environment. Yet, an individual self is unable to sense or see those outcomes because they are too gradual, tiny, large-scale, or long-term. The outcomes transcend everyday frames. An individual may not perceive that one "natural meaning" of burning a gallon of gas in the car is the addition of about 19.8 lb of carbon to the atmosphere. Rather, the driver learns that natural meaning only from belief in governmental or scholarly reports. In terms of natural meanings, then, we continually do more than we intend and much that we know not. Natural pathos is built into the simultaneous power of collective action based in part on shared ignorance. Pathos is part of human seeing and acting. Any single eye-sight is pathetic and needs continual refocusing.

Natural meanings are real, even if they are not seen or intended, that is, even if they are not part of personal or shared meanings. Ecological thought reflects a naturalistic move toward meaning. For example, deep ecology and the Gaia Hypothesis provide a powerful analogy for understanding the earth as an empirically functioning oneness, a unity from which symbolic personal oneness is a derivative. Deep ecology or Gaia makes the earth a certain kind of faith object. Any ecological whole is constructed from what passes for knowledge in the group from which I accept what is the earth for me, really.

Individuals' limits on knowing natural meanings that lie beyond sensory and cultural frames generate a third paradox, the Sociocultural Paradox. This paradox grasps the reality of society as a community whose actions probabilistically cause threats to the natural capacity of its environment to support that very society. Society enacts this paradox by organizing collective and individual action for national interests, institutional logics, and personal gains within temporal and spatial frames that do not adequately account for environmental effects. Nor do dominant sociocultural units (nation-states, military bureaucracies, economic organizations, education, churches) include natural environment effects as intrinsic components of their institutional logics. Furthermore, even though some of these organizations have knowledge-producing capacities that transcend individual frames, even the most effective knowledge-producing institutions do not foreknow all that is relevant for life-support systems.

Perhaps, in principle, adequate knowledge is impossible. What we take as scientific knowledge is based on universality, replicability, comparison, and controlled experimentation, whereas human interventions in the biosphere are more like a particular, one-time only, historical singularity whose future is outside the sights of experimental scientific certainty. Science is certain only of processes demonstrated with events that are now in the past. Life-support systems, however, address the future—a temporal realm beyond certainty, scientific or otherwise. In other words, whether single or aggregate interventions into biospheric processes will irreversibly alter their life-support capability lies forever beyond scientific certainty, except in the paradoxical and self-contradictory mode of "after the fact" (cf. difficulties in defining a commons, environmentalism, or ecology, Grizzle, 1994; Hagan, 1992; Hardin, 1968; McIntosh, 1986).

In light of the three paradoxes, we can reapply the social construction of reality perspective. Briefly put, three dialectical propositions ground the social constructionist perspective on what humans take as reality: society is a human product; society is an objective reality; humans are social products (Berger and Luckmann, 1966: 58). Furthermore, human social products take on a reality *sui generis* against both the social and natural processes that contingently generate and support those constructed products (1966: 50; cf. 192). Berger and Luckmann are aware of the human-nature dialectic, but they focus on society-body relationships, such as actuarial statistics on length of life that vary by gender, race, and class; nutrition, diet, and eating styles that differ historically and culturally; and the variety of sexual practices. Their constructionist assumptions inform the final thought in the substantive section of the book: "In the dialectic between nature and the socially constructed world the human organism itself is transformed. In this same dialectic man produces reality and thereby produces himself" (1966: 168).

Berger and Luckmann do not develop the realization that, although society is *sui generis* as a symbolically constructed object, it is not a reality or *genus* independent of the physical world. Society is not a free standing subsistent reality interacting only with human organisms. Society, as environmental sociologists and natural scientists repeatedly remind us, simply is *not* independent of the natural environment. Berger and Luckmann fail to add that the natural environment itself is materially and symbolically transformed as humans construct societies *and* technologies that physically alter their built and natural environments. This dual transformation amplifies the natural irony in the social constructionist thesis and in what is taken as knowledge of everyday life. There is no natural functionalism guaranteeing that both symbolic and physical transformations will endlessly support the species that enacts them. Indeed, an empirical picture portrays a species-based pathos in the logic and reality informing contemporary life. In bald-faced language, the probability is greater than zero that dominant institutions and life-styles are threats to future life.

In light of these paradoxes and the greater-than-zero probability of species pathos, I complement the social constructionist perspective with a "substructionist" perspective. That is, I aim at relating the socially *con*structed symbolic apparatus of selves and institutions with the environmental *sub*structure that physically supports such constructions. This transverse relationship cannot be definitively and exhaustively described nor proven scientifically for reasons suggested above. These reasons include: faith aspects of realities like imagined futures; limits of scientific knowledge about present conditions and projected futures; hierarchical and bureaucratic constraints on what we take as real and how we respond to it; and contested values that inform motives, institutions, and nation-states. Nevertheless, groups of scientists do, at times, focus their expertise onto an integrated interpretation of environmental threats by writing a letter to all who read (Union of Concerned Scientists, 1992).

The necessity of filling in scientific versions of the human situation is rooted in the realization that all descriptions, explanations, and interpretations of the natural environment and its relationships to human fate are themselves social constructions from institutional science and organizational policy. A primary responsibility of social scientists and citizens is to clarify natural meanings by disciplined sorting and evaluative ranking of cultural accounts about the world that is there. We must take a stand on questions like: Says Who? Whom do we believe? What do we do next? Cultural accounts are always constructions, and knowing how they are constructed is a necessary step in assessing their adequacy for moral action. How can we know the natural environment when every attempt at such knowledge is itself a social construction? This question emerges as central. Deconstruction of socially accepted narratives must be done in such a way that it leads to shared collective purpose and enlightened personal interests, not to fatalistic despair or irrational agnosticism.

Answers demand that every knower state clearly what socially available knowledge criteria he or she uses to rank accounts of natural meaning and what faith objects and moral futures that knower uses to fill in accounts and motivate action. One methodological path emphasized earlier is reasoning to ground in one's core values, such as sustaining an ecosystem supportive of human life and arguing purposes and interests on the basis of that core value (Milbrath, 1989). In the case of selves, institutions, and societies, both that which is indicated and the account by which it is indicated are social constructions. They are, as Berger and Luckmann argue, social constructions totally, *tout court* (1966). The young marine's eyes-closed eye-sight of his elbow bones illuminated in the light of a nuclear explosion that pierces both his arm and his eye lid demands that we work to integrate social constructions with physical outcomes.

The pathos of the human condition is built on the dual realities in transverse meaning that combines naturally given substructions and socially created constructions (the "two great models," Simmons, 1993). The American Way, the good life, the *summum bonum* is palpably built out of the same humble dust and dirt that lies under our streets, surrounds our potatoes, and reabsorbs our flesh and feces. Social scientists build their disciplines describing, explaining, and interpreting social constructions. Natural scientists do the same for the natural environment that is the substruction of human life. All scientists must help us relate the natural and the symbolic by recognizing the empirical priority of the physical world and the empirical power of our action on that world. So too must citizens in an ecological age. This challenge elicits a new understanding of self as an "ecological self."

7

Transverse Interaction and a New Self: Toward an Environmental Identity

A new self is emerging today. Philosophers and cultural analysts reflect deep concern for contemporary self-understanding, with new-found attention to the environment (Csikszentmihalyi, 1994; Gergen, 1991; Giddens, 1991; Naess, 1990; Solomon, 1988; Taylor, 1989; Thomashow, 1995; Wiley, 1995). Self-understanding in relation to a range of significant others is a central concern, and self-understanding in relation to the physical environment is at the heart of this concern.

I address two issues here. First, is it reasonable to believe that our moment in history is generating a new sense of self in relation to the natural environment? I mean a new self in the strong sense of the term, namely, a self-understanding with the potential to reorder our identities and actions. Second, if moderns do experience such a new self, are there empirically available cultural, institutional, and interactional sources for realizing that self in everyday life and investing it with new *environmental identities?* Environmental identities refer to experienced social understandings of who we are in relation to, and how we interact with, the natural environment as other. I believe the answer to both questions is, Yes. This chapter makes the case for a new environmental identity from a pragmatic social constructionist perspective (see chapter 1).

Previous chapters addressed aspects of a new self interacting with a re-sighted environment. Whatever else we think we are doing, we necessarily affect the environment. Such transverse interaction has routinely been out-of-focus, forgotten, or denied. Even the disembodied lives of virtual community members who interact only through electronic media and computer software are tripping energy, food, and sewage sources through their embodied selves. We saw in chapter 2 that the many meanings of environment limit our grasp of the total reality that supports life. In chapter

159

3, we discussed the tremendous spread of trippers in the last two centuries. Trippers are taken-for-granted tools for living. They are also instruments of transverse interaction that cause environmental responses with increasingly significant effects on survival.

The rapid rise of trippers adds up to deep and wide environmental effects. These worldwide effects justify thinking of our time as an Environmental Revolution that follows from the Industrial Revolution. Contemporary actions affect deep networks of material causes that determine environmental responses for generations to come. The material outcomes of anthropogenic global environmental change transform us into new persons: biospheric actors in the Environmental Revolution. *We interact within new historical forces in societies, institutions, and cultures that transform us from* **ecosystem** *selves into* **biospheric** *selves.*

Previous societies were more or less ecosystem actors. Their interactional effects on the environment could be absorbed within their limited ecological niches, like the BaMbuti pygmies living in African rain forests for upwards of five thousand years. Today's societies produce institutional and individual cumulative outcomes that affect the entire earth's biological, chemical, genetic, and physical systems. Simply switching on millions of computers affects the global environment through waste and pollution from energy generators. So it is with increasing numbers of instruments by which we live what we believe is the good life.

Material culture, including trippers, makes our standard of living physically possible and wraps our lives in what we believe is moral worth. We cannot live without trippers today; they are both the means and meanings of modern lives. As such, they are also the tools and symbols of a new self that comes into being as trippers, the environment, and selves merge into ways of living never before enacted. Life outcomes are no longer physically limited to local niches. Our throughsight sees us as biospheric actors. We learn to frame actions within one biosphere shared with everyone.

Modern selfhood is centering around a newfound awareness that we are now significant actors on the physical environment. Simply turning on the lights illuminates the room and adds a touch of pollution to the biosphere. We are biospheric actors. The Kantian axiom that actions gain moral worth to the degree that they are potentially universal must now include the earth that supports future life. Traditionally, acting as a member of my society was a primary source of self. The emerging environmental self, however, is based on the realization that the meaning of actions is primarily environmental and universal, and secondarily societal. Modern consciousness maps individual action on the Big Blue Marble, not simply on our local or national landscapes. Individual actions have social outcomes *and* environmental effects. Even culturally cherished decisions whether and how often to have children is being re-sighted within the biospheric frame that defines the earth as a commons necessary for all, including future generations. Using the earthly commons to fulfill only present preferences may threaten future good. Using the earthly commons to enhance a single generation's life may have self-destructive outcomes.

Re-sighting the human situation within an earthly commons or biosphere underwrites a new self. I illustrated new ways of seeing in discussions of lifescape reversals, trippers, and the rise of the industrial lawnscape. Here we focus on a new historical self based on universal implications of interaction between humans and the physical environment; formulation of a Generalized Environmental Other; concomitant awareness of self as environmental actor; and possible opposition between intended and actual outcomes of our actions. Selves are meanings we realize in our actions and in the responses we and others, including nature, make to our actions. A crucial question just outside our discussion is whether this new self will be able to move us beyond the moral minimalism and diffuse responsibility that characterize contemporary human-environment relations. To situate our discussion, let us review recent renditions of self-understanding.

Recent Renditions of Self-Understanding

Self is central to understanding the human situation. A central issue today is: how best understand the human person? Answers range from traditional religious or transcendent transformations of self as an apriori or immortal entity, to materialist or linguistic reductions of self to neuronal firings or the self-referential grammar of saying "I" (Harre and Gillett, 1994; Sacks, 1990).

For more than four decades, the Cold War polarized conflicting definitions of the person: radical individualism within market-driven capitalism versus reductionist collectivism within totalitarian state socialism. Since the breakup of the Soviet Union, individuals acting within technological capitalism is the reigning framework for self-understanding and economic analysis. Current conflicts based on religio-ethnic or regional identities take place within the larger capitalistic context for national and international policy. In addition, scholars are reframing self within an environmental framework based on new scientific data and ecological thinking. They argue that there is a historically new, at least in Western culture, and more adequate understanding of self as organism in relationship to environment. This relationship *is* the universal condition for human life. I use two axes for defining the modern self: a social axis ranging from individualistic capitalism to religio-ethnic collectivism; and a metaphysical axis ranging from symbolic constructions to physical forces (see chapter 1).

This chapter presents data and frameworks from environmental sciences to invite us to think of self in relation to the environment. From a social psychological perspective, self refers to a self-aware, experiencing person, an individual who serves as the underlying assumption for scientific and institutional analysis. This is our understanding of the person who confronts us in interaction; who answers and asks questions; and who lives in real space and time (see philosophical and historical reflections by Solomon, 1988; Taylor, 1989). Our lived experience emerges from overlapping social acts that move through stages such as impulse, manipulation, perception, and consummation. Social action underwrites scientific and experiential renditions of self. Each of us lives these phases of social action in which personal experience arises. These metatheoretical elements inform a dualistic model of the person as biologic individual and social self. Neither individual nor self is reducible to the other. Both together engage in transverse interaction. This re-sighting illuminates the contemporary challenge to formulate self-understanding adequate to interaction that sustains society even as it allows nature to sustain us.

Contemporary views of self move from the historical specificity of national identities to the theoretical universality of self-identity in a global environment.[1] Modern perspectives link the organically compelling experience of a fluid body that may be rejoicing, healthy, sick, or dying to cultural constructions of self understanding and environmental sustainability. I complement the inherited view of individual-in-society bodying forth a self with self-in-natural environment generating a new self-meaning. The foundational fact is that humans interact with the natural environment and other animals, human or otherwise. A new life politics is fashioning identities relevant to current challenges. Political meanings enter self definitions as identities that are realized in discourse (see Shotter and Gergen, 1989, for texts that identify self). Discourse alone, however, does not exhaust the realities of self experience. Discourse is realized in action. We are in the world first through our bodies. We keep transverse interaction in focus as we think about a new self.[2]

Changes in Our Sense of a Real Self Suggest a New Self

Ralph Turner argued that a historical shift from an "institutional" to an "impulsive" self occurred in the United States during the 1960s and early 1970s (1976). Framing self as social action, Turner suggests that a new self arises as definitive for a historical era if there are fundamentally different motivational accounts for how we act and how we think about ourselves. He characterizes social action as primarily motivated either by organic and individualistic impulses of the person or by institutional and cultural norms of society. During the 1960s, institutionalized norms of behavior from sex to politics were challenged by new-old impulses to make love, not war; to live simply, not richly; to turn on and drop out, not run the race. Turner's pragmatic approach leads to cultural understanding; but his substantive arguments, like all historical interpretations, are situationally limited and call for continual retelling.

It is historically fruitful to speak of new selves emerging in different socio-cultural contexts. It is scientifically fruitful to think of self as social action and to see self as impulsive or institutional. Both impulse and institution are symbolic transformations of organic responses in the first phase of the social act: impulse refers to individual needs and interests as sources for defining self, others, and action; institution refers to social norms and obligations as sources for such definitions. Attributing social acts to an individual, however, abstracts them from the interactional process that is both biographically and historically prior. Individual social acts—the oxymoron is accurate here—are part of interactional systems of responses. Social acts are moments within systemic interaction. Environmental and global thinkers within the scientific and policy communities insist that analysis eventually is systemic, that is, actions are moments within enveloping systems of interaction among organisms, communities, and physical environments.

Interactional meaning and self-definition construct the *other* that is relevant to the reconstruction of self. Redefining others is part of self-redefinition. To argue for a new self, we must define not only the initial impulse or institution phase of the social act that constitutes self, but also the other that makes either impulse or institution constitutive of the new self. Analysts locate social acts within interactional processes among self and relevant others, especially generalized social and environmental others, to reconstruct a self for our time.

George H. Mead urges us to consider additional phases of the social act, namely, manipulation, perception, and consummation. Manipulation of the physical object is a crucial process in the evolutionary narrative of human development and in the emergence of symbolic interaction (Mead, 1934; Reynolds, 1990). Humans handle their environments out of the brute necessity of assimilating matter as food, air, and water. The perceptual phase of the act is also necessary and universal. Throughout the evolutionary story, humans have perceived the environment in different, even contradictory, images and worldviews through which they temporarily adapt to and manipulate it (Evernden, 1992). Human perception, however, does not grasp long-term outcomes with the same vividness that it grasps immediate costs and benefits. Nevertheless, as technology enhances the power of perceptual and manipulatory phases of the social act, it also enhances the transformative power of consummation to have long-term cumulative effects on the environment. Human consumption is the final phase of a social act that is but one link in ever longer chains of consumption.

I focus on the perceptual phase of the act, our cognitive contact with the environment. How do we see what we think we see? Sociocultural influences shape what we think we know as unquestioned reality. No matter how certain we are today, our empirical knowledge is always for the time being, until anomalies or information lead to a new way of seeing. Mead's discussion of the perceptual phase of social acts moves toward what he calls a "total" social self, namely, an individual reconstructs the situation in terms of an organized set of attitudes, or a generalized other. The generalized other is a mental construction of collective reality that informs personal thinking and motivation. It is not a physical individual we see or touch. Think of the profit values driving American business or the etiquette rules for driving on interstate highways. We know these general values and rules and how to apply them to shopping and driving. We take them for granted, almost unselfconsciously, through the way we see and react to eighteen-wheelers at 70 mph or to credit cards at the grocery checkout counter.

So, too, each of us has a generalized understanding of the physical environment, a Generalized Environmental Other. My personal GEO frames the way I see and decide about interacting with the earth. Each individual's framing of interaction with the environment is a central part of personal realism. Frames are also shared cultural constructions. They are socially real as well. Our frames shape what we see, lead to situational interpretations, and motivate us to act in ways that generate physical responses back toward us by the forces our actions set in motion. Writ large, collective actions generate large-scale environmental responses.

Mead uses baseball to illustrate an individual's response to a generalized other. A competent shortstop responds to the ground ball by anticipating the organized responses of relevant others on the field. In doing so, the competent shortstop responds as a total baseball self in the double-play situation. This same cognitive-interactional process is involved in the emergence of a new environmental self. The analogy between a competent shortstop and a competent citizen is based on the social mind: we "think" in terms of our social location and the interaction patterns, social types, and paradigms for seeing that come with that social location. Sociocultural analysis shows that the way we see objects is, on the one hand, an outcome from socialization into inherited frames through which we look at the situation, and on the other, an ongoing process that can, in problematic situations, reconstruct itself.

Theoretical Sources of a New Self

Three theoretical sources underline the claim that a new historical self is emerging: mode of *interaction*; the *other* involved in the interaction; and the content of our *concomitant awareness* of self in action. The general

argument builds on both the social and physical realism of American prag-
matism and the interpretive constructivism of the sociology of knowledge
(Berger and Luckmann, 1966; Mead, 1934). Pragmatic social constructionism accepts the realist principle that the physical world is there independent of the ways we know that world and talk about it. The realist pole
rejects simplistic reductionism that says the world exists only as a construct
within a schema, narrative, or discourse. On the other hand, pragmatic
social constructionism denies naive certitude or cognitive reification that
leads us to think that we grasp the real world as it is or know all the relevant outcomes of our actions. Reductionism in either direction renders
moral reasoning an absurdity or a Cartesian conceit, since either we are
totally deluded about the physical world, or we have scientific certitude to
tell us how the physical and social worlds run and where each piece will be
at any moment. Such is not the state of the world nor of our moral situation.
We create moral careers in worlds of contingency, uncertainty, and anxiety.
We bequeath these moral and physical outcomes to those who come after
us, just as we inherited them from those who went before. To wish otherwise is to deny either the contingent reality of the physical and social
worlds or our limited but powerful knowledge of those worlds.

The first theoretical source of a new self is interaction. *Interaction*
generates selves. Different interactional modalities generate different selves.
Empirically speaking, humans have as many social selves as there are irreducible interactional modalities in which they participate. Interaction is the
way humans experience themselves as social, that is, existing simultaneously in two domains of reality. Interaction within different groups elicits
different self understandings. We act out different selves with our families
than with our teammates, in living rooms than in locker rooms, in waiting
rooms than in bathrooms.

Second, each domain of reality is defined by the relevant *other*,
whether a symbol, an individual, or a thing, involved in the interaction.
Each family member simultaneously knows self both as a self-defined individual and as an other-defined member of the family. I am a brother and
son, as well as citizen and shopper. After marriage, I add husband and
father to my self understanding as carpenter. Plural self-awareness arises
reflexively whenever self is involved in problematic interaction with family
members or with a 2×6 ceiling beam.

Third, in problematic and reflexive situations, self's existence is grasped
in the mode of *concomitant awareness* of self-in-action. Symbol users can,
in principle, experience themselves as being two things at once even as
they pursue a single course of action here and now. That about which self
is concomitantly aware becomes the substantive content or identity of self-
as-known-reflexively, that is, self as an object to self. Self is both socially
and self-consciously defined.

These three sources of new meanings for action and experience can produce a new self. Self is both a central meaning of, and course of action in, our lives. How we respond to ourselves and what we intend for ourselves subjectively defines the meanings of our lives. Like all meanings, who we think we are, how we feel about ourselves, and how we intend to act are dependent on interaction that makes meanings behaviorally real; others who externally define us and make us socially real; and concomitant awareness we have of ourselves in action that makes our experience real to us. Interactional meanings of self become socially real as we enact them in relation to defining groups that give public appreciation and plausibility to our lives.

Affirming groups are the reference groups within which we spend our days or which provide the frames and content for the way we think and feel about ourselves. Environmental reference groups and organizations exist at many levels from informal neighborhood toxic watches to bureaucratized national groups with offices in Washington, D.C., and on to international agencies within the United Nations or the Green Cross, headed by Mikhail Gorbochev. The emergence of environmental reference groups characterizes society in the twenty-first century (Jamison et al., 1990; Sale, 1993).

Concomitant awareness of self in interaction gives us a sense of present, past, and future. It makes possible the experience of time. A sense of living time makes reflexion possible, that is, self can return to particular actions and intentions in an ordered sequence through memory, even after the action or intention is past. Self can then relate presently interpreted past experience to imagined futures, whether consoling or terrifying. Recollecting the past to project an imagined future is possible because self is concomitantly aware of acting while engaged in the action. We grasp ourselves as situated and typically defined actors, that is, as newly *identified.* As we develop concomitant awareness that we affect the environment no matter what else we are doing, and as we do this in new groups that talk about what we do to the physical environment—then we become new selves with environmental identities.

We experience self through empirically available symbols applied by ourselves and others. Empirically available symbols are imposed or desired, accepted or resisted. Some we gladly seek, others are imposed against our will. Public and personal definitions support or threaten us and our implicated futures. Group definitions become real components of personal lives. They provide the factlike frames that make up the social meanings of selves in the many modes of interaction.

A Schema of Meanings Generated from Interaction

The following section presents a schema for emergent interactional meanings. It builds on the principle that the starting point and final grounding of meaning is interaction. I order levels of meaning according to definition and dependency around processes of interaction as follows:

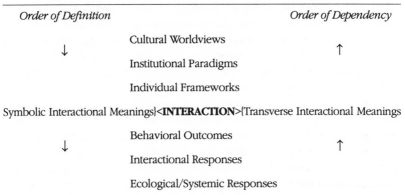

Figure 7.1 Interactional Orders of Definition and Dependency

Order of Definition   *Order of Dependency*

         Cultural Worldviews

  ↓   ↑

         Institutional Paradigms

         Individual Frameworks

Symbolic Interactional Meanings}<**INTERACTION**>{Transverse Interactional Meanings

         Behavioral Outcomes

  ↓   ↑

         Interactional Responses

         Ecological/Systemic Responses

This schema of interaction suggests parallelism and conflict between the orders of dependency and definition. Selfing is first a process of natural interaction. Through reflexivity, selfing and concomitant awareness of self in action generates an emergent symbolic object we know as self. To emphasize the pragmatic insistence that self emerges empirically from natural and then symbolic interaction with other selves, we speak of the social self. The somewhat paradoxical idea of a social self underlines the generative moment when the selfing individual, interacting with an organized community of other selves, internalizes an abstract but interactionally real Generalized Social Other.

The orders of dependency and definition depicted in Figure 7.1 suggest that if humans become reflexively aware of self in interaction with a Generalized Environmental Other, environmental selves emerge to complement social selves. There are historical instances of partial environmental selves. In ideal typical terms, however, earlier selves were involved in local ecosystem interaction that generated awareness of limited environmental self-efficacy and environmental self-understanding. Modernity, however, transforms local, rural, and agrarian populations into technological, urban, and industrial/service populations with biospheric outcomes just now being measured. Demographic, occupational, and technological transformation and growth provide the context in which meanings of environmental selfhood change as well.

Social philosophers and natural scientists sketch types of environmental selfhood. There are historical and substantive differences in the way groups see self-natural environment relationships, for example, ecofeminists, Earth Firsters, colonizers, and natural religionists (Albanese, 1990; Merchant, 1989; Orr, 1992). There are persons who identify themselves with groups organized around ideas of radical and deep ecology (Devall and Sessions, 1985; Naess, 1990). Different ways of seeing the earth inform group identities, social movements, and collective policies. Groups generating environmental identities exist worldwide from international bureaucratic organizations to local protest groups in traditional societies, especially among women.

The order of dependency illustrated in Figure 7.1 shows that symbolic interaction is grounded in interaction with the physical environment, both natural and built (Mead, 1934; Rose, 1962: ch. 1; Reynolds, 1990: 127). Interaction with the natural environment retains empirical priority: mind emerges from interacting and signaling bodies; and selves emerge from interaction among symbol-using individuals. Worldwide awareness of environmental changes are evident in redefinitions of national security, economic productivity, life-styles, and daily routines that turn the home into a recycling center and citizens into environmental agents.

There is a rich American tradition of nature writing from Henry Thoreau and John Muir to Annie Dillard and Barry Lopez. An interactionist argues that, though it is true that meaning is constructed in interaction with other selves, it is also true that meanings emerge in interaction with natural environments (Travisano, n.d.). Types of sensual meanings emerge through reflection on experiences fishing for lobsters and interacting with the boat, wind, ocean, rocks, narrow channels, and lobster pots. Interaction with the environment generates sensual meanings which evoke risk and reward in dealing with natural objects, like eating a wild mushroom that looks like a poisonous type (Fine and Holyfield, 1994).

Natural interactional meanings are real and basic. If the mushroom were misidentified, the eater may die. Humans always had such meanings. They are carried by our senses and are foundational for symbolic meanings. If tap water smells "funny" or a sprayed lawn smells "sharply," these atypical smells signal possibly serious problems, no matter how trivial they appear to someone who smells them as meaningless. Indeed, except for philosophical skeptics, before the modern mimicking of signs by virtual or artificial appearances in computer imagery, sensory meanings were definitive for daily life. Great cultural distances separate sensory meanings we see, feel, smell, and finger in the soil from virtual meanings we "see" through computer images of soil. Can we live so virtually that images replace sensory meanings as truthful? Can we grow real potatoes in virtual soil?

Symbols are so powerful, however, that they function like worlds in which humans think they live. Traditional peoples left the natural world to dwell in sacred places like heaven or the New Jerusalem. Contemporaries symbolically leave the earth to dwell in secular worlds they construct over electronic highways. We can experience virtual life in a virtual community that exists in no ecosystem anywhere on earth nor in heaven. Imagine moral and legal debates over a sensory male having virtual sex after virtual seduction with a virtual self who was a virtual female with a real male body. A virtual self contradicts an environmental self. A virtual self emerges from interaction with only virtual others. A virtual self enacts the skeptic philosophical conundrum that humans cannot refute the thesis that we are nothing more than isolated brains suspended in a vat, and we know nothing more than images unconnected to physical reality. Without immediate tacit knowledge of a real body living amidst a real earth, we are merely virtual selves in virtual vats.

Until now, humans and their ecological niches were incorporated into perceptions either of environmental constraints and opportunities within particular geographic regions or of life-supporting organic links in evolution from hunting-gathering to agricultural to industrial societies. Selves formed out of local or particular meanings remained partial environmental selves more or less adapted to the effects they had on the ecosystems at hand. In a word, historical meanings of self were for the most part appropriate to local environmental meanings. With possible exceptions such as Easter Island, the Maya, or the Hohokam, societies and environments have for the most part mutually *sustained* each other. Central to this book, however, is the claim that our global way of life has likely become unsustainable. The claim suggests urgency because a secondary claim is that dominant institutions are based on the presumption that business as usual is sustainable. Modern life is interwoven with action pathos. In a word, idealizations underwriting business as usual may not continue to support the current effects of self-environment interaction. Hence, we need a new self.

An individual self becomes more total or socially adequate to the extent that it acts in terms of meanings formed by the organized responses of generalized others. A new environmental self emerges as self interacts with an object that orients self's actions to the organized responses of ever more inclusive ecosystems as a Generalized Environmental Other. This GEO, as we mentioned, is an object of faith, but a faith in stark contrast with faith in virtual others constructed with computer images and in apocalyptic or transcendental others of world-denying religious frameworks. Yet, creative symbolic transformation makes it possible to turn even virtual and transcendental symbolic worlds into an enhanced sense of environmental self. Such symbolic worlds allow virtual and believing users to construct public definitions of self grounded in self-environmental relationships, as in computer simulations of earth as ecosystem, or in religious stewardship toward environment as God's loving creation.

The social reality of twenty-first-century environmental awareness is not based on the transverse interaction of hunting, gathering, agricultural, craft-linked, or industrial-service jobs. Rather, the new environmental self is based on generalized transverse interaction with an awareness of an ecological other. Today, we know earth as *a biosphere, a new symbolic other that includes the single functioning organization of living and nonliving interdependencies.* This systemic understanding of the shared fate of earth dwellers sees that the earth works like a living organism or mutually adjusting geo-chemo-biological systems such that nonliving and living beings sustain one inclusive system. Eliminate one central subsystem, for example, the production, distribution, and recycling of oxygen, and you eliminate layers of life needing oxygen and sustained by networks in which the oxygen cycle exists. Within an ecosystem, scientists speak of the continual relocating and restructuring of living and nonliving matter and the continual transformation of supportive incoming energy into degraded outgoing energy (Hagen, 1992). Think of the dynamics in a new pond that sustains cycles of aquatic life even as it evolves toward its own "death" as it turns into a marsh.

Self is empirically constituted by networks of others with whom or with which self interacts. Networks of interacting selves provide what Peter Berger calls "plausibility structures," that is, groups of confirming others who validate self in the context of a group's world view and the personal identities realized within that world view. The new environmental self explicitly includes organic and physical others within its plausibility structures. An integrated view of the social-natural world includes frames for experiencing self, perceiving others, seeing the world, and motivating action within an environmental identity.

Broadening Pragmatic Meaning to Include Self-Environment Interaction

Moderns are realizing anew that meanings are primarily *in nature.* If self is self-consciously aware of being at once a member of society and an actor within nature; of existing in two sets of meanings simultaneously; and of indicating such dual awareness to oneself, then a new self emerges along with new meanings of the environment. This new self bridges symbolic and natural meanings in a transverse way with one foot in the symbolic and one in the physical world—and increasingly aware of its slippery footing.

It is important to reflect on the sustainability and functionality of this spread-eagle stance. The symbolic power to construct interpretations drives a gap between the world that is there and the world that humans believe they see. The sustainability issue adds to this gap. Can we justify the assumption that no matter what we do to our physical surroundings, those surroundings will continue to support human life? The assumption of continual sustainability is not an empirical fact; it is a derivation from the idealizations, "I can do it again and again," and "the world will go on until further notice." Against the universality of these idealizations, history records breakdowns in the sustainability of societies. Nor is the sustainability assumption a philosophical certainty. Rather, it is a cultural construction that underwrites technological Progress and Control over the physical world.

The ruling belief is that intervention in, and control over, natural processes is the moral imperative that guarantees happiness and fulfillment. Until the late twentieth century, this cultural construction long grounded the hearts, minds, and policies of the Western self. Questioning this key construction and formulating alternative environmental awareness is part of the new twenty-first-century self. Indeed, one analyst refers to a newly emerging yet unspoken assumption akin to divine predestination or Greek fatalism, namely, twenty-first-century "industrial fatalism" (Beck, 1995). The tension between industrial progress and fatalism is the dis-ease of modern human-environment interaction.

Symbolic worlds can be autonomous and free from the constraints of the physical here and now. They have their own space-time forms and logics. Symbolic descriptions of the human condition, therefore, cannot guarantee sustainable progress between socially constructed realms and the physical world. The meanings of social action lie forever in the future, an empirical future that emerges and has at best a statistical link to intended futures. As Mead insisted, the *future* is always an *hypothesis*.

A future that sustains human life or one that ends it each has probabilities of coming to pass. Symbolic constructions are two-edged swords. This two-edged realization fuels ambivalence to technological power that both enhances and threatens species life. Although ideas are not limited by the body, paradoxically they contribute to the fulfillment or destruction of the body whose limits they do not share. The nuclear engineer's idea that it is safe to flip this switch may lead to a Three Mile Island nuclear crisis. These contingencies require reconstruction of the physical-symbolic mix of human action so that we can grasp their meanings.

Environmental awareness based on a single but dualistic self includes mixed symbolic-nonsymbolic meanings. Mixed meanings physically exist for biologic individuals, as well as within personal consciousness and the logics of social institutions. In short, *meaning is socially constructed, personally experiential, and behaviorally natural.* A broad understanding of meaning is essential to the argument of this book. We must think in terms of an expanded and realistic meaning.[3] As Figure 7.1 illustrates, physical life is prior to symbolic life in terms of dependency—mind depends on brain more fundamentally than brain depends on mind, though, in a deep paradox, minded beings can destroy the conditions for the survival of their brains, as Kurt Vonnegut caustically plays out in his evolutionary anti-utopia following the extinction of "big brains" in *Galapagos* (1985).

I build on the vital priority of nonsymbolic meanings from interaction with the natural environment rather than the experiential priority of institutional meanings. Our challenge is to form a new self with adequate natural meanings. As noted earlier, Mead sees an engineer building a bridge as engaged in a process that produces meaning by taking the attitude of the physical other. "An engineer . . . is taking the attitude of physical things. He is talking to nature and nature is replying to him" (1934: 185). Elsewhere, Mead notes that someone who steps not on a bridge but into a raging stream realizes the physical-symbolic duality of meaning as he intends to reach the far bank but fears being swept away.

> The rush of the torrent carries death to the man who rashly ventures into it. It has not that *meaning* unless in advance of his fatal plunge this outcome was present in its nature, and it is only in the organized conduct of men that the bare relatedness of events and things can pass over into meaning, that meaning can invest events and things. (1964/1929: 336, his italics)

Meanings are in nature, whether humans are aware of them or not. Humans consciously realize these natural meanings by their organized responses to them. The pure torrent both physically threatens death and offers life-supporting hydroelectric power. The second meaning does not undo the life-threatening meaning for a rash wader—a meaning learned by competent adults, but not genetically transmitted to newborns, much to the fear of parents who live near swollen streams. An innocent child swept away by the torrent unintentionally but really realizes one of its natural meanings. Occasionally dams break and death-dealing natural meanings of walls of water come to those who live downstream (Erikson, 1976). Finally, Mead argues that individuals achieve more total selves by relating to the *physical environment as a generalized other,* just as they relate to society as a generalized other.

> It is possible for inanimate objects, no less than for other human organisms, to form parts of the generalized . . . other for any given human individual, in so far as he responds to such objects socially . . . . *Any thing—any object or set of objects, whether animate or inanimate, human or animal, or merely physical—toward which*

. . . he responds, socially, is an element in what for him is the generalized other, by taking the attitudes of which toward himself he becomes conscious of himself as an object . . . and thus develops a self. . . . (Mead, 1934: 154 fn, italics added)

Natural meanings, *whether known or not* to human interactors, are foundational to other meanings. In Mead's terms, the biologic individual is prior to the self, and potential meanings in the physical environment are prior to the symbolic meanings of human-environment interaction. The likelihood of survival, as well as moral accountability, requires us to work toward a better grasp of natural meanings. Pragmatically, the metaphor of "grasp" implies that moderns learn better how to handle natural environments through symbolic transformations of behavior, that is, natural responses have to inform personal motives, institutional policies, and sociocultural norms and values. In a word, our intentional meanings need to be naturalized, even as those in nature are symbolized.

More on Three Types of Meaning That Make Up Self

I argue that natural interactional meaning undergirds symbolic interactional meaning. Contemporary understanding must make this foundation democratically clear and available for action. Consider three types of meanings, socially cognitive, personal experiential, and behaviorally natural, in relation to the natural environment. *Socially cognitive* meaning is conceptual, rational, and totally socially constructed. It is symbolic interactional meaning. In principle, such meaning is public, collectively shared, institutionally produced, and continually transformed. Its self-conscious prototype is science as pluralistic, ever growing, and continually reformable knowledge. An unselfconscious but powerful meaning is the unquestioned, taken-for-granted knowledge that informs everyday experience, perceptions, motives, and decisions. This mundane but real cultural knowledge sustains the sense of natural reality in everyday life. As the world moves deeper into environmental interaction, however, science must provide adequate everyday transformations of what we see and do. A firm empirical foundation provides the best chance for knowing the futures implicated in what we do. Empirical expectations can inform our motives as we reconstruct our actions. Intelligence emerges in problematic situations and conflicting impulses. A newly realized aspect of modern life is that everyday actions and valued decisions are environmentally problematic. To live authentically today, we take responsibility for acquiring adequate knowledge of the environmental outcomes of our actions. Environmental science provides one basis for anticipating such outcomes.

Personal experiential meaning is perceptual, aware, and partially socially constructed. It is interactional meaning informed by biographical meaning. Such meaning is personal and individual, but also public and intelligible since my life is part of group life. It is situated knowledge; the particular is seen as an instance of a universal. It is my seeing and interpreting the firey pink streaks in the sky as the "same" sunset that my family sees. This sameness is real, even though I know that the sun neither causes the color display each of us sees; nor is it really setting in the sky; nor does the sunset have the same meaning for other members of my family. Personal meaning of the sunset derives from the mix of transverse and symbolic experiences in each person's life. This is the meaning available to the individual in search of lobsters, a self who perceives the meaning of the wind, waves, rocks, sounds, and flags to "catch" a lobster just as other "lobstermen" do, and to return safely (Travisano, n.d.) A contemporary task is to align my personal meaning with empirical scientific meanings so that I act with greater awareness of the expected outcomes of my actions. I may not hide in innocent ignorance, or worse, deliberate ignorance—lest I be responsible for outcomes that I suspect lurk at the edges of my vision, but which I refuse to bathe in the light of my focused gaze.

Behaviorally natural meaning is in nature, possibly unknown, and physically caused. Whenever humans interact with each other or with physical others, they also interact with physical others that lie outside of immediate experience and perhaps outside of their symbolic grasp as well. Distant, future, or nonexperienced outcomes are explicitly emphasized in transverse interactional meaning. For example, to know my responsibilities for the trippers I turn on every day, I must know about their links to energy sources and to outcomes of their use. Knowledge of these links ties the empirical sciences of energy, pollution, and waste production to tripped objects like my car engine or my kitchen appliances. These meanings are not merely social constructions, though we always know them through socially constructed symbols, even those as solitary as daydreams and prayers. The environmental meanings of my actions are combinations of empirical science and personal experience. However, it is I who trip the meanings on the basis of what I think I see.

The presocial physical outcomes that are natural meanings of actions are available to socialized adults only indirectly and inferentially. The innocent eye of the presocial child is a mythic measure of what is forever beyond adult perception (Dillard, 1985). The myth refers to the meaning that humans, as biologic organisms, share with animals. It is the meaning of human interaction as animal interaction. As such, it is to some extent beyond our grasp, even when it is part of our past. This penumbra of ignorance around the total meaning of what I do, shadowed by the very concepts of reason, adds pathos to our lives and undermines simplistic naturalism as the answer to the environmental predicament.

The pathos of blind spots in environmental eye-sight flows from the paradox that natural meanings are known as real only through socially constructed meanings. The physical outcomes of actions do not announce themselves to us: we need to search for them through scientific instruments or data sources at our disposal. As constructed and communicated, furthermore, such meanings go beyond the sensory meanings embedded in the here and now. Environmental meanings are, as it were, generalized from a Particular Environmental Other in my personal interaction to a Generalized Environmental Other in our collective interaction. Only in the modern world is the earth, as an object of human action, seen as an empirical whole, an ecosystem, a biosphere, or a natural Generalized Other. This seeing is realized not only in the profound pictures of the earth rising and setting in outer space, but also in the networks of political, economic, and military interactions by which each person, group, and nation affects the life chances of all. This historically first-ever eye-sight is framed with first-ever worldwide movements, international environmental politics, and aggregates of space-age data documenting a changing global environment.

New Selves Are Situated as New Environmental Identities

Interactional dynamics generate definitions of what is being done, the business at hand. In addition to the business at hand, there is always an identity at stake: a personal identity imposed and resisted, presented and accepted, or reconstructed and rejected. Self is known as identified. Environmental selves are identified. They are accepted or rejected. In the past, environmental identities were traditional, rural, and limited to a local group or community. Today, postmaterialist environmental identities are breaking out of traditional frames, and social movements are rendering them universally plausible. Similar attitudes and identities are part of a widespread cultural shift in self understanding within industrial nations and, for different reasons, in Third World nations as well (Dunlap et al, 1993; Inglehart, 1990).

Personal identity is a tensed experiential and social psychological reality. On the one hand, it is an immediate and intimate sense of personal existence—I know myself, therefore I am. On the other hand, identities are social constructions—others know me, therefore I am. An identified person is a situated self at once presented to and addressed by others. The social psychology of personal identity captures the daily dialectic between experience and the objectified, the particular and the general, the private and the public, the individual and the group, the I and the Me. No one escapes this tensed reality. Everyone lives the dialectic of the I that I know and the Me that you know. Emergence of a new self implies the construction and experience of a new identity. We experience, and others construct, environmental identities in situations realized by: engaging in ecological identity work (Thomashow, 1995); membership in environmental groups and institutions (Jamison et al, 1990); shared environmental beliefs and attitudes (Dunlap et al., 1993); forms of environmental activism (Edelstein, 1988); contributing to environmental causes and organizations (Sale, 1993); and eyeing ordinary sights in ways that contradict conventional seeing, such as revulsion at the sight of a weedless, short, lush lawn.

Once experienced and imposed, environmental identities function within social action as historically selective mechanisms enabling individuals both to see a different environment and to respond differently to what they see and to themselves. A new identity is a framework for seeing the world differently and acting differently toward it. This selectivity function is analogous to that in the ox whose sensory apparatus selects the environment in such a way as to transform mere grass into grass-as-food. So too, a contemporary self with an environmental identity sees a new environment, which in turn affects responses to that selected environment (see the importance of self schemas for understanding self and motivating action, Markus and Nurius, 1987). Fashioning relevant identities is one way individuals contribute to the reconstruction of society. Everyday ideas such as, "throw out the garbage," is reframed as "feed the compost" or "recycle the cans." New sources of pollution or poison, like incinerators and radioactive dumps, work like anomalies generating lifescape inversions that change the way we see and feel our selves.

Indicators of New Environmental Identities

First-ever photographs, new words, social movements, and paradigm conflicts evoke new awareness of ourselves. This newness arises with images of earth as a single biosphere supporting all human life. Holistic constructions such as deep ecology or Gaia represent environmental self-understanding as part of a single living system. Other reconstructions are vying for public acceptance. Consider selected indicators, beginning with new images.

Images

If you are old enough, do you remember how you responded to two photographs in the last fifty years that image a new world? If you are too young, ask your parents or grandparents. First is the 1945 picture of the first thermonuclear explosion: the mushroom cloud linking earth-atmosphere, organism-globe, science-morality, and nation-species in ways that thoughtful persons, ethicists, military officers, political decision makers, terrorists, and international organizations are still unpacking. The mushroom cloud ties nations, armies, scientists, moralists, and each of us into a *destructive* picture of death, sickness, and environmental danger.

The second image is from 1968. It is a picture of the earth taken from outer space. The earth looks like a seamless Big Blue Marble with no socially constructed national boundaries. It is marked only by environmental processes of land-flora-water-cloud configurations. The earth we trod underfoot is seen as it is naturally: a single globe suspended in the vastness of space (Kelley, 1988). Additional images of earthscapes, for example, earthrise and earthset as the globe gradually slips over the horizon of the moon, communicate a oneness of origin and destiny, place and time, air and water that transcends national borders, monetary systems, languages, ethnicities, and ideologies. The photo links humans spatially and temporally in a shared fate on the earth as home to our species and all known life.

Earthlings who see and believe in that photo know themselves as sharing a fate in the oneness of a biosphere that bordered societies and conflicting cultures make us forget. These new images inform discourse that reconstructs how we should interact. Just as learning to imagine a world without war is fundamental for thinking about peace, so imagining the environmentally unified world is a step toward thinking how to live sustainably with it (Boulding, 1990). These images need to inform international civic culture.

Words

We construct new objects through linguistic coinage. Words structure thinking and frame seeing. Two crucial coinages are *ecology* in 1866, and the implicated word *ecosystem* in 1935 (McIntosh, 1986: 2, 193). They enable us to think of human life as sustained amidst complex empirical relationships with other living beings and the nonliving environment. Since then, "eco" words have spread through popular, intellectual, and scientific discourse: "ecosophy" for environmental wisdom; "deep ecology" for sustainable relations with the environment; and the political and educational challenges of "ecolacy" or "ecological literacy" for contemporary democratic citizenship.

A third word, *biosphere*, refers to a holistic and cyclic construct for thinking empirically about the human situation. It refers to the earth from a few miles beneath the surface to a few miles into space within which all life, as far as we know, exists. The term appeared in an 1875 book about the geology of the Alps Mountains. A Russian scientist was the first to use it in a modern sense (Margulis and Lovelock, 1989: 2). The term spread as a reference for the zone of life on earth. It indicates the interwoven nonliving and living components of a Generalized Environmental Other. Whatever else these words do in their narrative contexts, they carry a worldview based on holistic cyclic thinking as the larger context that integrates particular linear thinking. The terms work as lenses for seeing and as a glossary of environmental understanding.

Talk

Selves emerge in conversation as new meanings. As meaningful, selves are imagined, defined, and discursively enacted (Harre and Gillett, 1994; Perinbanayagam, 1991). Discourse or talk is always about objects, whether their ontological status be fictive or real, physical or symbolic. New forms and content of talk supply the concrete stuff for experiencing new identities. If new talk is linked with selves in newly defined situations, and such situated selves have new frames for interpreting natural others, then it becomes possible:

1. to construct additional new objects that exist for the first time and function as new others in the emergence of that new self, for example, I now think of myself as one organism within an ecosystem;
2. to formulate new speech categories and construct new texts of discourse such as ecological literacy, for addressing new objects like biosphere; and
3. to effect new interaction that grounds an ecological self.

Increasing use of "eco-talk" bespeaks the emergence of a new self.

Eco-talk supports new identities, motives, and actions. Eco-talk is heard in the polished "green ads" of transnational businesses; the "green talk" of governmental policy battles; the "green theology" of ecologians; and the "green politics" of new political parties and international eco-organizations (Porter and Brown, 1996). These discourses are met by the "green cries" of homeowners, workers, or farmers touched by pollution and poison. Rachel Carson first taught the nation to use eco-talk to voice more adequate interpretations for the use of pesticides. Lois Gibbs learned eco-talk as she struggled to understand and reconstruct her life lived along Love Canal. Dialects of eco-talk reflect such different ways of seeing as eco-feminism, eco-Christianity, and on to the "rational" calculations of risk assessment and profit making in eco-economics. Both supporters and critics of environmentalism use variants of eco-talk to make their cases (contrast Bailey, 1995; Brown, 1994). Once we eco-talk, our eyes are open to re-sighting not only the environment, but self and society as well.

Institutional Categories

Images and words inform institutional categories of what we take nature to be, how we reason about it, and how we should act toward it. New institutional knowledge teachs us to think differently about self and nature. New scientific and disciplinary specialties focus on self-environment relationships: ecology (McIntosh, 1986), environmental science (Miller, 1994), history of environmental worldviews (Oelschlaeger, 1997) environmental history (Simmons, 1993), environmental sociology (Catton and Dunlap, 1978), ecological education (Orr, 1992), environmental architecture (Fisher, 1993), environmental economics (Cronan, 1991), environmental ethics, and environmental art (Art Journal, 1992) in which artists design ecological landscapes that actually do environmental work, such as purifying polluted water. Initiatives in environmental psychology consider both built and natural environments and global environmental issues (Graumann and Kruse, 1990). Psychologists are developing an "ecopsychology" (Howard, 1993; Winter, 1996).

These new knowledge specialties are broader than university departmental disciplines and still not broad enough to grasp human-environment issues. The paradoxical need for new knowledge that is both more specialized and more generalized underwrites a move toward multidisciplinary and scholar-activist centers, for example, environmental study centers, ecological institutes, and funding initiatives that are multidisciplinary in the strong sense that they try to integrate natural and social sciences, moral analyses, policy formation, local activism, and futuristic thinking about the life chances of our children's children. Nations and international organizations are funding the study of a new domain of inquiry, "anthropogenic global environmental change," a central construct for seeing the effects of our actions on the life-support systems.

The difficulty of formulating a shared universe of discourse or integrative vocabulary reflects the newness of these developments. Similar difficulties are evident in the struggle for agreements in environmental regulatory law and policy formulations, as well as in increasing international cooperation and conflict over scarce environmental resources like oil, water, or land (Caldwell, 1990; Homer-Dixon, 1993). Just as athletes around the world acquire a general sense of an athletic self by training for and competing in the Olympic games that serve as a generalized other, so too, worldwide conferences, organizations, and conflict resolutions addressing human-environment relations realize a self in relation to a generalized other. Think of self in relation to events like the 1992 Earth Conference in Rio de Janeiro, the largest gathering of political leaders in history. Signatures of 172 heads of state on Agenda 21 at the Rio Conference symbolize shared environmental understanding as a possible basis for future cooperation (Sitarz, 1993).

Attitude Changes and Social Movements

Social movements often challenge institutional centers of power. As we noted, positive environmental attitudes continue to grow in both industrialized and less-developed nations.

A powerful development is that between women and environmental action in Third World contexts, even though men remain culturally and politically dominant. This gender-based dynamic highlights feminist arguments that core values and ways of seeing within patriarchal cultures conflict with values and perceptions needed for an adequate environmental self. In such contexts, changes in gender-based power arrangements are essential for effective environmental action. Women played a crucial role in redefining the meaning of logging in the Himalaya Mountains by actually hugging trees to stop loggers (Weber, 1989). Local environmental protests often led by women were pivotal in the dissolution of the Soviet Union. Widespread environmental disasters fueled local citizen opposition and brought people together in protest (Feshbach and Friendly, 1992).

Environmental movements in Western Europe are sometimes linked to political parties like the "Greens" in then West Germany. Green parties spread through Europe and show some visibility in the United States. Green thinking is particularly strong in Scandinavian countries. Young greens entered into Danish politics with striking drama. As the final plenary session of a natural history association was convening at the University of Copenhagen, a group of green students suddenly entered and:

> We locked them all in. We were about twenty people. After we had locked the doors, we cut off the ventilation and started to poison them. It was pretty violent. We got up on the stage and talked about air pollution. We burnt garbage and tobacco in large quantities. We poured waste water from a nearby factory in an aquarium with goldfish who slowly died. On the side walls we showed films about cancer and pollution and we had a loudspeaker with a traffic alarm blasting. We sprayed water in the audience from Emdrup lake. And we had taken along a wild duck which we covered with oil. 'Come and save it,' we screamed. 'You talk about pollution. Why don't you do anything about it?' Finally we cut off its head to end its suffering,

and we walked down along the first row of chairs so that all who were sitting there got blood on their clothes. After an hour we opened the doors and said that we wanted to start an environmental movement, and that the founding meeting was being held in the next room (Jamison et al, 1990: 66).

In Sweden, ecological thinking reached the center of national planning (Södergvist, 1986). Norway's Prime Minister, Gro Bruntland, chaired the United Nations committee that wrote the report emphasizing "sustainability" as a key contemporary issue (World Commission on Environment and Development, 1987).

In the United States, widespread yet local environmental problems work like a plague generating environmental identities in those linked as victims, activists, adversaries, or intellectuals. Action researchers simultaneously take a value position toward the problem and critically study its empirical dynamics. In sum, life in today's world is characterized by environmental identities defined by a global environment as the relevant other. To be modern is to see the environment as a shared life source that is endangered.

Further testing and time is needed to see if this new eye-sight translates into effective change. Reformulations of environmental issues in line with core values in a democratic society, like the right to know about danger and a fair chance to live in a safe environment, raise issues of environmental justice, including environmental classism and environmental racism. Justice perspectives highlight the social distribution of the costs of environmental degradation. Dangerous landfills, toxic incinerators, or radioactive wastes are likely placed close to poor, politically weak, and often minority communities (Bullard, 1990). No one expects the rich and powerful to allow such sitings in their backyards. Nor would the poor, if they had a fair alternative. Furthermore, environmental social costs like scarce water, soil, oil, and food, or siting of toxics and pollution often impact poorer nations and threaten international security and peace. A socio-moral perspective places environmental justice at the center of the modern predicament (Bellah et al, 1991).

Doing Personal Environmental Identity Work

All of us face the personal task of working out a sense of self adequate to the challenges of our time. The argument of this book is that human-environment relations are a shared challenge that is now front and center for us regardless of our political, moral, and ideological differences. Americans differ on deep and devisive issues. Yet, we all share common life-support systems. The real environmental conditions we share invite us to work toward environmental identities that interpret divisions in the context of what supports us all.

I assume we all desire an environment that supports our lives and, if we have children or love young people, the lives of those who come after us. We then must frame our desire for a supportive environment in a realistic and shared way of seeing where we are and how we act. Our eye-sight must include a focus that can range from our local personal scene to the global species sphere. This is the challenge George Perkins Marsh posed in 1864. It is a challenge echoed from American thinkers like Thoreau, Muir, Leopold, Carson, and answered in the findings of countless scientists generating empirical data that tell us how nature is responding to us.

In the previous chapter, I presented a Primer Paradigm with seven concepts as lenses through which all of us, regardless of our differences, can see human-environment relations. It integrates some of the ways of seeing that inform previous chapters, and that I believe are necessary, though hardly sufficient, for adequate environmental eye-sight today. In Figure 6.1, I start with the abstract idea of holism, then work from the most inclusive ecological domain of life, the biosphere, to more local domains or ecosystems, through population dynamics, and on to cultural, institutional, and personal views of human-environment interaction. This conceptual order is an "ecological" perspective, a top-down order that starts with the most inclusive abstract idea and works toward personal perspectives.

In this section, I reverse the order and start with personal experiences and ways "I" see the environment. This is an experiential order that starts with self. It is an "egological" perspective from an individual's or ego's point of view. An egological perspective is the heart of our inherited cultural world view. Culture codes "environment" as "the way *I* see environment," or the way *my* business or *my* nation sees environment. The utilitarian translation of an egological perspective is, "what's in it for *me* is the source of all value in the environment." Environment is only a resource for wealth that I can manipulate and transform any way I wish.

An egological perspective translates eye-sight into I-sight: my eye sees what I see. The landscape derives from my mindscape. Today's data, however, point to the need for more realistic eye-sight that fashions my mindscape in accord with the landscape, not the other way around (Orr, 1992: 86). Today's challenge is to ground egological perspectives by integrating them with an ecological perspective that explicitly recognizes the importance of the natural other, of a "thou" that includes nature. Objective eye-sight includes "thy-sight" as well as "my-sight."

The meanings of reality derive from interaction in which the other is a co-definer with self. I-sight is but one source of the meaning of what is really going on. Objectivity comes from seeing ourselves and the environment as though we were standing outside ourselves. It is as though I were both self-contained and "ecstatic," that is, both standing within myself and standing over there seeing myself interact. To understand the world, we decenter our egological perspectives, that is, we know reality by getting outside ourselves and seeing objects from the point of view of others as well as of self. In the basic process of role-taking, or "thy-sight," I see by putting myself in the place of the other. Even knowledge of self remains incomplete and likely erroneous if it does not integrate how others see us. Meaning demands thy-sight. We include the mutual other who or that, together with self, defines what is happening. My-sight alone is myopic. Combined with thy-sight, it gives us the binocular synthesis for solidly seeing what is out there. It makes I-sight into more objective eye-sight. So let us walk through the Primer Paradigm beginning with I-sight.

Personal eye-sight of the natural environment builds on youthful experiences. Alex Kotlowitz, for example, begins his gripping ethnography of two young black American boys struggling to grow up in the ghettoized "jects" of Chicago by describing their excited search for garter snakes in the "natural areas" alongside the railtracks that carry suburbanites to and from the Loop. Pharaoh, nine, and Lafeyette, eleven, find no snakes, but they discover three white eggs lying on the course dirt and spot a foot-long rat. Pharaoh sensed the tranquillity of a place shared with wildflowers and sparrows. Memory transformed it into a sanctuary for him (1992: 3–7). Well-off students in my classes, on the other hand, typically refer to woods behind their houses, summers spent lakeside, mountains hiked during vacations, family trips to the shore, national sites like Grand Canyon or Yellowstone, a favorite backyard tree, nearby farms, or a neighborhood pond.

Psychologists suggest that we all share the healing sense of natural imagery and the sense of loss at the sight of nature degraded. An environmental educator finds personal environmental self-understanding grounded in three sets of experiences: childhood memories of special natural places; feelings of loss at these or similar places destroyed; a sense of wonder at remaining wild places (Thomashow, 1995). Personal environmental I-sight is framed by mixed feelings of consolation and loss, wonder and threat, searching for the good life even as we leave behind the ground that nourished our youth. Ambivalence informs our relationship to the earth.

It is not likely that we destroyed those special childhood places or threaten remaining wild places that evoke mystery and awe. Students then ask Who and Why questions about how humans interact with the environment. They begin to answer these questions with various "They did it" responses. "They," it turns out, are sometimes neighbors but more frequently impersonal institutional actors like real estate speculators, mall developers, transportation engineers, local businesses, national chains, city utilities, airports, or even their own universities cutting down woods for parking lots or spraying toxics around their dormitories. Students' I-sights learn to include social seeing through the lenses of institutional logics: profit, power, parking, re-election, city services, or public roadways. A "politics of place" decides who does what with the environment according to the structure and use of power. Rows of mature trees are marked with X's and cut down to build four-lane roads or airport runways opposed by locals but imposed by the institutional power of city planners, suburban commuters, or mall merchants. If environmental eye-sights are shared, they sometimes lead to compromise as when a suburban developer protects wetlands or natural waterways that save someone's childhood places or future generations' wild places.

As students pursue understanding of human interaction with the environment, they spontaneously and with a touch of wistful resignation justify institutional logics with the general maxim, "Well, you can't stop progress." This oft repeated phrase reflects the dominant cultural way of seeing, a taken-for-granted formula that legitimates our particular historical worldview that "more is better": more people, roads, cars, malls, stores, clothes, and "things" in general. Economists teach their rational logic on the assumption that more is better. For example, Alan Blinder begins his invitation to economic reasoning with principles that he assumes are "noncontroversial." His first principle is that for most market products, "more is better than less" (1987: 16). My unreflective I-sight likely agrees with this formula—after all, I want a job to earn an income to live out the core values of freedom, health, and security for which I believe the sole means are dollars, and lots of them. So, my unreflective I-sight merges with the dominant cultural worldview that encodes an anthropocentric view of environment: humans are the source of all value, and environment has only use value as a resource for profit and consumption. Most likely, all of us were socialized into this worldview that drives the modern world.

In addition to motivating us as market players, however, our dominant cultural worldview paradoxically calls for the collection and communication of data that make us question its egological values and business as usual. Two simple questions point to another lense for looking at the noncontroversial primacy of "more." Can my town be home to ever more people? Can my local area support ever more consumption and receive ever more waste? For the first time in history, for example, we have reasonably accurate data on human population growth and the extinction of other species. The *fact* that human population reached one billion around the year 1810 and multiplied more than five times by 1996 with the expectation that at current growth rates it will double in about forty-five years and the *fact* that other species are becoming extinct and in tandom with growing human population invite us to integrate our individual I-sights with the outcomes of our collective interaction with earth.

I come to see myself and the environment within a dynamic interplay of collective and generalized responses. The moral dilemma is in part that I know my individual interactions as such have the tiniest, almost infinitesimal, outcome on the environment, so that I alone have no measurable effect. Yet, I must see my interactions as part of massive collective effects that indeed have significant effects on life-support systems. If, further, I believe that my local area has a knowable and finite capacity or upper limit to the number of people or amount of consumption/waste that it can sustain without destroying its life-support capability, then commitment to younger generations requires that I look at my actions through a frame that includes their tomorrow.

The next lense, ecosystem, helps integrate these insights. My-sight of the local area and neighborhood is transformed into thy-sight that includes seeing the outcomes of my actions from the point of view of other living beings, generations yet unborn, and the physical environment. I, you, and physical things are in fact parts of ecosystem dynamics of living and nonliving processes that rooted together in the physical world support each other's existence.

Dominant cultural ways of seeing blind us to the ecosystems that support us. A counter to such cultural blindness is to think of local ecosystems as a "bioregion," a word of apparently unknown origin that, once used in 1974, quickly spread to help us think environmentally about where we are and how we divide control over the earth (Devall, 1988). An obvious example is a river that depends on its watershed ecosystems, but which humans use as a political boundary. Many states in the United States, or the United States and Mexico, are divided by rivers transformed into borders. Yet these separate political units must make common decisions that destroy or sustain that river. The history of the Columbia and Rio Grande rivers contains continuous conflict among states and between the United States and Mexico. Think of the five Great Lakes "bordered" by two nations, eight states, and one province, not to mention Chicago, Milwaukee, Detroit, Toronto, and a host of smaller cities, towns, and counties. The idea of a bioregion, that is, my place defined by the life-support systems and forms of life that inhabit it, helps me reframe my and my neighbor's actions, and the identities of those who should govern ecosystems for whose sustainable good. I-sight learns to see ecosystems as support for our life, as our bioregion. Of course, thy-sight notes that many others live in it as well, from animals to unseen life forms like the six thousand miles of winter rye root hairs in a cubic inch of soil (Dillard, 1985: 164).

Educators suggest questions and practices for reframing where we live so that we can see the living systems that make my place into our space for living and nonliving others. A simple start is to answer questions derived from the colloquial challenge, "Where you at?" What are the typical weather patterns, or the once in a decade, or once in a half century weather events in your place? Does it make sense to build a house on a Mississippi flood-plain, on the eastern shore of Florida, or the outer coastal islands of Texas? These ecosystems are in floodplains and hurricane pathways. Relative to your turf, do you know where your water comes from and where it goes when you flush the toilet; can you name and spot five birds that live in or pass through your/their place; can you identify five edible local plants that grow naturally; do you know the history of local land use before European settlement and how it has been transformed since (Devall, 1988; Thomashow, 1995: 60ff.)? For contrast, visit your local supermarket and look at the fresh fruits and vegetables through a bioregional lens. Where do starfruit, guava, or kiwi come from? Whence the oranges and lettuce I buy in January in northern Indiana?

Just as I know that the socioeconomic world now interacts through global networks of communication, transportation, and markets, I become aware that ecosystems have interacted remotely or directly amongst them-selves since the birth of the earth. I-sight expanded into ecological thy-sight sees that humans affect local ecosystems just as other animals do. What is new is the breakout of technologically enhanced outcomes from large numbers of human animals amplified by their favorite cattle, both doubling in population in about forty-five years at present rates. Humans and their tech-nologies interact in ways that trip outcomes into the ecosystem of ecosys-tems, as it were. This enveloping system is the bioregion for all life. It is the "life commons" in which the powers of life and death are played out in the evolutionary dynamics that thus far support the human species. Individuals are born and die in biographical time; species emerge and go extinct in geological time marked by apparently sudden and widespread extinctions.

Previous species disappeared from natural dynamics. Today's species extinctions are influenced by activities of over five billions of humans and their preferred animal companions. How can this be? How can the cumula-tive outcomes of over five billion humans result in species extinctions and affect the conditions of life for all? These questions are at the heart of anthro-pogenic global environmental change. Scientists studying the state of the world are coming to a consensus that aggregate human activity is now a significant cause of change in the global life-support systems.

All humans everywhere depend on filtered sunlight, breathable air, drinkable water, arable soil, sustainable food sources, and available energy. Hence, the international concerns over humanly caused changes from burning fossil fuels that increases carbon in the troposphere and is linked to a warming globe; putting CFCs into the atmosphere and thinning protective ozone that filters harmful radiation from sunlight; increasing the acidity of rain and snow beyond the pH levels that support trees, frogs, crops, and human water use; eliminating habitats for increasing numbers of species; and the lack of ample alternative, safe, and sustainable energy sources. Once I integrate these global outcomes into my I-sight, the values informing my transverse interaction change as well. I may not see biospheric effects in my personal place nor even in my local ecosystem or bioregion. I must, as we discussed earlier, choose in whom and in what to put my secular faith about the state of the world. Whose narratives about the environmental outcomes that lie beyond my personal eye-sight do I accept as a basis for my eating, voting, and procreating?

Eye-sight that integrates a biospheric lens sees through beliefs and narratives about our material interaction to basic values and shared reasons. My-sight integrated with ecological sight brings us to philosophical and theological questions that humans ask at the boundaries of what they can measure, explain, or understand. The Primer Paradigm points to these boundary questions under the rubric of holism. I use holism in a broad sense to include the insight that all life, as far as we know it empirically, is interconnected; that values enter deeply into the way we see and act toward the earth; that humans share deep values of sustainability and commitment to future generations; and that humans differ, often violently, over more immediate values of identity, power, and territory. The common task is to find shared ways of seeing so that we can continue to reconstruct our lives and societies through sustainable interaction and adequate environmental identities.

Mitchell Thomashow summarizes the holistic challenge of environmental identity work as follows:

> we become increasingly aware of the tensions, contradictions, and distractions that pervade our lives. . . . We realize the necessity of balancing hope and despair, liberation and suffering, reflection and engagement. We learn how to find nature everywhere—how to see the ecological, political, and spiritual significance of everyday life. . . . There is no escape from this. It is the reality of our times, the landscape of our lives. (1995: 205)

Toward a Self for Our Time

A total self engages in transverse interaction with an identity based on images, attitudes, institutional categories, and talk for sustaining our shared lives. Selves with environmental identities reconstruct a new type of social interaction that bridges the symbolic constructed realm of social worlds and the physical causal realm of the world that supports all else. This ongoing fulfillment of self underwrites the only empirically available source of hope that humans have, namely, to reconstruct society into a just way of life that sustains a supportive environment. The pathos is that we never know all that we do until we have done it. Pragmatic truth lies in a partially unknown future.

Emergence of an environmental self and reconstruction of environmental identities raise further questions. How are different environmental identities distributed among populations both globally and societally? Do the life situations of First and Third World persons in different strata within their communities so focus eye-sight that members of this society or that social class do not see their actions linked to a Generalized Environmental Other? A profit-maximizing corporate cattle king may clear rain forest to supply beef for fast food franchises in the United States. A peasant subsistence farmer feeding a growing family may burn a rain forest to grow necessary food. Analogously, are the few privileged high-consuming wealthy, as well as millions struggling for subsistence in an underclass of poverty, able to see the world through a shared environmental framework that implicates a fair and environmentally sustainable solution to wastefully unequal life-styles?

In a word, discussion of environmental eye-sight raises empirical questions concerning the distribution of environmental identities over social strata and societies. Second, what are the everyday motives of persons with environmental identities compared to selves without such identities? What biographies and narratives are linked with environmental identities? Do leaders in business, military, educational, and religious institutions have environmental identities? What are the links between religious worldviews and responses to the environmental situation? How are age, gender, ethnic, and generational differences related to environmental beliefs and actions? How are environmental identities rewarded or penalized, taught to or hidden from youth? What costs and opportunities await persons with environmental identities in the occupational and political realms? What narratives give larger, even mythic, meanings to environmental issues and identities? How do we talk about environment to ourselves, our parents, our children, or our politicians? And how do we and others feel about what we say?

The way we talk about environment reflects the way we see it. And the way we see and talk about it shapes the way we think and feel about our relationship to it. Most of this book discussed emerging ways of seeing-thinking about environment. A full discussion of our environmental context requires another book to trace the central issue of how we see and *feel* about our relationship with the environment. Powerful emotions suffuse environmental identities (Thomashow, 1995). We draw energy and peace from pleasantly integrated childhood memories of special natural places that support our sense of self by evoking our animal sense of belonging where we physically are. On the other hand, sights of natural places destroyed elicit a sense of irreplaceable loss that causes a pain with no obvious balm. Pain without balm can fester into a loss of hope, a loss we experience as despair. Despair feeds depression.

Another route from deep loss is a turn to anger at those who took away that piece of our self. Smoldering anger can turn into burning rage, a contemporary type sometimes called "green rage." Some analysts argue that the only healthy response to impersonal environmental destruction is a rage that motivates radical action to defend life that cannot defend itself. Edward Abbey wrote accounts of a fictional "Monkey Wrench Gang" who pursue moral outrage through sabotage against giant bulldozers and "earthmovers" that dam rivers, clear forests, and level hills. If any of us feel anger or rage, we too need channels of sublimation to translate these powerful emotions into constructive action.

The challenge of sublimation faces those who sense environmental loss and internalize it as guilt. Some persons feel personal guilt, others feel family, ethnic, or species guilt. I or we are to blame for the loss. I or we are guilty. What then? I can remain fixed in guilt and drift into despair, or I can move from an inactive self guilty for the past to an active self responsible for a piece of the future. Pragmatic morality, like truth, calls for future responses to reconstruct my guilt, or pride for that matter. From an interactionist perspective, the moral worth of my feelings is what I do about them.

Besides a sense of loss, we see special "wild" places, that elicit meaning and joy. Joyful meaning fosters hope in workable futures. Workable futures generate personal motivation (Nuttin, 1985). As we talk about such futures, we make them into motives for explaining to ourselves and others the What and Why of the way we live. Questions addressed to the What and Why of our lives brings us beyond social psychology and into the realms of philosophy and religion.

The newness of these questions is generating "ecophilosophy," "ecotheology," and "ecospirituality." A recent wide-ranging anthology of religious views of nature starts within a section on "The Moment of Seeing" (Gottlieb, 1996). Religious ways of seeing reflect native autochtonous religious perspectives as well as new developments within traditional and mainline religions (McFague, 1987). The Coalition on Environment and Jewish Life, the Evangelical Environmental Network, the National Council of Churches, and the United States Catholic Conference, for example, have formed The National Religious Partnership for the Environment. This broad ecumenical effort attempts to focus their religious traditions on interpretations of and responses to environmental sustainability. For example, a new journal, *Green Cross*, was launched as an ecumenical Christian environmental quarterly with a biblical and activist orientation. The U.S. Catholic Bishops published a letter that calls parishes and individuals to a new way of interacting with the environment according to traditional biblical themes of responsibility for God's creation (U.S. Catholic Conference, 1994). A "consistent ethic of life" is empirically grounded in moral and political responsibility for a life-sustaining environment.

Modern politics of life builds on the viability of the human species as a core value. In personal terms, for those with children, this value may translate into concern for their children's survival and happiness. For those with no children, the value may refer to kinfolk or friends, and religious, moral, or professional commitments. All of us can look inside ourselves to find which, if any, values lead us to care for the environment so that those who come after us can pass on an earth that will support their children. How will the earth support a population likely to reach 11 billion by mid-century? Never in history has a generation had the means to transform life chances so significantly. Some may justify not bringing children onto an earth seen as less capable of supporting additional lives. Others believe that God wants an ever-expanding population of souls to be saved. We must come to grips with our own world views!

Whether aware of it or not, each of us engages in actions that impact the likelihood that our descendents will have a world in which to seek freedom and happiness with the reasonable expectation of their children inheriting the earth.

Notes

1. John Hewitt (1989) presents a pragmatic interpretation of self situated in the experience of American history. He sees American self-understanding stretched tensely across the axes of communitarian and individual identities, and optimistic and pessimistic self-definitions. He uses the idea of cultural "dilemmas" to grasp these tensions. There is little mention of relationships to the natural environment that played such an important part in the American story of how the West was "won." Anthony Giddens (1991) argues more generally that we are entering a period of high modernity that locates self-identity at the interface between the search for subjective security within objective conditions that make us anxious. High modernity is characterized by precarious social processes that define self as an inherently risky project. Physical life has always been risky, and modern society raises the environmental stakes to the limit that puts the social self at high risk also. Kenneth Gergen (1991) pictures postmodern persons as mosaics of ephemeral, saturated selves situated in criss-crossing webs of shifting relationships. The post-modern self is both liberated and threatened, creative and constrained, fabricated and fragmented. Susan Kreiger (1991), by contrast, depicts the sometimes successful struggle of women for an aesthetically grounded authentic self reflected in primitive and modern art and her own craft as a feminist writer-scholar. Robert Lifton (1993) discusses the tensions between other worldly apocalyptic versions of self understanding that turn their backs on the empirical world versus empirically-oriented versions that struggle to act creatively in their historical situation. Finally, Kathy Charmaz (1991) interprets embodied selves intimately mediated through bodies that are chronically ill unto death, a death that these contemporary sick selves continually redefine as they search for new meanings in self's final act. An all-encompassing view sees self as a continuing evolving process struggling to go on living within an absorbing flow of psychologically meaningful or semiotically generated experience (Csikszentmihalyi, 1994; Schwalbe, 1991; Wiley, 1995).

2. Earlier in this century, George H. Mead analyzed self-action into I and Me phases that are reflexively appropriated over evolutionary history by symbol-using biologic individuals such that they emerged as self-conscious persons. Meadian

selves are processual and rooted in evolutionary biology. Socially speaking, humans are continuously reconstructed through interaction and reflexion that ground the experiences we take as the stuff of individual life. Self reconstruction, combined with analysis of self-awareness, synthesizes pragmatist and phenomenological perspectives. Berger and Luckmann's (1966) social constructionist synthesis of these perspectives show how societies formulate motives and identities through which selves act out the relationships of organism and identity. Processes of motive and identity formation underlay the ongoing reconstruction of the person with a sense of a continuous and unique "substantival self." This sense is grounded in a reflexive and empirical grasp of one's experience as an historically verifiable, unified, and continuous self (Weigert, 1975). Substantival self is a complex of cultural assumptions; historical productions; social processes; experiential imperatives; and grounding it all, bodies interacting with the natural environment.

3. Pragmatically expanded meaning takes our discussion beyond typical boundaries of social psychology. Contrast this expanded meaning with the affective, reflex, or nonintentional meanings indicated by Herbert Blumer in both early and mature statements on nonsymbolic interaction (1936; 1969: ch. 1). Expanded meaning requires us to look in the natural world, and not only in personally or socially constructed realities.

Bibliography

Albanese, Catherine L.
   1990. *Nature Religion in America*. Chicago: University of Chicago Press.

Ammerman, Nancy T.
   1987. *Bible Believers*. New Brunswick: Rutgers University Press.

Arnheim, Rudolf
   1969. *Visual Thinking*. Berkeley: University of California Press.

Art Journal
   1992. *Special Theme*, "Art and ecology." Vol. 51 (2).

Bailey, Ronald (ed.)
   1995. *The True State of the Planet*. New York: Free Press.

Baldwin, John D.
   1986. *George Herbert Mead: A Unifying Theory for Sociology*. Beverly Hills: Sage.

Bandura, Albert
   1986. *Social Foundations of Thought and Action*. Englewood Cliffs: Prentice-Hall.

Barash, David R.
   1987. *The Arms Race and Nuclear War*. Belmont: Wadsworth Pubs. Co.

Baudrillard, Jean
   1981. *For a Critique of the Political Economy of the Sign*. St. Louis: Telos.

Baumgartner, M. P.
   1988. *The Moral Order of a Suburb*. New York: Oxford University Press.

Beck, Ulrich
   1992. *The Risk Society*. New York: Routledge.
   1995. *Ecological Enlightenment*. Atlantic Highlands: Humanities Press.

Bellah, Robert N., Richard Madsen, William M. Sullivan, Ann Swidler, and Steven M. Tipton
   1991. *The Good Society.* New York: Alford A. Knopf.

Bennett, John
   1993. *Human Ecology as Human Behavior.* New Brunswick: Transaction.

Berger, Peter
   1963. *Invitation to Sociology.* Garden City: Anchor Books.
   1980. *The Heretical Imperative.* Garden City: Anchor Press

Berger, Peter and Thomas Luckmann
   1966. *The Social Construction of Reality.* New York: Doubleday.

Berry, Thomas
   1988. *The Dream of the Earth.* San Francisco: Sierra Club Books.

Berry, Wendell
   1977. *The Unsettling of America.* San Francisco: Sierra Club.

Blair, Bruce G.
   1985. *Strategic Command and Control.* Washington: The Brookings Institution.

Blinder, Alan S.
   1987. *Hard Heads, Soft Hearts.* Reading: Addison-Wesley.

Blumer, Herbert
   1936. "Social attitudes and non-symbolic interaction." *Journal of Educational Sociology 9.* 515–523.
   1969. *Symbolic Interactionism.* Englewood Cliffs: Prentice-Hall.

Bormann, F. Herbert, Diana Balmori, and Gordon T. Geballe
   1993. *Redesigning the American Lawn.* New Haven: Yale University Press.

Botkin, Daniel B.
   1990. *Discordant Harmonies.* New York: Oxford University Press.

Boulding, Elise
   1990. *Building a Global Civic Culture.* Syracuse: Syracuse University Press.

Bracken, Paul
   1983. *The Command and Control of Nuclear Forces.* New Haven: Yale University Press.

Bradley, C.
   1994. "Using mulch helpful to plants, gardeners." *South Bend Tribune* (August 12): C 12.

Brown, Lester R. et al.
   1994. *State of the World.* New York: Norton.
   1995. *State of the World.* New York: Norton.

Brown, Phil
1992. "Popular epidemiology and toxic waste contamination: lay and professional ways of knowing." *Journal of Health and Social Behavior 33*: 267–281.

Buchanan, R.
1992. "Wicked problems in design thinking." *Design Issues 8*: 3–21.

Bullard, Robert D.
1990. *Dumping in Dixie*. Boulder: Westview Press.

Burch, William R.
1971. *Daydreams and Nightmares*. New York: Harper & Row.

Caldwell, Lynton K.
1990. *Between Two Worlds*. New York: Cambridge University Press.

Callenbach, Ernest
1977. *Ecotopia*. New York: Bantam.

Carson, Rachel
1962/1994. *Silent Spring*. Boston: Houghton Mifflin.

Catton, William R.
1980. *Overshoot: the Ecological Basis of Revolutionary Change*. Urbana: University of Illinois Press.
1994. "Foundations of human ecology." *Sociological Perspectives 37*: 75–95.

Catton, W. R., and R. E. Dunlap
1978. "Environmental sociology: a new paradigm." *The American Sociologist 13*: 41–49.
1980. "The new ecological paradigm for post-exuberant sociology." *The American Behavioral Scientist 24*: 15–47.

Charmaz, Kathy
1991. *Good Days, Bad Days*. New Brunswick: Rutgers University Press.

Chawla, Saroj
1991. "Linguistic and philosophical roots of our environmental crisis." *Environmental Ethics 13*: 253–262.

Chicago Tribune
1988. "Natural shocks uncut meadow brings fine, protests." (Sept. 18): *Home*, 6.
1993. "Ecology getting to be a habitat with golfers." (June 23): Section 1: 1,2.

Chilton, P.
1982. "Nukespeak: nuclear language, culture and propaganda." Pp. 94–112 in Crispin Aubrey (ed.), *Nukespeak*. London: Comedia Pubs. Group.

China News Digest
1994. April 8.

Cohen, Joseph.
  1989. "About steaks liking to be eaten." *Symbolic Interaction 12*: 191–213.

Cook, Gary A.
  1993. *George Herbert Mead.* Urbana: University of Illinois Press.

Cronon, William
  1991. *Nature's Metropolis.* New York: Norton.

Cross Currents
  1994. Special Issue on "Nature as Thou." Summer.

Csikszentmihalyi, Mihaly
  1994. *The Evolving Self.* New York: Oxford University Press.

Daly, Herman E. and John B. Cobb
  1990. *For the Common Good.* Boston: Beacon Press.

Darwin, Charles
  1975. *The Origin of Species.* New York: Norton. Originally published in 1859.

Demerath, L.
  1993. "Knowledge-based affect: cognitive origins of 'good' and 'bad'." *Social Psychology Quarterly 56* (2): 1346–147.

Denzin, Norman K.
  1989. *Interpretive Interactionism.* Newbury Park: Sage.

Devall, Bill
  1988. *Simple In Means, Rich In Ends.* Salt Lake City: Gibbs Smith Pubs.

Devall, Bill and George Sessions
  1985. *Deep Ecology.* Salt Lake City: Gibbs Smith Pubs.

Dillard, Annie
  1985. *Pilgrim at Tinker Creek.* New York: Harper and Row.

Douglas, Mary
  1970. *Purity and Danger.* Baltimore: Pelican.
  1986. *How Institutions Think.* Syracuse: Syracuse University Press.

Douglass, G. K.
  1985. "The need for agricultural awareness." Pp. 9–21 in Gordon K. Douglass (ed.), *Cultivating Agricultural Literacy.* Battle Creek: Kellogg Foundation.

Dowd, Douglas
  1989. *The Waste of Nations.* Boulder: Westview.

Dunlap, Riley E. and William R. Catton, Jr.
  1983. "What environmental sociologists have in common." *Sociological Inquiry 53*: 113–135.
  1994. "Struggling with human exemptionalism: the rise, decline and revitalization of environmental sociology." *The American Sociologist 25*: 5–30.

Dunlap, Riley E., and Angela G. Mertig (eds.)
1992. *American Environmentalism.* Philadelphia: Taylor and Francis.

Dunlap, Riley E., George H. Gallup, Jr., and Alec M. Gallup
1993. *Health of the Planet.* Princeton: Gallup International Institute.

Dunn, L. A.
1994. "Provocations: deterring the new nuclear powers." *The Washington Quarterly 17*: 5–25.

Eckberg, D. L. and T. J. Blocker
1989. "Varieties of religious involvement and environmental concerns: testing the Lynn White thesis." *Journal for the Scientific Study of Religion 28*: 509–517.

Edelstein, Michael R.
1988. *Contaminated Communities.* Boulder: Westview.

Edwards, M.
1994. "Chornobyl." *National Geographic 186*: 70–115.

Eisley, Loren
1978. *The Firmament of Time.* New York: Atheneum.

Eliade, Mircea
1961. *The Sacred and the Profane.* New York: Harper and Row.

Erikson, Kai T.
1976. *Everything in its Path.* New York: Simon & Schuster.

Evernden, Neil
1992. *The Social Creation of Nature.* Baltimore: The Johns Hopkins University Press.

Eyerman, Ron and Andrew Jamison
1991. *Social Movements.* University Park: Pennsylvania State University Press.

Eyre, D. P. (ed.)
1992. "The Army: geostrategic concerns and environmental considerations." *Report of Conference by Strategic Studies Institute*, U.S. Army War College, and Hoover Institution on War, Revolution, and Peace. March 5.

Feshbach, Murray and Alfred Friendly, Jr.
1992. *Ecocide in the USSR.* New York: Basic Books.

Fine, G. A. and L. Holyfield
1994. "Secrecy, trust, and dangerous leisure." Unpublished paper, University of Georgia.

Firey, Walter
1945. "Sentiment and symbolism as ecological variables." *American Sociological Review 10*: 140–148.

Fisher, T.
  1993. "Editorial: The paradox of 'green' architecture." *Progressive Architecture*
  74 (March): 9.

Ford, Daniel
  1985. *The Button*. New York: Simon and Schuster.

French, W. C.
  1989. "Crabgrass wars." *Commonweal* (August 11): 421–422.

Freund, Peter and George Martin
  1993. *The Ecology of the Automobile*. New York: Black Rose Books.

Gallagher, Carole
  1993. *American Ground Zero*. New York: Random House.

Garfinkel, Harold
  1967. *Studies in Ethnomethodology*. Englewood Cliffs: Prentice-Hall.

Gergen, Kenneth J.
  1991. *The Saturated Self*. New York: Basic Books.

Giddens, Anthony
  1976. *New Rules of Sociological Method*. New York: Basic Books.
  1991. *Modernity and Self-Identity*. Stanford: Stanford University Press.

Globe and Mail, The
  1994. "The lawn as polyester leisure suit." Editorial (July 16): D6.

Goffman, Erving
  1959. *The Presentation of Self in Everyday Life*. New York: Doubleday.
  1974. *Frame Analysis*. New York: Harper and Row.
  1983. "The interaction order." *American Sociological Review 48*: 1–17.

Gold, A. J., W. R. DeRagon, W. M. Sullivan, and J. L. Lemunyon
  1990. "Nitrate-nitrogen losses to groundwater from rural and suburban land
  uses." *Journal of Soil and Water Conservation 45(2)*: 305–309.

Gore, Al
  1992. *Earth in the Balance*. Boston: Houghton Mifflin.

Gottlieb, Roger S. (ed.)
  1996. *This Sacred Earth*. New York: Routledge.

Graumann, C. and L. Kruse
  1990. "The environment: social construction and psychological problems." Pp.
  212–229 in Hilde T. Himmelweit and George Gaskell (eds.), *Societal
  Psychology*. Newbury Park: Sage.

Greeley, Andrew
  1993. "Religion and attitudes toward the environment." *Journal for the
  Scientific Study of Religion 32*: 19–28.

Greider, Thomas and Lorraine Garkovich
1994. "Landscapes: the social construction of nature and the environment." *Rural Sociology 59*: 1–24.

Grizzle, R. E.
1994. "Environmentalism should include human ecological needs." *BioScience 44*: 263–268.

Guth, J. L., L. A. Kellstedt, C. E. Smidt and J. C. Green
1993. "Theological perspectives and environmentalism among religious activists." *Journal for the Scientific Study of Religion 32*: 373–382.

Hagen, Joel B.
1992. *An Entangled Bank*. New Brunswick: Rutgers University Press.

Halstead, J. M., W. R. Kerns, and P. D. Relf
1989. "Lawn and garden chemicals and the potential for groundwater contamination." *Ground Water Issues and Solutions in the Potomac River Basin/Chesapeake Bay Region*. Dublin, OH: National Water Well Association.

Hardin, G.
1968. "The tragedy of the commons." *Science 162* (December 13): 1243–1248.

Harré, Rom, David Clarke, and Nicola De Carlo
1985. *Motives and Mechanisms*. New York: Methuen.

Harré, Rom and Grant Gillett
1994. *The Discursive Mind*. Thousand Oaks: Sage.

Harte, John, Cheryl Holdren, Richard Schneider, and Christine Shirley
1991. *Toxics A to Z*. Berkeley: University of California Press.

Harwell, Mark A.
1982. *Nuclear Winter*. New York: Springer-Verlag.

Hecht, M. E.
1975. "The decline of the grass lawn tradition in Tucson." *Landscape 19*: 3–10.

Hewitt, John
1989. *Dilemmas of the American Self*. Philadelphia: Temple University Press.
1991. *Self and Society*. Boston: Allyn and Bacon.

Hochschild, Arlie
1983. *The Managed Heart*. Berkeley: University of California Press.

Homer-Dixon, T. F.
1993. "Across the threshold: empirical evidence on environmental scarcities as causes of violent conflict." Unpublished paper. University of Toronto.

Howard, G. S.
1993. "Ecocounseling psychology: an introduction and overview." *The Counseling Psychologist 21*: 550–559.

Howard, G. S., E. Delgado, D. Miller, and S. Gubbins
1993. "Transforming values into actions: ecological preservation through energy conservation." *The Counseling Psychologist 21*: 582–596.

Hughes, E.C.
1962. "What Other?" Pp. 119–127 in Arnold M. Rose (ed.), *Human Behavior and Social Processes.* Boston: Houghton Mifflin Co.

Hundley, Jr., Norris
1992. *The Great Thirst: Californians and Water, 1770s–1990s.* Berkeley: University of California Press.
1993. "Letter to the editor." *Los Angeles Times.* Sunday, March 14: M 6.

Hynes, H. Patricia
1989. *The Recurring Silent Spring.* New York: Pergamon Press.

Inglehart, Ronald
1990. *Culture Shift.* Princeton: Princeton University Press.

International Peace Research Association
1989. Special issue on "Ecological security and peace." *IPRA newsletter 27* (January).

Jackson, John B.
1984. *Discovering the Vernacular Landscape.* New Haven: Yale University Press.

Jackson, Kenneth T.
1985. *Crabgrass Frontier.* New York: Oxford University Press.

Jamison, Andrew, Ron Eyerman, Jacqueline Cramer, with Jeppe Laessoe
1990. *The Making of the New Environmental Consciousness.* Edinburgh: Edinburgh University Press.

Jenkins, Virginia S.
1994. *The Lawn: A History of an American Obsession.* Washington, D.C.: Smithsonian Institution Press.

Johnson, C. L. and A. J. Weigert
1980. "Frames in confession: the social construction of sexual sin." *Journal for the Scientific Study of Religion 19*: 368–381.

Kelley, Kevin W.
1988. *The Home Planet.* Reading: Addison-Wesley.

Kennedy, Paul
1993. *Preparing for the Twenty-First Century.* New York: Random House.

Keyfitz, N.
1993. "Are there ecological limits to population?" *Proceedings of the National Academy of Sciences 90* (August): 6895–6899.

Kierulff, S.
1991. "Belief in 'Armageddon Theology' and willingness to risk nuclear war." *Journal for the Scientific Study of Religion 30*: 81–93

Klausner, Samuel Z.
1971. *On Man in His Environment.* San Francisco: Jossey-Bass.

Kotlowitz, Alex
1992. *There Are No Children Here.* New York: Anchor Books.

Krieger, Susan
1991. *Social Science and the Self.* New Brunswick: Rutgers University Press.

Kuhn, Thomas S.
1970. *The Structure of Scientific Revolutions.* Chicago: University of Chicago Press.

Kurtz, Lester R.
1988. *The Nuclear Cage.* Englewood Cliffs: Prentice-Hall.

Lanier-Graham, Susan D.
1993. *The Ecology of War.* New York: Walker.

Latimer, Thomas L.
1991. *Written Statement, Senate Subcommittee on Toxic Substances, May 9.*

Leopold, Aldo
1970. *A Sand County Almanac.* New York: Ballantine.

Lewis, J. D., R. McLain, and A. J. Weigert
1993. "Vital realism and sociology." *Sociological Theory 11*: 72–95.

Lifton, Robert J.
1993. *The Protean Self.* New York: Basic Books.

Lifton, Robert J. and Richard A. Falk
1982. *Indefensible Weapons.* New York: Basic.

Lindsey, Hal
1977. *The Late Great Planet Earth.* Grand Rapids: Zondervan.

Los Angeles Times
1993. "Drought is over, Wilson declares." Thursday, February 25: A 1.

Lovelock, J. E.
1987. *Gaia.* New York: Oxford University Press.

Lyman, Stanford M. and Marvin B. Scott
1970. *A Sociology of the Absurd.* New York: Appleton-Century-Crofts.

Margulis, L. and J. E. Lovelock
1989. "Gaia and Geognosy." Pp. 1–30 in G. Mitchell B. Rambler, Lynn Margulis, and René Fester (eds.), *Global Ecology.* Boston: Academic Press.

Markus, H. and P. Nurius
1987. "Possible Selves: the interface between motivation and the self-concept."
Pp. 157–172 in K. Yardley and T. Homess (eds.), *Self and Identity.* New York:
John Wiley.

Marsh, George F.
1864/1965. *Man and Nature.* Cambridge: Harvard University Press.

Marty, Martin E. and R. Scott Appleby
1992. *The Glory and the Power.* Boston: Beacon Press.

Maszak, M.
1988. "Minding the missiles." *Psychology Today* (June): 52–56.

McCall, George J., and J. L. Simmons
1978. *Identities and Interactions.* New York: Free Press.

McCarthy, E. D.
1984. "Toward a sociology of the physical world: George Herbert Mead on
physical objects." *Studies in Symbolic Interaction 5*: 105–121.

McFague, Sallie
1987. *Models of God.* Philadelphia: Fortress Press.

McGuinnis, J.
1970. *The Selling of the President 1968.* New York: Pocket Books.

McIntosh, Robert P.
1986. *The Background of Ecology.* New York: Cambridge University Press.

Mead, George H.
1934. *Mind, Self, and Society.* Chicago: University of Chicago Press.
1938. *The Philosophy of the Act.* Chicago: University of Chicago Press
1964. *Selected Writings.* Indianapolis: Bobbs-Merrill.
1982. *The Individual and the Social Self.* Chicago: University of Chicago Press.

Melucci, Alberto
1989. *Nomads of the Present.* Philadelphia: Temple University Press.

Merchant, Carolyn
1983. *The Death of Nature.* New York: Harper & Row.
1989. *Ecological Revolutions.* Chapel Hill: University of North Carolina Press.

Meyrowitz, Joshua
1985. *No Sense of Place.* New York: Oxford University Press.

Milbrath, Lester W.
1989. *Envisioning a Sustainable Society.* Albany: SUNY Press.

Milgram, Stanley
1975. *Obedience to Authority.* New York: Harper and Row.

Miller, G. Tyler
1994. *Living in the Environment.* Belmont: Wadsworth.

Mills, C. Wright
1961. *The Sociological Imagination.* New York: Grove Press.

Morin, R.
1992. "Giving the green light to the environment." *Washington Post National Weekly Edition.* June 15–21: 37.

Naess, Arne
1990. *Ecology, community, and lifestyle.* New York: Cambridge University Press. Translated and edited by David Rothenberg.

National Academy of Sciences
1990. *One Earth, One Future.* Washington, D. C.: National Academy Press.

Nelson, C. E.
1989. "Skewered on the unicorn's horn: the illusion of tragic tradeoff between content and critical thinking in the teaching of science." Pp. 17–27 in Linda W. Crow (ed.), *Enhancing Critical Thinking in the Sciences.* Washington: Society for College Science Teachers.

New York Times
1965. "The Beautiful Dandelion." Editorial, (Sunday, April 27), Section 4: 16.
1990. "Smiles, golf carts and lethal footballs." (June 3): 1, 12.
1991. "Lawn herbicide called cancer risk for dogs." (Sept. 4): Section B: 7.
1994. "California and the politics of drought." Sunday, June 26: E 2.

Norton, Bryon G.
1991. *Toward Unity among Environmentalists.* New York: Oxford University Press.

Nuttin, Joseph
1985. *Future Time Perspective and Motivation.* Hillsdale: Erlbaum.

OECD
1991. *Environmental Indicators.* Paris: Organization for Economic Co-operation and Development.
1991a. *The State of the Environment.* Paris: Organization for Economic Co-operation and Development.

Oelschlaeger, Max
1991. *The Idea of Wilderness.* New Haven: Yale University Press.

Olsen, Marvin E., Dora G. Lodwick, and Riley E. Dunlap
1992. *Viewing the World Ecologically.* Boulder: Westview Press.

Ophuls, William and A. Stephen Boyan, Jr.
1992. *Ecology and the Politics of Scarcity Revisited.* New York: Freeman.

Orr, David W.
1992. *Ecological Literacy.* Albany: SUNY Press.

Osgood, Charles E., G. I. Suci, and P. H. Tannenbaum
1957. *The Measurement of Meaning.* Urbana: University of Illinois Press.

Otto, Rudolf
1958. *The Idea of the Holy.* New York: Oxford University Press.

Paehlke, Robert C.
1989. *Environmentalism and the Future of Progressive Politics.* New Haven: Yale University Press.

Perinbanayagam, Robert S.
1991. *Discursive Acts.* New York: Aldine de Gruyter.

Piller, Charles
1991. *The Fail-Safe Society.* New York: Basic Books.

Polanyi, Michael and Harry Prosch
1975. *Meaning.* Chicago: University of Chicago Press.

Pollan, Michael
1989. "Why mow? The case against lawns." *The New York Times Magazine* (May 28): 23–27, 41–42, 44.
1989a. "Weeds are us." *The New York Times Magazine* (November 5): 49, 96–99.

Ponting, Clive
1991. *A Green History of the World.* New York: St. Martin's Press.

Porter, Gareth and Janet W. Brown
1996. *Global Environmental Politics.* 2nd Edition. Boulder: Westview.

Rathje, William and Cullen Murphy
1993. *Rubbish!* New York: Harper Perennial.

Reisner, Marc
1993. *Cadillac Desert.* New York: Penguin.

Reynolds, Larry T.
1990. *Interactionism: Exposition and Critique.* Dix Hills: General Hall.

Rheingold, Howard
1993. *The Virtual Community.* Reading: Addison-Wesley.

Ridgeway, C.
1991. "The social construction of status value: gender and other nominal categories." *Social Forces* 70(2): 367–386.

Rochberg-Halton, Eugene
1986. *Meaning and Modernity.* Chicago: University of Chicago Press.

Rose, Arnold (ed.)
1962. *Human Behavior and Social Processes.* Boston: Houghton Mifflin.

Sacks, Oliver
1990. "Neurology and the soul." *The New York Review of Books 37* (November, 22): 44–50.

Sale, Kirkpatrick
1993. *The Green Revolution.* New York: Hill and Wang.

Schnaiberg, Allan and Kenneth A. Gould
1994. *Environment and Society.* New York: St. Martin's Press.

Schroeder, Fred E.
1993. *Front Yard America.* Bowling Green: Bowling Green State University Press.

Schutz, Alfred
1962. *The Problem of Social Reality.* The Hague: Nijhoff.
1970. *Reflections on the Problem of Relevance.* New Haven: Yale University Press.

Schutz, Alfred, and Thomas Luckmann
1989. *The Structures of the Life-World, Vol. II.* Evanston: Northwestern University Press.

Schwalbe, M. L.
1991. "The autogenesis of the self." *Journal for the Theory of Social Behaviour 21*: 269–295.

Selcraig, B.
1993. "Greens fees." *Sierra* (July/August): 70–77, 86–87.

Shotter, John and Kenneth J. Gergen (eds.)
1989. *Texts of Identity.* Newbury Park: Sage.

Shulman, Seth
1992. *The Threat At Home.* Boston: Beacon.

Simmel, Georg
1968. *The Conflict in Modern Conflict and Other Essays.* New York: Teachers College Press.

Simmons, I. G.
1993. *Interpreting Nature.* New York: Routledge.

Sitarz, Daniel
1993. *Agenda 21.* Boulder: Earthpress.

Sivard, Ruth L.
1991. *World Military and Social Expenditures 1991.* Washington, D.C.: World Priorities.

1993. *World Military and Social Expenditures 1993*. Washington, D.C.: World Priorities.

Söderqvist, Thomas
1986. *The Ecologists*. Stockholm: Almqvist & Wiksell International.

Solomon, Robert C.
1988. *Continental Philosophy Since 1750: The Rise and Fall of the Self*. New York: Oxford University Press.

South Bend Tribune
1993. "New habits." Editorial, April 24: A 8.
1994. "City's mowing crew mistakes 'nature scaping' for patch of weeds." September 25: F2.

Standard and Poor's Industry Surveys
1993. "Appliance fundamentals." 2: T-96.

Stein, Sara
1993. *Noah's Garden*. Boston: Houghton Mifflin Co.

Stevens, W. K.
1994. "Severe ancient droughts: a warning to California." *New York Times* (July 19): B5,B9.

Stine, S.
1994. "Extreme and persistent drought in California and Patagonia during mediaeval time." *Nature* (16 June): 546–549.

Stokes, R. and J. Hewitt
1976. "Aligning Actions." *American Sociological Review 41*: 838–849.

Stone, G. P.
1981. "Appearance and the self: a slightly revised version." Pp. 187–202 in G. P. Stone and H. Farberman (eds.) *Social Psychology Through Symbolic Interaction*. New York: Wiley.

Taylor, Charles
1989. *Sources of the Self*. Cambridge: Harvard University Press.

Thomashow, Mitchell
1995. *Ecological Identity*. Cambridge: MIT Press.

Thompson, James
1985. *Psychological Aspects of Nuclear War*. New York: Wiley.

Time
1991. "Can lawns be justified?" (June 3): 63–64.
1994. ""Proliferation: formula for terror." (August 29): 46–51.

Tobias, S.
1988. "Armed and dangerous." *Ms.* (August): 62–67.

Travisano, R. V.
   n. d.. "Small time lobstering out of Narrow River: transverse interaction and a generalized environmental other." Unpublished paper. University of Rhode Island.

Tuan, Yi-Fu
   1982. *Segmented Worlds and Self.* Minneapolis: University of Minnesota Press.

Turnbull, Colin M.
   1962. *The Forest People.* New York: Simon and Schuster.

Turner, R. H.
   1976. "The real self: from institution to impulse." *American Journal of Sociology 81*: 989–1016.

Union of Concerned Scientists
   1992. *World Scientists Warning to Humanity.* 26 Church St., Cambridge, MA.

U.S. Catholic Conference
   1994. *Renewing the Face of the Earth.* Washington, D.C.

U.S. Department of Commerce
   1993. *United States Industrial Outlook '93.* Washington: U.S. Government Printing Office.

U.S. Environmental Protection Agency
   1988. *Lawn Care For Your Home.* Chicago: Office of Public Affairs.
   n. d.. *Questions and Answers on Lawn Pesticides.* Washington, D.C.: Office of Pesticides and Toxic Substances.

U.S. General Accounting Office
   1990. "Lawn care pesticides' risks remain uncertain while prohibited safety claims continue." Report to the Chairman, Subcommittee on Toxic Substances, Environmental Oversight, Research and Development, U.S. Senate RCED 90–134.

U.S. Senate
   1990–1. "The use and regulation of lawn care chemicals." Hearing before the Subcommittee on Toxic Substances, Environmental Oversight, Research and Development. Senate Hearing 101–685. Washington: U.S. Government Printing Office.

Van Der Leeuw, G.
   1963. *Religion in Essence and Manifestation.* New York: Harper and Row.

Van Impe, Jack
   1984. *America, Israel, Russia, and World War III.* Royal Oak, MI: Jack Van Impe Ministries.

Veblen, Thorstein
   1979. *The Theory of the Leisure Class.* New York: Penguin.

Vonnegut, Kurt
1985. *Galápagos.* New York: Laurel.

Walter, E. V.
1988. *Placeways.* Chapel Hill: University of North Carolina Press.

Walton, John
1992. *Western Times and Water Wars.* Berkeley: University of California Press.

Weart, Spencer R.
1988. *Nuclear Fear.* Cambridge: Harvard University Press.

Weber, Thomas
1989. *Hugging the Trees.* New York: Penguin.

Webster, D.
1994. "One leg, one life at a time." *The New York Times Magazine,* January 23: 27–33; 42; 51–52; 58.

Weigert, Andrew J.
1975. "Substantival Self: a primitive term for a sociological psychology." *Philosophy of the Social Sciences 5:* 43–62.
1983. *Social Psychology.* Notre Dame: University of Notre Dame Press.
1988. "Christian eschatological identities and the nuclear context." *Journal for the Scientific Study of Religion 27:* 175–191.
1991. *Mixed Emotions.* Albany: SUNY Press.
1991a. "Transverse interaction: a pragmatic perspective on environment as other." *Symbolic Interaction 14(3):* 353–363.

Weigert, Andrew J., J. Smith Teitge, and Dennis W. Teitge
1986. *Society and identity.* New York: Cambridge University Press.

Weigert, K.
1990. "Experiential learning and peace education: on visiting Greenham Common women's peace camp." *Peace and Change 15(3):* 312–330.

Whorf, Benjamin L.
1956. *Language, Thought, and Reality.* Cambridge: MIT Press.

Wiley, Norbert
1995. *The Semiotic Self.* Chicago: University of Chicago Press.

Wilson, E. O.
1984. *Biophilia.* Cambridge: Harvard University Press.

Wiman, B. L. B.
1991. "The world of perceptions versus the world of data: notes towards safe-failing the energy equation." Pp. 171–186 in Kei Takeuchi and Masatoshi Yoshino (eds.) *The Global Environment.* New York: Springer-Verlag.

Winter, Deborah, D.
1996. *Ecological Psychology.* New York: Harper Collins.

World Commission on Environment and Development
1987. *Our Common Future.* New York: Oxford University Press.

World Resources Institute
1994. *Environmental Alamanac.* New York: Houghton Mifflin.

Worster, Donald
1977. *Nature's Economy.* New York: Cambridge University Press.

Young, Michael
1988. *The Metronomic Society.* Cambridge: Harvard University Press.

Zurcher, Louis A.
1983. *Social Roles.* Beverly Hills: Sage Pubs.

Index

Note: Page numbers in **bold type** reference non–text material

Lawns
as big business, 123
care of, EPA on, 121
definition of, 122
lawn–care services and, 118
motivational power of, 118
as source of identities, 126–128
as status,
    dichotomies that generate, 114–117
    methods of giving, 112–14
    struggling with life, 111–29
    see also Industrial lawnscape
Lawnscapes, identity/status of, 122–123
Lemmas, ecological, function of, 7
Leopold, Aldo, on taking the long view, 14
Life, self and, 13
"Lifescape inversion"
    described, 57–58
    Rachel Carson and, 58–59
Logics, defined, 139
Lopez, Barry, 168

M
Marsh, George Perkins, on human life and the environment, 1–2
Mead, George H., 67
    on human capacity, 32
    notion of sociality by, 25
    on phases of the social act, 163
    on physical–symbolic duality of meaning, 172–73
    self-other paradigm, 20–23
    on selves and evolutionary time, 47
    social act described by, 24
    on symbolically organized human society, 153
Meaningful objects
    described, 5
    in nature, 26
    pragmatic axiom on, 36
Meanings
    arise from interaction, 15
    physical-symbolic duality of, 172–73
    pragmatic axiom of, 36

pragmatic lemma and, 39
    self and, 173–75
    see also specific type of meaning
Milbrath, Lester, on "dominant social paradigm," 52
Military trippers, 77–79
Mixed interaction, defined, 23
Moral minimalism, suburbia as, 119
Morality, knowledge recipes and, 36
Muir, John, 168

N
National Aeronautics and Space Administration (NASA), 6
Natural environments, 150
    air, 98
    definitional formula of, 61–62
    definitions of, 48–50
    meaning tree for, **51**
    mutual sustainability of, 56–57
    described, 45
    "dominant social paradigm" of, 52
    emerging alternative paradigm, 53
    framework for seeing/talking about, 47–50
    personal experience and, 150–151
    seeing the, 43–62
    soil as, 99
    sun, 97
    trees, 100–101
    trippers in, 63–90
        everyday life, 68–75
        industry, 75–77
        interpreting responses to, 66, 80–81
        military, 77–79
        nuclear weapons as mega, 79–80
        understanding, 16
    views of, 52–53
    water, 98–99
Natural meanings
    behaviorally, 174
    described, 15
    discussed, 15
    social meanings and, 17, 30–31
Natural objects, inversion of, 96–97